THE

HISTORY
OF THE
UNITED STATES

TOLD
IN ONE
SYLLABLE
WORDS.

New York McLOUGHLIN BROTHERS

Published by:
Chagrin Falls Alumni Association
400 East Washington Street
Chagrin Falls, Ohio 44022
440.247.4387
www.chagrinfallsalumni.com
cf_alumni@lgca.com

First Printing December 2005
ISBN 0-9771225-0-6
Library of Congress Control Number: 2005930383

Design, layout and graphic presentation by:
Tag Art Studio
Terry Taggart, class of '62
www.tagartstudio.com

HISTORY OF THE
CHAGRIN FALLS
SCHOOLS

Volume I
1833-1960

by Tom Mattern

Chagrin Falls High School Class of 1955
Chagrin Falls Schools Teacher 1965-1990
Chagrin Falls Alumni Director 1990-2004

To Theresa—
May the next step in
your life be as
successful as your
last and your fond
memories of CFHS
remain strong.
Best Wishes,
Tom Mattern
Go Tigers!!!

"School days, school days, dear old golden rule days…"

The Fancy Dress Party 1912

Dedication

This history is dedicated to the graduates of Chagrin Falls
High School who have helped make this community, state, nation
and world a better and safer place to live, and to the educators
who provided them the opportunity.

iv

Contents

PART I   One-room Schoolhouses Emerged Throughout The Village

A school board was established-consolidation led to a Union School -
the 19th century ended with the schools having an excellent reputation....

pages 1-50

*"Last Friday evening I got the
inhabitants of the district
together and delivered them
an address on school teaching."*

Rev. L.D. Williams, teacher   Page 5

*"...the school taught by a
Miss Hemmingway, who was so kind
to her pupils as to warm the benches
for them on cold mornings...."*

Austin Church, student   Page 12

v

"A school meeting will be called on Tuesday evening, June the 12th (1849), at early candlelight at the North School House...."

School Board minutes   Page 13

"There shall be no talking or whispering in the hours of school without permission to do so."

Board of Education rules   Page 18

"The School Board has gotten up some handsome diplomas for those graduating from the High School. Hugh Christian receives one this commencement."

Chagrin Falls Exponent, May 18, 1879   Page 23

"With sadness we record the death ...of little Erwin Luse, aged 6 years... The cause has been authoritatively ascribed to the rash act of the principal of his school bumping Erwin's and playmates heads together as a mode of correction, thereby causing an ulcer in the brain."

Chagrin Falls Exponent, February 9, 1882   Page 25

"...nothing could have been more pleasing to our citizens, as well as the board, teachers and scholars, than the open house reception at the new building on New Year's Day."

Chagrin Falls Exponent, January 7, 1886   Page 28

PART II The Early 20th Century Brought New Buildings

The curriculum was broadened -
interscholastic athletics were expanded....pages 51-118

"One of the most auspicious occasions in the history of Chagrin Falls and one highly interesting and attractive to her citizens, was the public ceremony of laying the cornerstone of the new high school building...."

Chagrin Falls Exponent, July 12, 1914   Page 51

"Gifford (Raymond "Pete") proved to be one of the most efficient cheerleaders Chagrin Hi has ever had. Quiet and unassuming, yet enthusiastic, he succeeded in swaying the sidelines, to the strong support of their men by their hearty cheers."

1922 Annual   Page 62

"The Friendship and Hi-Y Clubs feeling that religion is an integral part of the life of high school, students are seeking to emphasize that endowment."

1924 Annual   Page 62

*"We, the pupils of the Chagrin Falls
High School, have decided to draw
up a petition… to have coach
Theodore Gurney back again."*

School Board minutes, April 1928   Page 76

*"The 1932 basketball game with Orange
wound up in a free-for-all…Players were fighting,
spectators were on the floor fighting and
Mr. Sands, Mr. Gurney and the Orange
coach trying to quell the crowd."*

Memories, Robert Cathan '33, student   Page 87

*"I am sending this letter to inform you of the
fact that the local Bowling and Recreation Parlor has
been working elementary school boys from 4 o'clock
in the afternoon to 12 and 1 or 2 o'clock in the morning."*

Letter written by Superintendent Lewis Sands
to the chief of police, Alvin Smith March 15, 1944   Page 104

PART III The 1950's Brought Progressive Changes In Curriculum

New schools were built at the old fairgrounds - teachers were encouraged to improve their proficiency - the schools remained committed to excellence....pages 119- 147

"The Chagrin Falls Exempted Village School has been designated as a hospital center by the Civilian Defense Organization and an $8000 allotment has been assigned for equipment and supplies."

1953-1954 Student Handbook   Page 122

"We Were Young Tigers... Young women of the fifties, we did it all for you; but we were young tigers, and truth be known, we did it for a bit of glory, too...."

Jon Fitzpatrick '54, student   Page 127-128

" You handled them with a paddle, and you didn't call home and ask pop for permission to whale him one; you just hauled off and fired him one and that was it."

Norm Fry, teacher   Page 132

"The Chagrin School Board of Education passed a motion to name the new elementary school in honor of the Superintendent Lewis Sands....
The school will be called 'Sands Elementary School.'"

Chagrin Falls Exponent, August 24, 1956 Page 136

Acknowledgments

On several occasions, as the book was in its early stages, I mailed copies to respected local historians, Kathy Watterson, Annie Gumprecht and Yolita Rausche. I wanted to make sure that I was moving in the right direction before I went any further. With their acknowledgements that I was factually correct, I continued. Yolita provided me with more detailed architectural information concerning the first schools located on the Philomethian Street property. You will find those specific details throughout the book. Yolita and Chagrin Falls Preservation always do their homework thoroughly. I wish Annie were still alive to see how I added some of her colorful historical tidbits to the book.

The Chagrin Falls Historical Society and Laura Gorretta were excellent sources of information. While Laura was writing <u>Chagrin Falls - An Ohio Village History</u>, we were in constant communication, always helping each other with particular historical facts and issues. We know that you can't separate the history of the village and its schools. They grew together.

Alumni Association secretary, Marilyn Wyville, continuously inspired me to write this history. She kept the pressure on me for years. Upon mentioning a certain fact or relating a particular story, she would say, "Write that down!" Thanks, Marilyn, for all of your help with typing and proofreading. She turned poorly-written sentences into neatly typed pages.

I owe Brian McKenna '88, our new alumni director, and our new alumni secretary, Connie Bridges Miralia '83, a much-needed thank you for their patience during the transition process, while I struggled to complete the book.

Barbara Bullock Hubbard '52, as usual, was a very competent proofreader and helpful editor. Her loyalty to the Alumni Association since its inception is greatly appreciated.

Scanning of photographs for the book began in the capable hands of Julie Andrews. Though an Orange High School graduate, she is becoming a real Chagrinite!

Reed Carpenter '62 spearheaded the production of this book. He was instrumental in the photo collection process and is the master of many skills. Terry Taggart's '62 professional services have made this book's design, layout and graphics an outstanding and unique publication. His artistic ability is well known in the Chagrin Falls community.

Last of all, I owe much to Superintendent David Axner for allowing the Chagrin Falls Alumni Association to grow as it has. Without his support through the years and the encouragement of previous superintendents, Arlene Rieger, Jake Hudson and Ruth Ann Plate, it could have "withered on the vine." I thank them for continuously nourishing it so that it didn't.

Author's Note

I have tried to make this history as accurate as possible concerning names, dates, locations and events. There were times when pursuing accuracy was difficult. I am certainly open to criticism and corrections. Confirmation still remains sketchy as to where, for example, some of the early schoolhouses were first built and how long they existed. Even the original board of education minutes failed to describe specific locations. On most occasions, I used the date or location that had best evidence of fact. Once again, if necessary, a discussion of needed corrections is encouraged. Many quotations in the book display the phrase "copy undisturbed from original source." It seemed appropriate to keep the quotation as original as possible to help understand the proper context. I did not use them where I did not feel they were necessary.

Introduction

The will of the people of the Chagrin Falls community to provide a strong education for its children is the most important link to its educational history. The close ties and pride from the community for its schools has been demonstrated for over 170 years. Today's students and those responsible for their education remain part of the fabric of the history of the Chagrin Falls Schools.

Future president of the United States, James A. Garfield, was often called upon to speak at holiday celebrations in Chagrin Falls. On one such occasion he stated: "These pioneers know well that the three great forces which constitute the strength and glory of a free government are the family, the school and the church. These three they planted here . . . "

(James A. Garfield, Chagrin Falls, 1873)

First Annual

The Annual

THE ANNUAL

1918

C. F. H. S.
1911

...HAM, "Bill"
... Glee '17, '18, '19, 20;
... Football '18, '19, '20;
... Debating (Pres. '20),
...ness Manager.

...aters and a very good one.
...ery dignified but you'd be
...en he forgets his dignity.
...Basket Ball players this year.
...all field. Philip, like a few
...boys of our class has quite an affinity for
...oom.

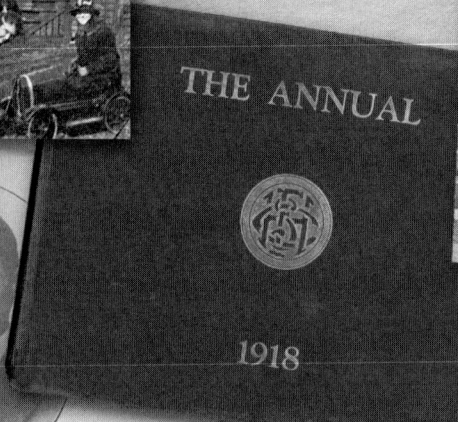

ARLIE CLINE, "Cliney"
English Course. Football '19-'20, Track Manager, Boys' G... Phidelphian Debating, Editorial Boar...

Arlie, our ...... prominent member of the Senior ...... fond of visiting the Junior roo...... the hall at the drinking fountain...... room door with "her". He is alwa...... somewhere, running into whoeve...... is away. Nevertheless, Arlie is a ...... minute.

...Scientific 9, 20;
...yone De...

...nny, laug......
...d student...... been a
...to lose o...... is go-
...... grad-
...And pleasant, too, to...

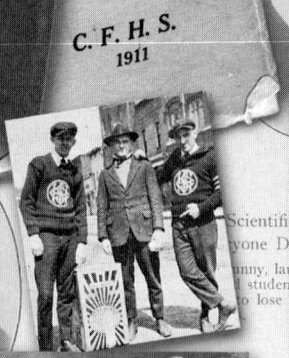

LEOTA...
Scientific Cours...
Glee '20, Phidelphi...
bate, Editorial Boar...

Leota is what you...
...any responsible work...
one to serve, for ...
...make things go. ...
...and her good scho...

...etic and sure to
...many activities
...success for

...VE, "Jas"
... Glee '20, Track '17,
...ting, Triangular De-

...lads who is full of live-
...erests included this year.
...rath, and mischief, and
...strong in the latter. During the lat-
...enior year Babe seems to be taking up
...We wonder why?

The Old

...PES, "Bill"
...Club '20, Basket B...
...'19-'20

FRANC...
Commercial ...

The New

...ve that:

...ings ye sing
...miles ye wear,
...aking the sun shine
..."

One-room Schoolhouses Emerged Throughout The Village

A school board was established-consolidation led to a Union School - the 19th century ended with the schools having an excellent reputation.

Chagrin Falls was first settled by pioneers from New England (circa 1833). These early pioneers were seeking a location that could provide them waterpower for various industries. With the river providing sufficient waterpower and surrounding virgin forests to provide lumber for building, Chagrin Falls became a thriving mill town with a vision of becoming an industrial center between the Youngstown/Warren area and Cleveland. The name of the river and village comes from an Anglicized version of the name of a French trader, Francois Seguin, who traded with Native-Americans in this area in the mid 1750's. Some early historical documents referred to the area as the "High Falls."

Noah Graves is considered one of the founders of the village. He later was a member of one of the first Chagrin Falls Boards of Education which originated in 1849. As the number of families grew in those first few years, the education of their children was a major concern. Socrates once proclaimed that, "There is only one good, knowledge; and only one evil, ignorance." Education became the way to combat the evil of ignorance.

In early colonial Pennsylvania, it was mandated in one province that all twelve-year-olds "be instructed in reading and writing…" and taught a useful trade or skill so that "the poor may work to live, and the rich, if they become poor, may not want."

The exact location of early

schoolhouses is a difficult task to substantiate. Even the original board of education minutes failed to describe specific places. Several important early histories did write of schools, for example, existing on West Washington Street (then named Pearl Street), Cottage Street, Maple Street and others. However, the board minutes often referred to them as the schoolhouse near "Gardner's House" or "Church's property" or the "schoolhouse on the north side of the river," or "schoolhouse on the south side of the river." Specific dates were difficult to establish as to when they existed and for how long. Henry Church, Jr., the second child born in Chagrin Falls and the carver of Squaw Rock in the South Chagrin Reservation of the Cleveland Metro Park System, drew sketches of some of those early schoolhouses. They are the only pictorial record of the first schools in Chagrin Falls.

The first schoolhouse was built in Chagrin Falls around 1835 (the actual date is uncertain). It is thought to have stood on the east side of Main Street, approximately where the I.O.O.F. (International Order of Odd Fellows) building (Dink's Restaurant) is located. However, there is some question that it might have been situated to the west of Main Street, which is now North Franklin Street. The debate in location is due to the fact that the Geauga and Cuyahoga County line in the early 1830's was actually Main Street itself. Chagrin Falls was considered a Cuyahoga County village. Since the Geauga County line was moved eastward in 1841, it matters little as to whether it was east or west of Main Street.

The schoolhouse was constructed of slab wood among the forest of trees in the center of the village. A student described the school as being "in the

This is a sketch by Henry Church, Jr. of what is thought to be the first schoolhouse in the village. It was located where the I.O.O.F Building is located on East Main Street.

woods in the heart of our village." What is now Triangle Park was probably part of the children's playground.

Miss Almeda Vincent, daughter of the village's first doctor, was the first teacher at the schoolhouse and was paid 50 cents a week. As all early teachers did, she "boarded around," meaning that she would live with the families of her students. The first schools were not free, but were supported in part by public monies. Also, the parents agreed to pay an arranged amount for the education of the young students.

It should be noted that one historical source placed the first school in Chagrin Falls on East Cottage Street. Possibly Noah Graves provided funds for this school which may have been moved and remodeled into a residence that is still standing today. Noah's daughter, Mary, is thought to have been the teacher.

Plans for building a college in the village were mentioned in several early histories of Chagrin Falls. It was to be located on the hill northeast of the village between East Cottage and East Summit Streets and was chartered in 1838 by the Ohio Legislature as the High Falls Primary Institute. Perhaps the aftermath of the financial panic of 1837 might have cancelled that ambitious plan, for the school of "higher education" never occurred.

After the first schoolhouse was built, other families organized their own learning centers and became the instructors. Most of the early one-room schoolhouses in the village were small in nature, poorly heated, often dirty and with slab benches. A few were church

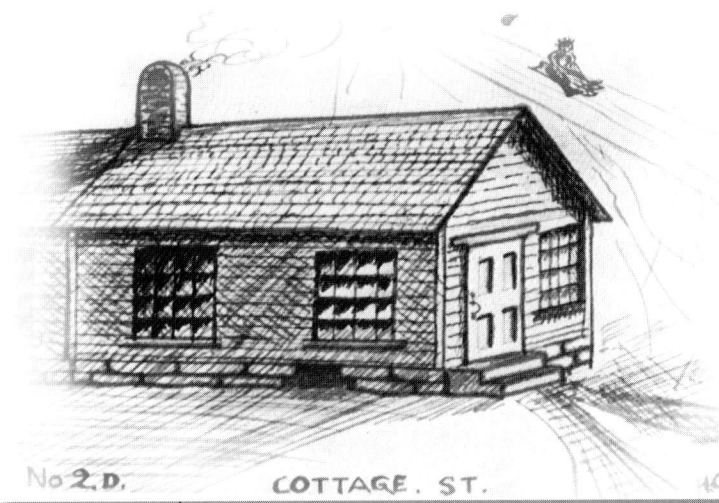

affiliated. These learning centers were located in various areas of the village. The success of these early schools often depended on the skills and popularity of the teacher.

An early schoolhouse was located at the end of "school lane," an alley between Orange Street and East Cottage Streets. That alley is the present Valley Lutheran Church driveway and parking area.

Austin Church, born in Chagrin Falls in 1838, attended school until he was seventeen, remembered attending this district school (circa 1840's-1850's). In his written reminiscences (1911), he included a humorous story about a teacher at this school, Mr. Ives (copy undisturbed from original source):

This Mr. Ives was an oldish man and I remember one day he wanted to leave the school for a few minutes and he spoke to one of the older scholars (Foster) to take charge of the school. Foster went out on the floor for business but kept his eye on Mr. Ives through the window. Soon as the old man was out of sight Foster says 'School is dismissed' and when the teacher came back not a soul was in the house nor in sight. Next day the school convened as usual. Foster was asked to stand up. 'Foster, I want to ask you why you dismissed school yesterday when I left it in your charge.' 'You left it my charge and I had a right to.' After looking at each other for a moment Ives says, 'Take your seat.'

At another time in the early spring the side door was open but snow was on the ground and good sliding and one of those warm first days of spring. My brother and two other boys got on a long sled at recess and came down the hill at breakneck speed and to play a little joke ran the sled right into the open door. Things didn't work out as they expected. The moment the sled struck the bare floor; it stopped so suddenly all three went bobbing across the floor. The sled was left in the door, they on the other side of the room. That schoolhouse and the hill has a history of their own and the old oak tree up near the top where we used to get permission to go in the shade and study.

No 3. D.   North. St.   H.C.

Another schoolhouse was located at the corner of North Street and High Street. That location is presently referred to as Franklin Park.

No4. D.   WASHINGTON. ST.   H.C.

Yet another schoolhouse was built on East Washington Street near South Main Street on the south side of the river One historical source credits the Bible Christian Church, often referred to as the "English Church", for building this school. This congregation was composed of English immigrants who arrived in the village around 1845. Their church was built in 1851 on Bell Street near the present day Federated Church.

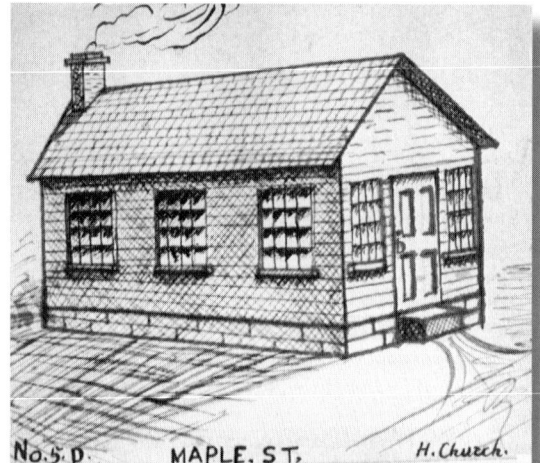

No. 5. D.   MAPLE. ST.   H. Church.

Another early historical reference referred a schoolhouse located on the northwest corner of Maple Street and Water Street. This school was eventually moved and is presently part of a residence on Olive Street.

Most historical sources claim that the most popular early schoolhouse was located in 1837 on the second floor of the "Robert Barrow home" on Pearl Street which is now named West Washington Street. This school is thought to be the present residence at 55 West Washington Street. This "select school" (private school) was conducted by Reverend Lorenzo D. Williams. He and his wife Olive moved to Chagrin Falls in 1837.

Reverend Williams wrote a letter dated November 18, 1837 to his parents in Monroe County, New York, with a description of a situation in regard to this school:

We commenced our school on the 2nd of this month but the inhabitants, feeling themselves unable to support a district and a select school at the same time, solicited us to take the Dist. School under our supervision so as to secure the public money. Thinking that this would be the better course for a while, till we get our names up as teachers, we have consented to do so for 3 months at 40$ per month and board ourselves. Small wages to be sure, but we shall be certain of our pay, and as we are allowed to take in scholars from out the dist. We shall be preparing for a better school by & by, if we choose to teach. The Dist. School. commences Monday

next. Last Friday evening I got the inhabitants of the dist. together and delivered them an address on sch. teaching. It took very well. We shall receive about 45$ public money.

To help his meager income as a teacher and part-time minister, he requested from the federal government the position of Postmaster of Chagrin Falls. The appointment was granted, and L. D. Williams became the first Postmaster of Chagrin Falls in 1839.

Reverend Williams was licensed to preach and perform the sacraments of the Methodist Church. His "select school" was later integrated into a newly chartered seminary by the state legislature in 1839. He is named as one of the incorporators. This school was conducted in the interest of the Methodist Episcopal Church but under private ownership. It was named the Asbury Seminary, probably in honor of Bishop Asbury of the Methodist Church. Reverend Williams became its first principal. The seminary was a framed building built on the west side of Philomethian Street. The word "philomethian" apparently derives from the Greek word "philomethan," meaning "love of learning."

In the Geauga County newspaper, The Geauga Republican and Whig, Volume I, September 9, 1843, an article appeared announcing the opening of the new school:

ASBURY SEMINARY

at Chagrin Falls

This large and commodious building 33 feet by 70 feet is erected for the school and the lower story, consisting of a large chapel, one room for young ladies and two other recitation rooms will be completed by the commencement of the term, and the whole edifice will probably be

No.6.D.   ASBURY SEMINARY.

finished by the quarter following.

Instruction will be given in all the branches usually taught in seminaries of learning.

Particular attention will be paid to students who intend to teach. A suitable course of instruction will also be adopted for such as wish to qualify themselves for business life. Those desiring to enter college will be able at this institution to take a thorough preparatory course.

The French will be taught at the Department of Languages. Chemistry will be illustrated by experiments.

The following persons constitute the Board of Instructors:

Rev. L.D. Williams, Principal

Rev. M. Mattison, A.M., Prof of Languages

The Asbury Seminary was built in 1843 on Philomethian Street. It was originally thought to be a preparatory school for Allegheny College, a Methodist school in Meadville, PA. However, the college has no record of such a connection. The building was torn down for salvage in 1893. This sketch of the school was done by Henry Church, Jr.

Reuben H. Harris, A.M., Professor of Mathematics

Mrs. Almedah Boothe, Preceptress Asbury Seminary

Boarding can be obtained at low prices.

There is some thought that the seminary acted as a preparatory school for Allegheny College in Meadville, Pennsylvania; however, Allegheny College has no record of such a connection. The Asbury Seminary, as in most early seminaries, also offered teacher training and business courses.

The Reverend Williams later became a professor of natural sciences and mathematics at Allegheny College and was appointed vice-president of Allegheny College in 1857. While serving as vice-president until 1863, he also served as a chaplain with the 111th Pennsylvania Volunteers in the Civil War. He and his family had been active abolitionists before the Civil War.

Reverend Williams died on October 14, 1878. Three days later, as the hearse waited for his coffin in front of his home in Meadville, Pennsylvania, his wife fell dead next to his coffin. On October 18, 1878, a double funeral took place. It was largely attended by faculty, students and alumni of Allegheny College and the citizens of Meadville. His importance in the early history of the Chagrin Falls Schools was clearly noted in his obituary in the local weekly newspaper, Chagrin Falls Exponent.

In 1848 an Asbury Seminary student, Newton S. Sheldon, wrote the following letter to his cousin describing the school and village of Chagrin Falls (copy undisturbed from original source):

Dear Cousin,   December 9, 1848

I now sit down to pen you a few lines as I am not very busy today as our school does not keep. One reason that I have delayed such a length of time is that Newel wrote to you a short time after I received your letter and another is that I thought I would wait until I found out where I was going to spend the winter. I left home two weeks ago today and came out here and commenced school the following Monday at the Asbury Seminary with Mr. G.B. Hawkins as Principle and Mrs. E.M. Wilson and Mrs. Marsh as assisting teachers. The school is quite large, consisting in all of about 100 scholars. In the chapel there is about 75 scholars of which 15

are gentlemen and 10 are ladies. Mrs. Marsh has the charge of the other 25 which are principle small scholars. The 75 study in the chapel under Mr. Hawkins and go into the recitations room and recite to Mrs. Wilson as she hears recitations through the whole day. In the forenoon she hears 1st a class in Geography and Mental Arithmetic ½ hour and 2nd Adams Arithmetic ¾ hr., 3rd Reading ¾ hr., 4th 1st Class in Browns Grammar ½ an hour and ½ an hour is devoted in the morning exercise to calling the roll, reading a chapter in The Testament and prayer.

In the afternoon 1st recitation 2nd class in Grammar ¾ hr., 2nd Astronomy ½ do, 3rd Algebra ¾ do, 4th Writing and Drawing ½ do, 5th French and Music ½ do. Mr. Hawkins hears recitations in Philosophy, Perkins 2nd Edition Arithmetic, Latin, Geometry, Phisiology, and shows the scholars when they want help. I am studying Adams Arithmetic, Brown Grammar, Astronomy, Algebra and Philosophy. There is 40 and 50 in one class studying Adams Arithmetic, 20 or 30 Grammar, and 6 in Astronomy, and 9 in algebra, and 10 in Philosophy. I wish you were here to write compositions with the rest of us for be it—remembered that the gentlemen have to write a composition and declaim every other Saturday (which is wholly devoted to reading compositions and speaking pieces) and each lady has to read a composition and jointly produce a pamphlet form called the ladies miscellany which they have to sustain with pieces of their own composing. They choose one of their number every two weeks to recite the pieces off into this pamphlet, and read it the same day their compositions are read and declaiming done. If they do not present a composition, he very pleasant and gives me an

Schools

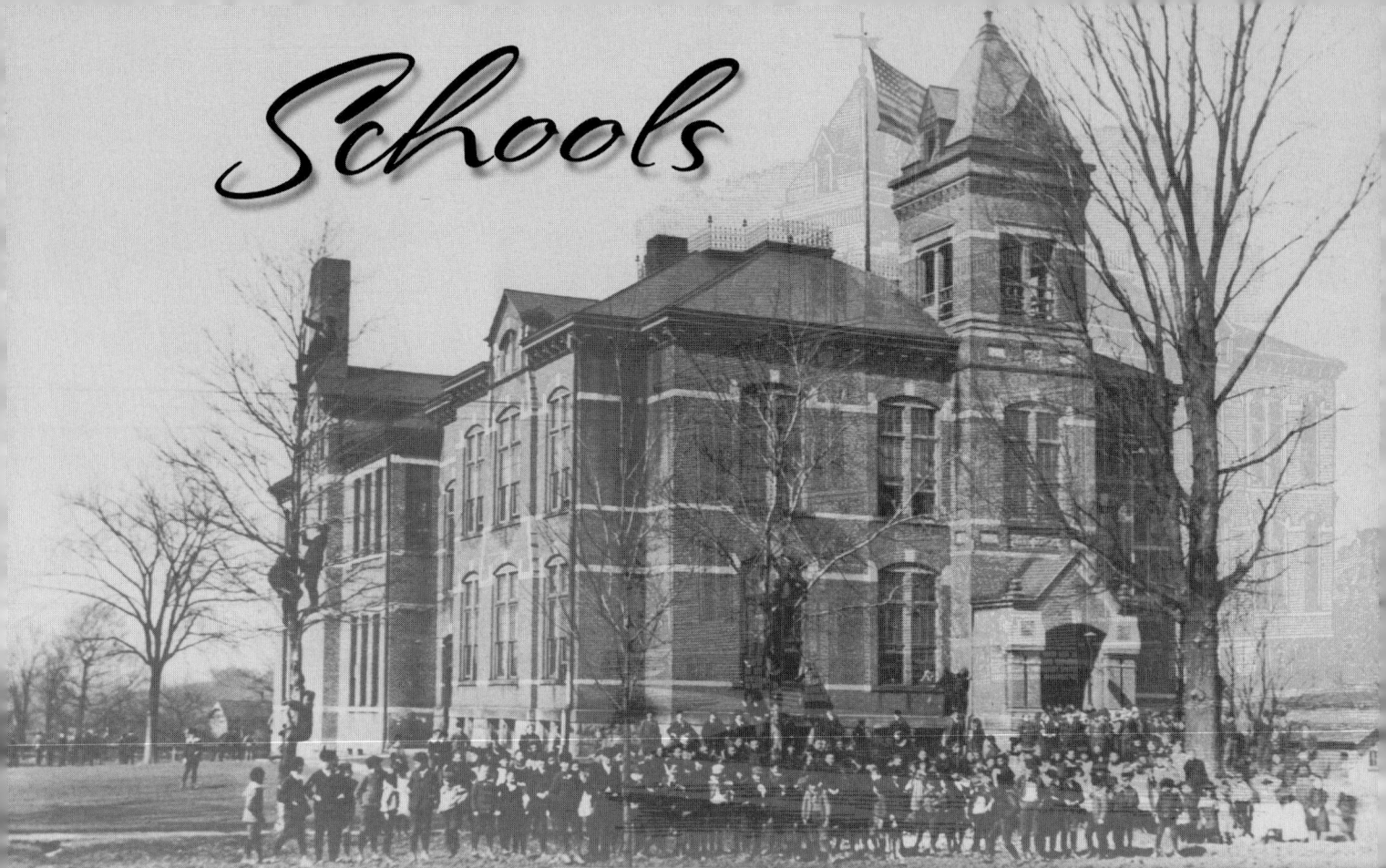

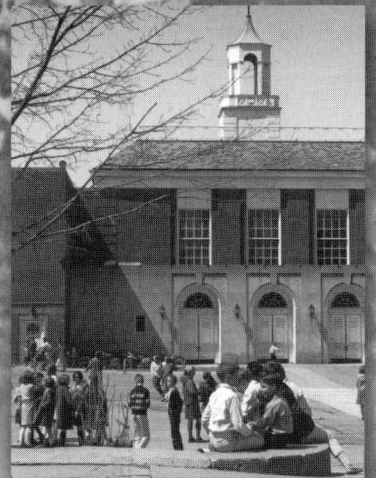

opportunity of studying all of the time, only when I am occupied at recitations. As I believe you were never here at the falls, I will try to give you a brief description of the place. Its populations is about 1500 inhabitants, it is not far from 15 miles to Mantua from here, and is situated a little north of west from Auburn. The village is situated on the banks of the Chagrin River and the most business part of it is down in the hollow, the banks being quite high after you get back a little short distance from the stream. As you come into the village from any direction, you cannot see the place until you get almost into it for when you get onto the top of the hill, you can look down upon the whole village, and as the houses are mostly painted white, it looks both neat and handsome. The water privileges was what laid the foundation of the place, though the stream is not very large, but there being quite a fall in the water gives a place for 8 dams within one mile, which supply water for some 10 or 12 mills and factories. In one place there is a natural falls where it pours over a projecting rock about 10 feet. The place contains 2 taverns, 6 stores, a number of groceries and shops of all descriptions. There are also three meetinghouses, Methodist, Presbyterian and a union house belong ½ to Baptist and Protestant Methodist. The Seminary is situated in the east part of the village upon the hill. It is quite a large building, being 30 x 70 feet on the ground and 2 stories high. It is painted and has a belfry and a bell. The south end of the lower story is done off into a large room called the Chapel. Then there is a hall running through from east to west, and on the north end, there is a large recitations room for the scholars and a room where the assistant teachers live. The upper story is not done off at all. I believe that I have given you as good as a description of the place here as time and paper will allow

From your affectionate cousin
Newton S. Sheldon

I do not know for certain whether I shall be here more than 5 months or not.

Franklin Walters was a 21-year-old carpenter in 1853, who worked for his father, Reuben Walters, in the Chagrin Falls area. Reuben had another son who was a doctor in the village for a long period of time who occupied a house at the corner of South Main Street and May Court. Records indicate that Walters Road was named after this family.

Franklin kept a diary in 1853 and 1854. In it he described working with his father in helping to finish the second floor of the Asbury Seminary. He noted in his diary: "This forenoon went over and helped get new bell up into the belfry. It is a fine one, weighing 95 lbs."

That "Seminary Bell" is the bell that was put into the new Chagrin Falls Union School belfry on Philomethian Street in 1885. When that school was torn down in 1940, the bell was put in storage in the boiler room of the new 1940 addition to the 1914 high school building facing East Washington Street. In 1965 after the new high school building and gymnasium were completed at the old fairgrounds on East Washington Street, the bell was placed inside an outdoor structure and used as a Victory Bell at the Friday night football games.

John Blazer '67 remembered the following in regard to the bell's installation:

I don't recall how the idea for the Victory Bell originated; it could have been something as simple as a remark by the building's custodian, John Hlad, to my mother, Naomi Blazer, who worked in the middle school principal's office at the time. Regardless, it became a topic of discussion in the high school Student Council of which I was a member.

The job of planning fell to me. The construction labor for the pad and piers was donated by my neighbor Stuart Wendl, a mason. I think the clapper was removed and kept in Coach Quesinberry's office so that the bell would only be rung at the appropriate times.

I recall one football game victory rally in the fall of 1965 or 1966 when a well-meaning, spirited, but misguided classmate couldn't wait for the clapper and he rang the bell by striking it with a brick, leaving scars on the bell.

Ultimately, in 1968, the bell was stolen, later recaptured and then stolen again in 1970. Mike Solether '69 has written the following about the first recapture of the Chagrin Falls Victory Bell:

I can't remember the exact date or complete circumstances for this event,

but I do remember the following:

It was the fall of 1968. The Chagrin Falls Tigers were not having a good year on the gridiron. Seems Coach Piai couldn't motivate his players to the level of his past teams. It wasn't that they weren't trying, but the Chagrin Valley Conference was changing. The other communities were growing and we were not.

There had to be something done to revitalize the spirit. Earlier in 1968 our Victory Bell was stolen. Yes, that was it! Find the bell, present it at a pep rally and all would change for the better.

Under the leadership of Ken Melby '69, the investigation began. After a short while it was learned that a band of Solon Comets had taken the bell. Ken had found out the name and address of one of the perpetrators.

One Thursday afternoon after school, the word went out. We were going to bring our bell back home. The football players could do this then, as practice on this day was done under the lights at night. All who wanted to show a display of force were asked to participate. About 40 people assembled in the senior parking lot. Our destination was a home in the area of Miles and Harper Roads. Let's go!

When we arrived, we stood outside the house. Ken knocked on the door. A sheepish teenager answered the door. A conversation took place. Satisfied, Melby turned and walked down to us. The bell is in a field off Cannon Road.

Here we went again. At the farmhouse we were greeted with the same result. 'The bell is in that field,' the boy said. After a short hike, we found what we were looking for. Mission accomplished!

The next day at the pep rally, the Victory Bell was presented to the high school. We all cheered! It didn't matter, though. We still lost the game that night. All in all, we only won two games the entire season. But we now had our bell returned to its proper home.

The Victory Bell was again stolen a few years after its return. It is now up to another class to do the work to find it and return it to its proper home.

The bell was taken once again in the fall of 1970. It is thought to have been stolen the week of the West Geauga or Kenston football game. The search continues for our beloved historical bell.

Confirmation remains sketchy as to when some of these early schools were first built or when each closed. To add to the uncertainty of locations and dates of existence of our early schools, Austin Church wrote in his reminiscences:

A lady by the name of Angeline Earl taught several terms of school in a room over Mr. Waldron's shoe store on the north side of the river (circa 1837). Some of the residents of the place remembered attending a school in the "Bryant" house on Cottage, the school taught by a Miss Hemmingway, and who was so kind to her pupils as to warm the benches for them on cold mornings and to present them with pieces of crimped pink paper as rewards of merit for conduct.

Austin continued:

To return to 1840 we find there was a district school taught by Miss Sarah Bancroft, in a slab shanty with slab benches on the lot now owned by Miss Fowler on Orange. I went to a select school in the Town Hall, one or two terms taught by "Priest" (Rev. E.D.) Taylor (circa 1850) and one or two

terms to Darrus Layman who taught a select school in the old Philadelphia block and where I learned more than in all the others put together.

Some district schools often had different teachers for spring, summer, fall and winter terms. Teaching was not a preferred profession, but women found it a job that they could easily acquire.

Champion Library Hall was built in 1847. It provided a public lecture room and a gallery for library books. It is presently the Chagrin Falls Township Hall. The building was built as the village's first library thanks to Aristarchus Champion, a Yale graduate, lawyer, benefactor, philanthropist and a land speculator from Rochester, New York, who built the Greek Revival Town Hall and donated 600 to 800 volumes of books. He was the nephew of Moses Cleaveland, the founder of the city of Cleveland. The building was also used as a lecture hall for community events. It was frequently used by Chagrin Falls Abolitionists before the Civil War.

In 1856 Aristarchus Champion, for some unexplained reason, lost interest in the village, removed his books from the library and returned them to Rochester, New York. He left the building to his agent, Royal Taylor.

In 1850 the Reverend E. D. Taylor of the Congregational Church and his wife were teachers at an excellent "select school" in the newly built Champion Library Hall on Main Street in the village. C. T. Blakeslee in his manuscript, <u>History of Chagrin Falls and Vicinity</u>, written in 1874, wrote:

This building was occupied for a few years soon after it was erected, by Rev. E. D. Taylor and lady, for a private school, and the influence they had over our children and youth,

under their instruction there if no
other good had been experienced
from the erection of that hall, would
abundantly pay for its cost. Our
coming generation had enjoyed only
such advantages as a new settlement
could furnish for their general
improvement, when Mr. Taylor came
here, as pastor of Congregational
church, where he only received a
small and insufficient salary for the
support of his family. Both himself
and his estimable lady were well
qualified to teach; not in the school
room merely, but as a christian
gentleman and christian lady, their
influence both in the school room and
out of the school room was morally
and educationally elevating, and
their influence over their pupils in
this respect, is still manifest as they
had grown up to maturity. Besides
some we have heretofore mentioned, a
number of others speak of that school

as the place where they first felt those
aspirations after a useful manhood
and womanhood, which they are now
trying to realize.

In 1849, when the Ohio legislature
established a state-wide education
system, it decreed local boards of
education. Therefore, a volunteer,
self-appointed Chagrin Falls Board
of Education was formed. The first
organizational meeting was held May
25, 1849, when Stephen Smith was
appointed its first president. The board
had $31.67 in its fund. As a result of
that meeting, they posted the following
announcement throughout the village:

A school meeting will be called
on Tuesday evening, June the 12th, at
early candlelight at the North School
House then and there to vote for or
against the purchasing of sites and
erection of two or more schoolhouses

and such other business as of right come before the meeting.

At that June meeting, the citizens of the village voted to build two or more schoolhouses and to raise $1,000 to purchase sites and build the schools "as soon as is necessary and practicable." According to the original board minutes:

". . . that $500 be raised as soon as may be for the erection of schoolhouses, and also that we call for a tax of four mills on the dollar for school purposes and that four schools begin on the first of July or as soon after as is convenient."

That first book of minutes from the Chagrin Falls Board of Education is presently located in the Chagrin Falls Schools' Historical Preservation room.

Four teachers were immediately hired with a salary of $1.50 per week and told to acquire "room and board" within the village. Often, families took turns providing a room and meals for the "schoolmarm" or "professor" as some male teachers were called. Dr. A. H. Harlow was hired to teach the high school.

The length of a school term seemed to vary by the school. The young scholars did not have to attend the schoolhouse nearest their residence; they could attend the school that they liked best.

On many occasions school was an on-again, off-again sort of thing. In some more rural areas, school terms began and ended at times which would leave the children free to work on the family farm during the busy planting and harvest times. Children attended school during the summer and winter, while the school was closed in the spring and fall. Because of this, some youngsters quit high school or started to school at the age of six but did not graduate until they were 21 years old.

It should be noted that these early teachers had to undergo the scrutiny of a board of examiners to see if they were qualified to teach at a district school. The first board, appointed in 1849 by the board of education, consisted of General Alanson Knox, a lawyer; C. T. Blakeslee, who later wrote a history of the village in 1874; and Dr. A. H. Harlow, who became superintendent of schools from 1857 to January 1860.

General Knox had been a member of the Massachusetts Militia before moving to Chagrin Falls in a covered wagon in 1840. In 1845 he became the first treasurer in the newly formed Chagrin Falls Township.

Dr. A. H. Harlow administered his own select school in the village, the Chagrin Falls Commercial Institute. The school had a very extensive curriculum. At one time, the future President of the United States, James A. Garfield, was a student in this school.

The Harmonial Institute was another school of higher learning that existed during this era. It was established in 1857 by several distinguished residents of the village. Its classes were conducted in the Town Hall.

In 1849 the board of education adopted McGuffey's Eclectic Reader and Ray's Arithmetic as the primary textbooks for the schools.

By March 1850, there was $557 in the school fund and $441.20 in the building fund. Things, at least financially, were looking up, but there were other problems. The first annual report was read in May 1850, in which "the schools were represented as not being in a very flourishing condition." What the problem or problems were remains unknown.

Noah Graves, one of the founding fathers, was elected to the board of education at that meeting along with Phineas Upham. A year later, Abel Fisher was appointed to replace Graves, "who has neglected to attend the meetings of the board or qualify for office." All must have been forgiven just a year later when he was elected to a three-year term.

Interestingly, by 1850, almost all the log cabins in the immediate area of Chagrin Falls had been replaced by framed houses.

For a few years in the early 1850s, it was quite probable that Lysander and John Hamlin, who went on to become very famous and make a fortune from selling "snake oil," attended schools in Chagrin Falls before moving on to Chicago. Their names are in the school board's first 1850 census. The product was Hamlin's Wizard Oil, and it became one of the best-known liniments in the country. They toured America in special wagons and while conducting circus-like shows, sold their cure-all liniments.

Several years later, during a board meeting on May 15, 1852, it was resolved, "that the board be requested to appoint a superintendent of schools and pay a reasonable compensation for his services." Thus, one week later, on a motion by board member, Noah Graves, Royal Taylor was appointed superintendent for the ensuing year and examiner for three years. Royal Taylor was a land agent for Aristarchus Champion.

Since 1852, twenty-eight people have served as superintendent of the Chagrin Falls Schools with W. S. Hayden performing the duties on two different occasions. At one time, he attended a district school in the village. Until the superintendency of Dr. Robert Finley in 1958, all superintendents were teachers and at some time during their tenure did some classroom teaching. Most

of them preferred to teach and did so voluntarily. However, in contracts with earlier superintendents, it was a part of their contract that they teach so many classes per day. Superintendent L. N. Drake (1916-1920) successfully coached men's basketball and baseball. A list of the superintendents in the 1800s and the dates of their tenure follows:

Royal Taylor: May, 1852-1855

L. D. Mix: May, 1855-Nov., 1855

A. T. Allen: Nov., 1855-1857

Dr. Harlow: 1857-Jan., 1860

Jas. Vincent: 1860-1864

W. S. Hayden: 1864-1871

Geo. F. Wright: 1871-1876

C. C. Hubbell: 1876-1878

C. F. Stokey: 1878-1879

W. S. Hayde: 1879-1883

C. W. Randall: 1883-1887

R. M Collins: 1887-1888

F. P. Shumaker: 1888-1901

In organizing the schoolhouses throughout the village, the board in October 1852 resolved the following:

...that spelling, reading, writing, grammar, geography and arithmetic may be taught in the various primary schools in this village during the next fall and winter, and that those scholars who attend the select (private) schools shall be entitled to a reasonable share of the public monies, the amount to be determined by the board of education, provided that board of education may determine what scholars shall attend such select (private) schools.

When the first public schools were established in the eighteenth century, geography was not one of the subjects taught. It was well into the nineteenth century before physical and world geography were added to

Circa 1900's
East Cuyahoga County
Fairgrounds
Union Fair Association
Purchased Fairgrounds
in 1873 -
photo circa 1900's

Fairgrounds

the curriculum. Chagrin Falls was considered a progressive school because geography was part of the curriculum in the school system's first years.

Spelling was certainly emphasized. Austin Church remembered having interscholastic "spelling downs":

> Later as I grew older, our school and a school at Bentleyville used to match each other for spelling down, as we called it. A number of times our school would walk down to the Bentleyville School always in the evening and then get whipped in spelling down. And they used to come up and visit us at home and whip us right at home. The sequel of it was that they had one of the best spellers in either school. Mary Kent was always on her feet to the last. Years after, she married Col. Pritchard who figured in the capture of Jeff Davis.

During the American Civil War, Union General Benjamin F. Pritchard was responsible for the capture of the President of the Confederate States of America, Jefferson Davis. Davis was attempting to flee from capture dressed in women's clothing. General Pritchard was a resident of Chagrin Falls for some years before the Civil War and had attended Reverend Taylor's "select school" at the Town Hall for a few terms.

In February 1853, the board reported that Royal Taylor received eight dollars a week for his work as superintendent of schools in 1852, and in April, the board voted to raise teacher salaries to two dollars per week.

In 1855 the first library books were bought for the schools. Until this time library books were borrowed from village residents. In the early 1850s William Waldron, owner of a local drugstore on Main Street, rented his own books to the school board.

Also in July 1855, for some mysterious reason, the board minutes read: "Unanimously resolved that school not be discontinued for the present."

Teacher salaries were raised to $2.50 per week in April 1856. In May, the board voted to "pay superintendent for each visit he has made to school (13)."

In July 1857, the board of education established some new rules which all teachers were expected to enforce, in addition to "all rules and regulations as appropriate to teachers generally." These new "rules for students" were as follows:

1. *There shall be no talking or whispering in the hours of school without permission so to do.*

2. *There shall be no moving around the room, hitching upon the seats or unnecessary noise shall in any case be allowed.*

3. *Scholars shall be required to attend with assiduity to their studies during the hour of school, and at recess shall not remain out over five minutes and when out shall not be permitted to holler and make unnecessary noise, shall go into no neighbor's yard without permission, shall not be permitted to do any injury to any of the buildings connected with the school property inside or out.*

4. *Any scholar refusing to submit to and obey in any particular the foregoing rules shall be dealt with and punished as the teacher thinks most suitable and proper.*

Repeat offenders were to be reported to the superintendent and expelled unless "reformation, improvement and more were promised." The board required all teachers to enforce these rules to maintain their employment as teachers. If found not enforcing these rules, a teacher could be dismissed.

Clarence A. Vincent, D.D., wrote in his manuscript, <u>Chagrin Falls and Vicinity from 1865 to 1880</u>, concerning the difficulty for teachers to keep order in the early schools, especially at recess time:

It was a difficult task to keep the boys from rushing pell-mell down the aisle, pushing one another over the seats and slamming the door in the face of the boy following. Most teachers had the pupils march out, and even then, when they drew near the door, it was difficult to hold them from rushing.

My aunt who taught in the fifties (1850s) was greatly sought after because of her powers of disciplining. The trustees supported a teacher who enforced discipline.

Vincent continued:

Having later taught in such a one-roomed schoolhouse, I give credit to the ability and patience of most of the teachers of that early day.

He concluded with a comparison of the one-room schoolhouse to the newly organized "high school" in 1858:

The high school at Chagrin Falls had the advantage of having the pupils at that grade together and of a recitation room for the assistant principal in addition to the main room where usually the principal taught. The schools in most of the villages were very much alike. They were not graded as they came to be later. They would fit a person in a way to enter the middle preparatory classes at colleges.

For many of those early teachers, their job was more than teaching the three R's. They were also the school nurse, social worker and guidance counselor. They policed playground fights, supervised recesses and coped with some parents who saw no need for their children to have an education of any kind.

A school census was taken in 1858, and according to the September 20 board minutes, the result was: "north side of river - 72 males, 75 females and 2 colored females; south side of river - 91 males and 105 females. Total 345. (Ages 5-21.)"

In 1858 the Asbury Seminary was closed and purchased by the board of education for public school purposes. The citizens of the village voted to pay $1,300 for the Asbury Seminary and "to tax themselves for the purpose." The seminary was in need of work, and after much renovation (windows repaired, walls plastered, chimneys moved, the outside painted, well dug, walls papered, two cold stoves installed, gateways repaired, a fence made and chairs and/or desks installed), the seminary opened as the new "Chagrin Falls High School" on December 20, 1858. However, the building was always referred to as the "Seminary." The board then began to consolidate village schoolhouses into a "Union School."

Westel W. Hunt, a tuition student from Russell Township at the Chagrin Falls Union School (formerly Asbury Seminary), wrote an essay in 1859 describing the early years of the history of Chagrin Falls. The following is a portion of the essay, reprinted in the August 18, 1933 <u>Chagrin Falls Exponent</u>:

. . . Standing on the hill that stretches itself along north of the town

we now behold a beautiful village spread out before us. Looking to the East we see that the upper part of the town—the paper mill now in the course of construction. Turning your eyes in different directions you behold foundries, machine, cabinet and mechanic shops of various descriptions. Nor is this all, for here is situated one of the great wonders of the age. The shoe peg factory that furnishes shoe pegs to the thousands scattered up and down our land who use them. Various other articles for the comfort and use of mankind are manufactured here. . . .

Westel went on to fight for the Union cause in the American Civil War. His military career took him from Chancellorsville and Gettysburg in the East to the Tennessee campaign in the West and finally, as an ambulance driver in Company B, Fifth Ohio Volunteer Infantry. He accompanied Sherman on his "March to the Sea."

At the Battle of Gettysburg on July 3, 1863, he wrote in his journal:

The sound of musketry was getting pretty loud and everything would indicate a hard time of it today...We were told to take the place of another regiment that had been engaged some time ... We fired as fast as we could load for a few minutes, but after the excitement was over, began to look around to see if anything could be seen to aim at...Very heavy musketry was heard in some part of our line all day and cannonading was very lively part of the time.

The heavy fighting was undoubtedly Confederate General George Pickett's final charge - the turning point of the Battle of Gettysburg.

Though there is no record that A. H. Williams from Chagrin Falls

attended any select or district school in the village, the 18-year-old gave his young life for his country at the Battle of Gettysburg. He died defending the Union position holding Cemetery Hill on July 2, 1863. Whoever held that height had an opportunity to win the battle. The Union Army continued to hold the hill, and after the failure of Pickett's charge on July 3 at Cemetery Ridge, Confederate General Robert E. Lee finally retreated from Gettysburg on July 4, 1863. His army was never again a threat to win the war. However, the Civil War continued for two more bloody years.

In 1859 the board of education voted to pay male grammar school teachers seven dollars per week and female teachers five dollars per week. This discrimination in salary would continue for many more years. The superintendent's salary was set at five hundred dollars per year. Also in

1859, the board appointed a committee to purchase books "for such scholars as are not able to furnish their own." This practice existed well into the 20th century.

The old schoolhouses were sold in 1859. "Southwest schoolhouse was sold for $155, schoolhouse No. 3 for $75, and schools one and four for $190."

Schools were closed in May 1861, for "one week in consequence of the presence of small pox." On several occasions in its history, the

THE CHAGRIN FALLS HISTORICAL SOCIETY

schools were closed because of the threat of diseases.

According to board minutes, the first disciplinary case appeared on September 11, 1869, when two students were brought before the board after being suspended by the superintendent for "inebriation." The next violation brought before the board was a week later when a student left school to "drink beer." It is noted that the board allowed all three to remain in school with a promise of better behavior.

At the September 18, 1869 board meeting, "it was voted that the board meet regularly upon the first Saturday evening of each month." There must not have been much weekend entertainment in the little village at that time. The board meeting concluded with the statement: "Parents are showing more interest in taking care of their horses and cattle each day and think little of visiting our schools."

As with many pioneer communities, school was first regarded as a luxury and not a necessity. Pioneer families were more concerned with survival and had very little time to devote to book learning.

By 1870 there were 10 manufacturing companies using the water power of the Chagrin River to operate their industries. The Ivex Paper Mill on Cleveland Street was the last remaining mill in Chagrin Falls, closing in 2004.

In June 1870, W. S. Hayden resigned as superintendent because he was "not inclined to accept the offer of $900 per year." The board decided not to offer him the $1,000 he requested and made an offer of $925 and refused to accept his resignation. He remained superintendent for one more year. Then, in 1879, the well-liked and highly regarded educator (with hurt feelings obviously healed), was hired once again and served as superintendent until 1883. Hayden was so admired by his former students, they formed a society in his honor. A column in the May 7, 1903 Exponent was titled "A Permanent Organization of the W. S. Hayden

Triangle

Students Effected—Reunions of the Society to be Held Annually," written by Virginia Curtiss Smith, secretary of the organization.

In 1873 the Union Fair Association of Chagrin Falls purchased 34 acres on the south side of East Washington Street to build a half-mile horse racing track with a wooden grandstand. One year later, because of the new track, Chagrin Falls was selected as the location for the Cuyahoga County Fair. It is the site of the present grade 7-12 school campus on East Washington Street. At that first Cuyahoga County Fair, as an added attraction, a $10 purse was awarded to the winner of a footrace once around the new half-mile track. The winner was Tom Bright of Chagrin Falls with a time of 2:38.5. Today, 130 years later, Chagrin Falls' athletes still run on a portion of that original track.

The school board introduced a five-mill levy in May 1875, "three-fifths to be used for teachers and two-fifths for incidentals." They needed the money for the school board treasury. The levy failed and the next year the board of education had to borrow money to pay teachers. On September 1, 1875 the board showed a balance on hand of $9.91 after paying "teachers, superintendent and other expenses."

In 1878 the school board did invest in renovations of the deteriorating old school. The Exponent continued to urge the community to build a new school. However, the board of education did not have the funds.

As early as 1878, according to the February 7 board minutes, establishing a "kindergarten school" was discussed. However, it was not until 1939 that a kindergarten program became permanent.

Due to overcrowding in the "Union School" (the former Asbury Seminary) on Philomethian Street in 1881, the basement of the Chagrin Falls Methodist Church on South Franklin Street was secured for the teaching of the first and second grades of the Chagrin Falls Schools. The Chagrin Falls Township Hall basement was used for first grade pupils in 1882. It would not be the only time that such village facilities were used for teaching.

In 1882 the state of Ohio decided that all teachers had to pass an examination on United States history. The May 18, 1882 Chagrin Falls Exponent stated it nicely to teachers: "So look up the history."

The Chagrin Falls Board of Education took upon itself the responsibility to award its first diploma in 1879. The recipient of that diploma was Hugh Christian. He was the only member of the graduating class.

In the May 18, 1879 Chagrin Falls Exponent, the following appeared in regard to graduation:

The School Board has gotten up some handsome diplomas for those graduating from the High School. Hugh Christian receives one this commencement.

The newspaper continued in its June 5, 1879 edition:

The spring term closes Friday of the week. Hugh G. Christian graduates being the first of our schools to receive a 'sheepskin'.

The newspaper concluded in the June 12, 1879 edition:

The Board of Education, teachers and scholars of the High School met at the sitting room of T.W. and M.V. Scott's Bank last Friday P.M. when

Hugh G. Christian graduated from our high school. He read a scholarly essay after which the diploma was presented with appropriate remarks. Mr. Christian then presented Prof. Stokey (superintendent) with an elegant photograph album. The professor replying with much feeling. I.W. Pope made a short speech suited to the occasion.

In the mid to late 1800s, teachers in surrounding communities began to organize a "Teachers' Institute." Teachers would meet with an opportunity to discuss common problems and to listen to invited speakers discuss relevant topics dealing with education.

In a January 1880 Exponent, the newspaper recommended in an article on an upcoming Orange Teachers' Institute:

There is nothing better for our schools than these institutes, and those teachers who do not avail themselves of these benefits arising from them will soon find themselves behind the times.

Over one hundred years later this educational concept continues.

In the late 1870s and early 1880s a private business school was located in Chagrin Falls. The curriculum consisted of penmanship, bookkeeping, telegraphy and business arithmetic. The November 21, 1878 Chagrin Falls Exponent stated, "The teachers bring the best of recommendations from the Spencerian Business College of Cleveland." It was referred to as the Chagrin Falls Business Institute. By the mid 1880s, it was gone.

During this period of time, there was even a special school for women in regard to teaching writing. As the local newspaper advertised, "Ladies burdened with household cares have found it impossible to attend to this art." Thus, a night school was established in 1878 for that purpose. Even a special "singing school" was instituted for children on Saturdays in 1878.

As noted in the August 25, 1881 Exponent:

The cost per pupil for the school year in 1881 was $9.30. The market price for eggs was 12 cents a dozen, butter was 18 cents a pound and

apples were 30 cents a bushel.

The first woman to graduate from Chagrin Falls High School was Ella Whitlock, class of 1882. She was the only graduate that year.

In the June 8, 1882 <u>Chagrin Falls Exponent</u>, the following appeared in regard to graduation:

The schools of Chagrin Falls closed on Friday, June 2. Literary exercises in the afternoon consisted of essays, recitations and music and graduation exercises by Miss Ella Whitlock, who on that day completed the course of study prescribed. The year has been unusually prosperous and glad as all are to have vacation come, the break up is filled with sadness to teachers and pupils.

Also in 1882, a young woman by the name of Alice J. Russell was hired to teach in the Chagrin Falls Schools. She attended Chagrin Falls Schools, but there is no record of her graduating. However, she attended normal school at Hiram College and a college in Ada, Ohio. She retired in 1925. Most of her 43 teaching years were in the first grade. She has the longest full-time teaching career in the history of the Chagrin Falls Schools.

Found in the 1915 yearbook was a dedication to Alice J. Russell:

In token of our loving appreciation of her whole-hearted, unselfish service, which has endeared her to the hearts of hundreds of Chagrin Falls High School graduates, we, the Senior Class of 1915, dedicate the <u>Annual</u> to our first grade teacher, Miss Alice Russell.

When she retired she was given a short letter of appreciation from the board of education for her service to the schools. A copy of that letter is in the Chagrin Falls Schools' Historical Preservation Room.

Once corporal punishment was the norm in schools for even minor infractions. In the February 9, 1882 <u>Chagrin Falls Exponent</u>, the following paragraph appeared:

With sadness we record the death at Mr. J. H. Luse's, Orange, Thursday night, February 2nd of little Erwin Luse, aged 6 years and 10 months, son of Shelby L. Luse of Brooklyn, Ohio. The cause has been authoritatively ascribed to the rash act of the principal of his school bumping Erwin's and playmates heads together as a mode of correction, thereby causing an ulcer in the brain.

The Philomethian Street School / Chagrin Falls Union School was built in 1885 and torn down in 1940. It was located on what is now the playground on Philomethian Street. Note that this circa 1890's photo shows a corner of the old Asbury Seminary School on the left and is the only known photo of this building.

The February 23, 1882 <u>Chagrin Falls Exponent</u> continued:

Why is that in all the reports of the case sent us, the name of the teacher who pounded the two boys heads together, and evidently causing the death of the Luse boy, has been withheld from the public? And we would also like to inquire whether any legal proceedings have been instituted against him, or whether any are likely to be? It seems to us that where a school teacher uses sufficient violence in correcting a scholar to cause his death, something should be done to teach him and others a wholesome lesson.

It seemed possible that the child was a tuition student in the Chagrin Falls School District. Members of a Luse family did attend Chagrin Falls schools at various times in the late 1800s and early 1900s. Ironically, an Erwin L. Luse graduated in the class of 1925.

Finally, the editor of the <u>Chagrin Falls Exponent</u>, in its March 2, 1882 edition, added the following:

Explanation in the Luse Boy Case Editor, <u>Exponent</u>

In reply to your inquiries

The Union Schools Catalogue of the Rules, Regulations and Course of Study of Chagrin Falls, Ohio adopted by the Board of Education May 1889.

concerning the death of Erwin L. Luse, I will give the facts and you judge for yourself. About the last of November, while coming out of his recitation room at recess, he and his little chum threw their arms around each other and were passing out of the hall when the principal saw them, and stepping up, struck Erwin on the head with a book which he had in his hand and struck his little chum with his other hand. During the striking Erwin was knocked against the building, and when found by his brother, he was crying bitterly and complained that his head ached. From that day until the day of his death when he passed to the unknown shores, he complained of his head."

Thankfully, though all the details were in the <u>Chagrin Falls Exponent</u>, Erwin L. Luse was not a tuition student in the Chagrin Falls Schools. The teacher involved was Mr. W. P. Cope, the principal of the Brooklyn, Ohio schools. What happened to W. P. Cope remains a mystery. Interestingly, a family by the name of Cope attended the Chagrin Falls Schools in the early 1920s. Corporal punishment remained a legal form of discipline for many years.

In 1885, with the demand for more educational facilities, a new beautiful brick Romanesque Revival school building was built on Philomethian Street next to the old Asbury Seminary for a cost of $12,870. It was designed by Cleveland architect, H. B. Smith. It was named the Chagrin Falls Union School. However beginning in the early 1900's the students and community began to refer to it as the Philomethian Street School.

The Asbury Seminary was actually moved south of its original foundation on Philomethian Street to make room for the new schoolhouse. The June 4, 1885 Chagrin Falls Exponent had this to say about moving the seminary:

The work of moving the old school building was nearly completed last evening. It is to be placed within a few feet of the south line of the lot, making room for the new building on the ground formerly occupied by the old. The work of moving progresses favorably and the building will not be injured to any great extent, although it was feared at one time that owing to the sagging of the ends the contrary would be the result.

Program of the 1ˢᵗ Commencement Exercises of Chagrin Falls High School, M.E. (Methodist Episcopal) Church June 10, 1887.

The January 7, 1886 Chagrin Falls Exponent had the following article about a community open house at the new school:

House warming at the new school house as announced in the last issue of The Exponent, the social event of the New Year was the open house reception given by the board of education. About 700 of our citizens inspected the new building. All were seemingly well pleased with the structure and thought it substantially built and furnished, especially fitting it for school use.

Professor Randall (superintendent) and lady teachers that will be transferred from the old building assisted the board, who were all present, in receiving refreshments, consisting of coffee, tea, fruit and cake, furnished by the wives of the board were served to about five hundred, the lady teachers presiding at the tables. Epicures were profuse and enthusiastic in their praise.

The most thoughtful pronounced the several appointments of the building all that could be expected

1890 High School Graduation Class

from the money expended, reflecting credit upon the building committee, who may feel justly proud of the result of their untiring efforts.

Professor Randall and his corps of teachers have the confidence of those most interested in education. Our citizens are awake to the condition our schools have been in and will see their present prosperous condition is continued. We venture to say nothing could have been more pleasing to our citizens, as well as the board, teachers and scholars, than the open house reception at the new building on New Year's Day.

Franklin P. Shumaker replaced R. M. Collins as superintendent of schools in 1888 and remained in that position until 1901. He later filled the offices of mayor of Chagrin Falls and state senator as well as being a member of the county board of education.

As school began in early September 1890, the Chagrin Falls Exponent announced a change in the course of study. An English course was added to the high school and Latin became an elective course. The article proclaimed that Chagrin Falls students "are now accepted by the best colleges in the state." The Chagrin Falls Schools were advertised as an excellent college preparatory school.

In 1891 the school board took a progressive step forward and added music to the school curriculum. C. E. Judd was employed as the first music teacher at a salary of three dollars per week.

1895 High School Graduation Class

Another item of business at this board meeting was a letter from a teacher, Miss Anna M. Brugh, requesting changes in the seating arrangement in her classroom and an advance in her salary. School desks were bolted to the floor and could not be moved unless unbolted and rearranged. According to board minutes, the new seating would be arranged to meet her request, but no advance would be made in her pay.

By 1892 twelve Chagrin Falls High School graduates were pursuing a college degree. Until 1892 there had only been thirty-eight graduates.

A 750-seat Assembly Hall (auditorium) and four elementary schoolrooms in the Georgian Revival style were added to the Philomethian Street School in 1892 at a cost of $12,000. Cleveland architect S. R. Badgely, who specialized in church and college architecture, designed this new addition. However, the $12,000 was found to be insufficient, and on January 7, 1893, the board of education petitioned the state legislature to empower the board to issue $4,000 in bonds to complete the new school building. House Bill #1581, passed by the General Assembly of the State of Ohio on March 17, 1893, authorized the Chagrin Falls Board of Education to issue bonds in the amount of $4,000 to finish and furnish the new building additions.

While the Town Hall was too small to hold some of the community events, the new Assembly Hall on the first floor was large enough to accommodate both school and community events. According to school board minutes, September 20, 1914, the Assembly

Hall had recently been used by the Congregational Church, W.C.T.U. (Women's Christian Temperance Union) and the Woman's Suffrage Party. Each organization was charged one dollar for janitors' fees and one dollar for the use of electric lights. High school commencements were held in the Assembly Hall with an admission charge of 10 cents. As a result of the 1892 addition to the

Philomethian Street School, the Asbury Seminary, no longer needed, was sold for salvage in 1893 for $100 to O. H. Gleason and H. Henderson. The woodshed was sold to William Hutchings for seven dollars. The entire Chagrin Falls school system from primary school through high school was now housed in this building. It had a capacity for approximately 300 students. Since 1843 a school has existed on the Philomethian property.

Four large stones with 1885 PUBLIC SCHOOL written across them were located several years ago in a flower garden at 125 May Court in the middle of the village. They belonged to the old Philomethian Street School that opened its doors to the students of Chagrin Falls in 1886. This beautiful brick building was torn down in 1940 to make way for the elementary school addition to the 1914 high school building facing East Washington Street. It is the present intermediate school. Today, those golden pieces of Chagrin Falls Schools' history remain in the possession of the Chagrin Falls Alumni Association.

How the stones arrived at 125 May Court is an interesting story. After asking how they ended up at that

location in the alumni newsletter, Tiger Tales, January 1, 1998 issue, Amy Patterson '74 wrote the following:

In your current 'From the Director' column in Tiger Tales, you ask how the Philomethian School stones came to rest in a May Court flower bed. Having grown up in that house at 125 May Court, I can shed some light on your query.

According to my mother, Shirley Mickelson (now of Ashtabula), my late father, John Neil Patterson, with the help of an esteemed C.F. public school employee, Jess Rankin (our May Ct. neighbor) placed the stones on rollers and moved them to our backyard to edge the flowerbed. This occurred around 1960. My mother can't recall how they got the stones, just the difficulty of moving them. Given that Mr. Rankin was principal at Philomethian, perhaps he gave them to my parents.

My mother was sad to leave the stones and flowerbed when she moved out in 1978. Hope this fills in some blanks.

At the October, 1893 board meeting, some parents appeared to complain "in presence of the teachers, that some pupils are being promoted faster than others." No comment was made on how the matter was settled.

Appearing in the Geauga County newspaper, The Geauga Times Leader, on March 4, 1978, were the following two examples of tests which had to be passed by high school graduates applying for teacher certification in 1894:

GEOGRAPHY
Saturday, March 17, 1894
See directions on Physology [sic] list.
1.   What is meant by the culuminating [sic] point of a grand division? Name one.
2.   What are Capitol and Metropolis?
3.   Make a map of New York State naming the boundries [sic] on the map.
4.   Give area of Texas, U.S., Europe, and the Indian Ocean.
5.   Name two rivers of Utah and two cities of Wyoming.

C. F. Easton

GRAMMAR
Saturday, March 17, 1894
1.   Name the departments of grammar.
2.   Give examples in sentences of verbal noun, and subordinate clause.
3.   Give examples of substantive and of objective clause.
4.   What is the difference between parsing a word and governing it? Do not ask the examiner about this.
5.   Give the inflection of the verb WHIP, potential mode, passive voice, present perfect tense, negative progressive form.

C. F. Easton

By 1895 electric lights were installed in the Philomethian Street School by the Chagrin Falls Electric Company, J. W. Hutchinson, President, with two electric lights put into the superintendent's office in 1896. An initial request for a telephone was denied at that time.

In March 1895 the schools were closed because of anxiety concerning scarlet fever.

The Chagrin Falls High School class of 1896 had nine graduates. The class of 1996, one hundred years later, had 127 graduates. The total school enrollment in 1896-1897 was 326 students; the 1996-

Front Row Howard Mc Lane- Burr Peterie- -Ray Honeywell- Frank Bayard
Second Row Neal Bright-(Fred) Cameron-Forrest March-Clade Hill- Lute Harris- Petric (Basil)
Third Row Roy Smith — Ralph Stillwell- Ed. Henderson

1898 1st football team

1997 school year had an enrollment of 1,874 students.

The first football game played by Chagrin Falls High School took place at Washington Park on November 6, 1897. Washington Park was located at the old Cuyahoga County Fairgrounds, presently the middle school, high school and "Rec" Center campus. The game was attended by 35 people with an admission charge of 10 cents. Chagrin's opponent was the Geauga Seminary team from Chesterland, Ohio. An interesting footnote is that former U.S. President James A. Garfield attended the Geauga Seminary during his high school years after learning some of his ABC's in Chagrin Falls. Chagrin was easily defeated by a score of 10-0. From 1893-1897 a touchdown was worth 4 points, a field goal 5 points, a point after touchdown 2 points and a safety 2 points.

One year later, in 1898, Chagrin Falls High School played its first regularly scheduled football season under the guidance of Coach Lute Harris and team captain Ray Honeywell. New uniforms were purchased and the colors orange and black were adopted by the team. The season ended with a record of 2 wins and 3 losses. At the conclusion of the season a banquet was given by school superintendent, F. P. Shumaker, at the Falls Hotel on South Main Street just south of Triangle Park.

Lucius F. "Lute" Harris, an honorary member of the Chagrin Falls Schools' Athletic Heritage Hall of Fame, and first football coach, was an avid booster of all high school athletics well into the 1900s. He formed what might be considered the first Booster Club and was responsible for the school colors, orange and black. Lute awarded gold footballs and gold basketballs to varsity athletes at their annual athletic banquets. Several are displayed in the Chagrin Falls Schools' Historical Preservation Room.

Lute once played second base for the old Cleveland Spiders, the precursors of the Cleveland Naps and the Cleveland Indians. He was a close friend of the legendary Connie Mack of the Philadelphia Athletics, whom he entertained on occasion in Chagrin Falls, along with the entire team of Philadelphia Athletics.

Marjorie Black Bottomy '37 wrote of more memories of Lute's relationship with the Philadelphia Athletics in the January, 1995 alumni newsletter, Tiger Tales:

In the August, 1994 newsletter, there was an article written by Jim Vittek about Lute Harris and his role in baseball. In the late 20s, Lute sponsored a baseball team, the "Harris Juniors." Paul Bottomy was a member along with Philip Harris, Barney Hoopes, Cloyd Pealer, Glen Hern, Bud Rood, Art Stenman, Pete Reitz, Bill Reitz, Howard Simmons, Norman Edic, and Raymond Brown. We still have a large photo taken by local photographer, Walter Robinson, of the team in their uniforms with Lute Harris.

On some Sunday mornings, some of the Philadelphia Athletics would take the car from Cleveland to Chagrin to visit Lute for Sunday brunch. The "Harris Juniors" would always show up to play catch with their heroes. Paul remembers playing catch with Lefty Grove, Mickey Cochran, Jimmy Fox, and looking, with a great deal of awe, at Connie Mack. Jim Vittek '67 conjured up a great deal of happy memories with his article.

Ballgames were often played on a field east of Evergreen Hill Cemetery on South Franklin Street where the

Harris farm is still located.

An interesting story about Lute while he was a student in the Chagrin Falls Schools appeared in the February 15, 1952 edition of the <u>Chagrin Falls Exponent</u>. The incident occurred (circa 1884) during a spelling bee at the school:

One remembered spelling bee, with chuckles, featured F. P. Shumaker, the principal, Miss Alice Russell, the teacher, and Mrs. F. A. Kupfer conducting a spelling bee. A bad boy, L. F. Harris, dared to hit the principal with a spitball.

No mention was made of any punishment.

By 1898 the tax rate in Chagrin Falls Village, including the school tax, was $3 per $100. It was the second highest rate in a list of 39 Cuyahoga County subdivisions. The Chagrin Falls' rate included one dollar for schools.

Before the 19th Amendment to the U.S. Constitution was adopted in 1920, allowing women the right to vote, the Ohio legislature in 1894 passed a bill giving women the right to vote in school board elections. In April 1895, two women, Mrs. W. S. Gates and Mrs. H. S. Kent, were candidates for the Chagrin Falls Board of Education. Neither was elected, but Mrs. Gates came within 19 votes of election. Out of 587 votes cast in that election, 250 were cast by women. However, equality for women took a big step forward in Chagrin Falls in 1898 when Mrs. E. T. Robens became the first woman elected to the Chagrin Falls Board of Education.

By the latter half of the 1800s and into the very early 1900s, the teaching profession dramatically opened up for women, mostly young women possibly looking for something to do before finding a husband.

The turnover of young women teachers was so great that many school employment contracts specified that dating was forbidden, or that the female teacher could only socialize one night a week. Even though a young woman married, pregnancy would mean automatic dismissal.

In the early 1900s, all it took to become a teacher was completion of a two-year course at a state "normal school." Kent State University opened its doors in 1915 as the Kent State Normal School. In the 1920s, a "normal school" existed in Chardon, appropriately named Chardon Normal School.

Some of the very early teachers were as young as eighteen, barely older and often smaller in stature than many students they taught.

Enthusiasm for athletics at the high school was displayed early in the school's history. Football coach, Lute Harris, charged eighty cents for a round-trip ticket to Willoughby, Ohio, to watch the orange and black play Willoughby High School in 1899. Willoughby beat Chagrin, 5-0. However, the game had a dramatic ending! A dispute over rules occurred in the second half, and the Chagrin Falls team refused to continue playing. Captain Ray Honeywell '00 took his team off the field, claiming that Willoughby's team was not comprised of high school players. This type of situation was not uncommon in the early days of interscholastic high school sports.

By the end of the 19th century the Chagrin Falls schools had an excellent reputation. The Union School (often referred to as the Philomethian Street School) and its surrounding property was the center of much village activity. Many non-residents wanted to send their children to Chagrin Falls to be

Plays

educated. It was possible to do so by paying $1.80 tuition per month in 1900. Students could board locally. Those students who attended the high school could follow the English course or Latin course. They were required to pass two rhetorical exercises each term and reviews by the superintendent. Several colleges at that time, including Mount Union in Alliance, Ohio and Ohio Wesleyan University in Delaware, Ohio, had free tuition scholarships for the seniors graduating the highest in their class.

A certificate was presented to Raymond W. Honeywell '00 at his high school graduation, stating:

Upon presentation of this certificate Raymond W. Honeywell, first honor student of the Class of 1900 in Chagrin Falls High School, will be granted a free scholarship in the Ohio Wesleyan University, Delaware, Ohio, good for the completion of the College Course. This certificate is not transferable, and does not include incidental or laboratory fees.

J.W. Bashford, President

The local newspaper (1874-1963), Chagrin Falls Exponent, featured the schools in its December 31, 1896 edition.

Its headlines stated:

*Chagrin's Schools
Magnificent Building Superbly Equipped
With Modern Appliances*

Enterprising And Progressive Management....

*Efficient And Popular Teachers....
Something Our Citizens Are Proud Of
In Chagrin Falls*

Thus, the 19th century ended with its schools the pride of the community as it remains in the beginning of the 21st century.

The first Chagrin Falls High School Alumni Association was organized April 11, 1890 by the class of 1889. The first banquet was held June 14, 1890 at Punderson Lake. After the banquet of 1901, which was held at Superintendent F. P. Shumaker's home, the meeting place of the alumni was at Assembly Hall in the Philomethian Street School.

In the early 1900s, the freshmen at the high school were nicknamed "flats." Webster's Dictionary uses such words as tasteless, dull and a simpleton in describing "flat." However, as the school district moved into the 20th century, it continued to grow in student

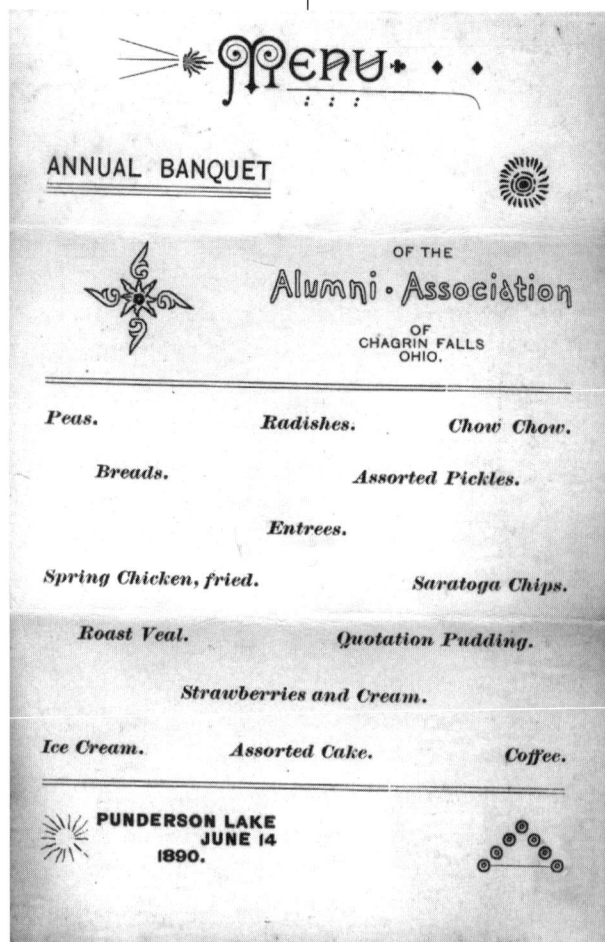

Menu

ANNUAL BANQUET

OF THE Alumni · Association
OF CHAGRIN FALLS OHIO.

Peas.	Radishes.	Chow Chow.
Breads.		Assorted Pickles.
	Entrees.	
Spring Chicken, fried.		Saratoga Chips.
Roast Veal.		Quotation Pudding.
	Strawberries and Cream.	
Ice Cream.	Assorted Cake.	Coffee.

PUNDERSON LAKE
JUNE 14
1890.

1890 banquet menu of the 1st Chagrin Falls Alumni Association.

population and quality of education even though the freshmen remained "flats."

Also in regard to freshmen, the 1953 <u>Zenith</u> stated:

The senior was born for great things,
The junior was born for small.
But no one has yet found the reason
Why the freshman was born at all.

In the spring of 1903 there was "Trouble in River City" over the issue of social dancing by the high school students. From a column titled, "Terse Local News" in the May 7, 1903 edition of the <u>Chagrin Falls Exponent,</u> there appeared a short paragraph that unsettled the social fabric of Chagrin Falls. Very simply, the paragraph expressed that the young people of Chagrin Falls had "gone dancing mad." It stated that there had been a recent week in which there were five dances in six evenings. The paragraph concluded with this intriguing statement: "If people will dance they will have the 'fiddler' to pay."

On Sunday morning, May 17, 1903, the Reverend S. L. Boyers of the M. E. (Methodist Episcopal) Church of Chagrin Falls followed up the <u>Exponent's</u> paragraph by delivering a sermon that severely denounced dancing and those indulging therein. The sermon created a great deal of controversy among the citizens and students of Chagrin Falls. Some were even censuring the Reverend Boyers for having attacked dancing.

As news of the sermon spread, an article appeared in the May 20, 1903 <u>Cleveland Plain Dealer</u> and was titled,

"Sermon Caused Big Row - Chagrin Falls' Pastor Criticized Dancing and High School Graduates Are Angry." According to the <u>Plain Dealer</u>, the Reverend Boyers made a scorching reference to dancing in his sermon and remarked, "that any young woman school teacher who attended dances was not fit to be a teacher." The graduating class of 30 students had been holding club dances during the winter months. The reverend's sermon did not please them. He had been invited to deliver the invocation on commencement day, and the graduating students asked Superintendent D. W. McGlenen to remove him from the program. He refused. As a result, "classmen and women" threatened to boycott the graduation until the invocation had been given, even though 800 invitations had been sent out. Many students went so far as to threaten a boycott of the M. E. Church.

Upon learning of this criticism, the Reverend Boyers announced that he would preach the following sermon on Sunday, May 24, 1903: "The Public Dance of Chagrin Falls." He invited the parents, students, and citizens of Chagrin Falls to attend. As a result, two other churches gave up their services to attend the M. E. Church.

In his sermon, the Reverend Boyers attacked dancing as a health problem (getting hurt trying to "outshine" each other) and an economic problem (too much money spent on clothes, creating debts for one's family).

He thought dancing destructive to the social life of Chagrin Falls, taking

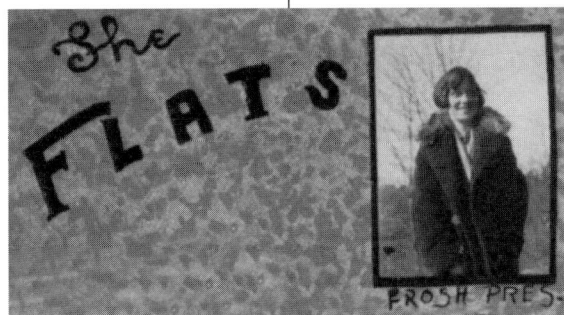

1903 Baseball Team

away from more intellectual things. The Reverend Boyers was not accusing anyone of doing anything immoral, but was insinuating that "dancing leads to immorality." He further declared that dancing was injurious to the spiritual life of the churches and schools of the village. Finally, he blamed the dancing scandal on the parents, the school teachers who attended the dances, and the students themselves.

On Thursday evening, June 4, 1903, the commencement exercises were held in Assembly Hall at the Philomethian School. The invocation was given by Reverend Boyers and the main address by Dr. Morgan Wood, pastor of Plymouth Congregational Church in Cleveland, without incident. The largest class through 1903 to graduate from Chagrin Falls High School had left its mark on the social history of the village—dancing was here to stay!

Also in the spring of 1903, the baseball team had an interesting confrontation with the Chardon High team involving baseball and chewing tobacco. An excerpt from the sports page of the May 10, 1903 Chagrin Falls Exponent stated the following concerning the high school baseball game between the two schools:

> *The features of the game were the half-hour 'chewing match' before the game, the pitching of Sprague of Chardon, and the $6 collection from 200 people present at 3 cents per head, of which Chagrin finally got $3 after a verbal scrap.*

The chewing match before the game was won by Chardon High School. Distance and accuracy were the keys in this important pre-game activity. Chardon outplayed the home team at every point and won the game 18-9,

but they also proved themselves to be the most "unreliable and disagreeable players the Chagrin boys have ever encountered."

As the Chagrin team began its trek home, they hollered, "Come down to Chagrin, Chardon High, for the return game, and we guarantee you will be treated like gentlemen." For unknown reasons, the return game was never played. Maybe Chagrin Falls High School was getting too good with their baseball skills and tobacco chewing.

D. W. McGlenen replaced F. P. Shumaker as superintendent in 1901 and remained in that position until 1908. He later served as mayor of Chagrin Falls from January 1912 to January 1914. After serving as mayor he founded an interesting business dealing with education. The 1914 <u>Annual</u> described the business as follows:

> *His business consists mainly of the collection and classification of the names of high school Seniors throughout the United States. These names he furnishes to the various colleges, who use them for advertising purposes. He also collects the names of college Seniors. He does business with more than half the colleges in the United States, including many of the most noted universities.*

An interscholastic literary league was formed in 1903. It consisted of high schools in Burton, Chardon, Garrettsville and Chagrin Falls. The first contest was held in Assembly Hall on Friday evening, February 20, 1903. Each school had four contestants. The competition was in the following categories: vocal solo, essay, piano solo, recitation and oration. Each school provided a judge who graded the

contestants from all of the schools but their own. Assembly Hall was filled to capacity, and when Superintendent McGlenen of Chagrin Falls announced the winner, the spectators from Garrettsville High School went "nearly wild."

The February 26, 1903 Chagrin Falls Exponent concluded:

The contests not only furnish a very high grade entertainment for the communities in which they are held, but it is sure to develop literary, oratorical and musical work among the members that they would not otherwise acquire. The citizens of Garrettsville, Burton, Chardon and Chagrin Falls are to be congratulated on the fact of each having enterprising and up-to-date managements at the head of their schools in the persons of their respective superintendents and it is to be hoped that all future contests will be as successful in all respects as that which was held in Assembly Hall last Friday evening.

The first orange and black basketball team was organized during the 1903-04 school year. It was managed by teacher and future school superintendent Ezra Teare. The coach was a student from Hiram College. The first basketball teams were very successful. For example, in 1911 the Chagrin Falls High School men's basketball team defeated the Western Reserve University Dental School 27-23. The following year they defeated the Hiram College freshman team 46-12. Their record was 15 wins and 3 losses.

In the early 1900s, as the Cuyahoga County Fairgrounds grew to approximately 54 acres, improvements were continually made. The most significant was the construction of a permanent concrete grandstand in 1913. This is the very stadium Chagrin Falls

1ST. & 2N. GRADE BLDG. CHAGRIN FALLS

High School uses today. Ninety years later it still remains Chagrin's home for rooting the Tigers on to victory.

Also during the 1913 football season, the orange and black overwhelmed Hudson High School by a score of 84-0 in the first game of the season and finished with a record of 5 wins and 1 loss.

On January 26, 1905, as a preliminary to the high school basketball game between Chagrin Falls and Burton, the girls of Chagrin Falls High School played an exhibition game with the girls from the community of Orange. Final score of the girls' game: Orange 2, Chagrin Falls High School 0. In the following boys' game the score was Chagrin Falls High School 70, Burton High School 2.

In 1907 the Chagrin Falls School District was granted a charter from the Ohio Department of Education entitled "First Grade High School," meaning that it had met successfully all of the requirements required by the state to be an excellent high school. It qualified

The 1st- and 2nd-grade building was built in 1909 and torn down in 1940.

as a four-year high school; therefore, there were no graduates in 1908. Since many surrounding schools were three-year high schools, many students from surrounding school districts paid tuition to do "post-graduate" work at Chagrin Falls High School. For example, Lewis Messenger graduated from Auburn's three-year high school in 1924 and also received a diploma from Chagrin Falls High School in 1925. Also in 1908, baseball was reorganized as a high school sport.

By 1909 it became necessary to provide more classroom space. A separate wood-frame, two-classroom building for first and second grades was built on the southeast corner of the Philomethian Street property. The cost was $2,947 with an additional $492 for taking care of the plumbing in the new school. It was known as the "Little White Schoolhouse."

By 1910 there were 2,194 books in the Chagrin Falls Public School Library.

Students
YEARBOOK

1923

1948

1913

1914

1915

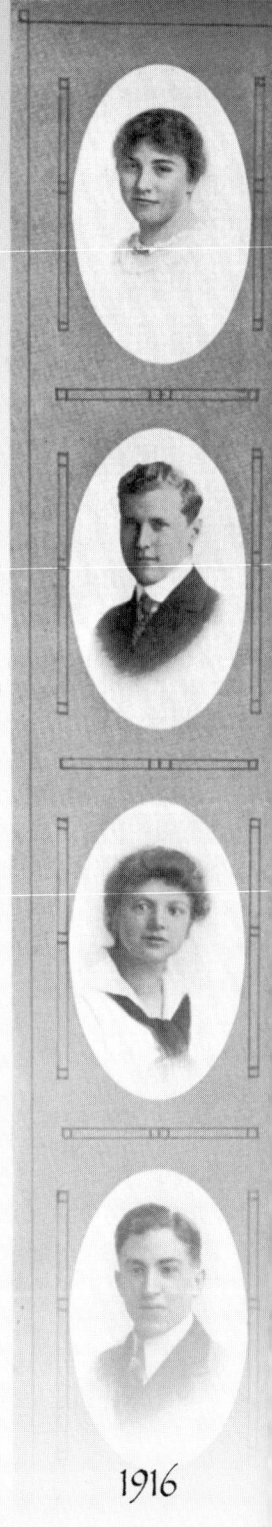

1916

1921

1922

C F

H S

'26

1926

1927

Seniors '32

C F H S

1932

1920

Not only were students reading in 1910, but they were doing a lot of writing. In 1910 more than twenty million pencils were sold, mostly to school children.

A year later, the first Chagrin Falls yearbook was published by the class of 1911 and added to the school's library. It was named Annual.

Financial problems halted play on the football field. No football was played from 1901-1903 and 1905-1911. According to the 1912 yearbook, Annual, "football not played on account of lack of funds."

The First Annual

of

The Chagrin Falls High School

Published by The Class

of 1911

However, the orange and black did participate in the 1904 football season and were undefeated with 4 wins, outscoring their opponents 61-6.

The 1911-1912 basketball team was very successful with a record of 15 wins and 3 losses. Adding to its success, according to the 1912 Annual, was the fact that "Chagrin Falls feels proud of its athletic teams for they do not enjoy the services of a coach as do many larger high schools."

According to the September 19, 1912 edition of the Chagrin Falls Exponent, the school board purchased over an acre of land just west of the Philomethian Street school grounds and a lot on East Washington Street adjoining it for $2,500 with bonds sold for payment. The paper stated:

"This furnishes a much enlarged plot of ground for use as a playground, for utilization in the teaching of agriculture, arrangement of athletic sports, etc. and also gives a much nearer route to the school building from downtown. It furnishes several distinct advantages."

This land would later be used for building the new Chagrin Falls High School building in 1914 facing East Washington Street. It remains part of the present Chagrin Falls Intermediate School.

In the 1911 Chagrin Falls High School yearbook, Cora M. Sanders, class of 1890, wrote the following early history of the first Chagrin Falls High School Alumni Association:

The Chagrin Falls High School Alumni Association was organized April 11, 1890, for the purpose as stated in the Constitution, of promoting acquaintances among the Alumni and the interest and immediate success of the Chagrin Falls High School.

The first officers of the Association were Geo. B. Haggart, Pres., Miss Lena L. Pratt, Rec. Sec'y.

Previous to the class of '89, by whom the Association was organized, there had been ten graduates, Hugh Christian in '79; Theodore Modroo and James Short, '81; Ella Whitlock Dudley '82; Geo. Haggart, '87; and the class of '88 containing four members: H. C. Cleverdon, Lewis Richards, Fred Gates and Lucy Foster. June 14, 1890, the first banquet and

44

1904 Football Team. 1st row: M. Burnett, J LeRoy, C. Robinson, P. Hall, V. LeRoy, C. Page. 2nd Row: H Dripps, C Bradley, G. Hintz, Ezra Teare, W. Scott, N. Bright, V. Wilmont.

reception for new members was held at Punderson Lake, the Class of '90 becoming members at that time. At the same time, it was decided to hold a reception or affair of a social nature each June.

In '91 and '92 the banquets were held at Punderson Lake, but in '93, it seemed the desire of the majority to make it a more formal function, and Hotel Irving (where Key Bank is located today) was selected as the place of meeting. This proved quite satisfactory and several receptions were held at the Irving House.

One of the most enjoyable events in the history of the Association occurred June 21, 1901, when in response to an invitation extended by Supt.

Shumaker, the annual reception was held at his home (the present Chagrin Falls Village Hall). A most delightful evening was spent.

Since that date, the Assembly Hall (located in the old Philomethian School, torn down in 1940), has seemed the most desirable place for the receptions. The last meeting held June 28, 1910, resulted in the election of the following officers: Pres., Harry Stroud; Vice Pres., Madaline Harris; Cor. Sec'y., Helene Dripps; Rec. Sec'y., Lilon Pugsley; Treas., Vernie Fuller.

The Association has an enrollment of over three hundred, nearly every profession being represented. Each year adds a class to the membership. It also adds to the list of names that

will respond to roll call no more.

All activities of the society in the past have been in a social nature, but suggestions have been made that the Association assume responsibilities along other lines.

Realizing that with a rapidly increasing membership, the society should become a potent factor in raising the educational standard among the young people, another year may find some of the suggestions acted upon.

Cora later taught in the Chagrin Falls Schools for 37 years as a sixth-grade teacher and for many years as elementary school principal. She retired in 1929.

In 1912, for the first time in nine years, Chagrin Falls High School played football and finished with 2 wins and 0 losses. The coach was Ralph Gibson who also was the high school principal.

The year 1912 was a great one for music at the high school. The first Boys' Glee Club and the first Girls' Glee Club were organized.

Also, the first high school orchestra performed at the Assembly Hall in the Philomethian Street School.

As the demand for more educational facilities continued to grow, on September 12, 1913, the board of education passed a "resolution of necessity," to build a new high school at an estimated cost of $38,000. The

46

The first high school Boys' Glee Club. Dan Taber, Robert Richardson, Merrill Reed, Ralph Coombs, Sam Ridge, Harley Coombs, Carlyle Harris, Claude Oberlin, Carlton Lowe, Mr. E. C. Miller, Clarence Waite, Maurice Shumaker, Owen Carlton, Warren Parker, Sim Shepard, Turner Kline, Fred Page, Reveley Beattie, Joe Mattis, Harry Halsey, Harold Bright

original amount was not sufficient for the job and the board asked for an additional $12,000. The election resulted in a vote of 120 for the levy, 117 against. The board proceeded to sell the bonds and finish and furnish the school building.

Snow days always brought a cheer

The first high school Girls' Glee Club Mona L. Sanderson, Mary B. Iredale, Miss Lila E. Coit, Georgiene G. Hutchinson, Joyce L. Sheffield, Edna F. Wrentmore, Muriel E. Nichols, Louise C. Brewster, Lucile W. Stoneman, Olive A. Robens, Helen Brewster, Aleata J. Johns, Bernice L. Ober, Darline C. Phinney, Irene L. Davis, Bernice G. Fleming, Mary F. Kent

The first high school Orchestra. Standing: T. B. Kline, First Violin; H. H. Davis, Second Violin and E. C. Miller, Instructor & First Violin. Seated: H. H. Halsey. Pianist; C. W. Huggett, Second Violin and O. A. Goodwin, Second Violin

from students and teachers alike. Possibly the first snow days occurred in 1913. According to information included in a Christmas card from the Stem family in the Ruth Scott Noble's '20 Christmas card collection was the following (copy undisturbed from its original source):

On the second week end of November, 1913, it snowed and snowed until by Monday morning all the inhabitants of Chagrin Falls were snowbound and the business district and locals were abandoned. When the merchants could eventually get to their stores they were soon sold out of food, boots, and snow shovels. (There was no automatic snow plows in those days. Everybody shoveled.) School was closed for a week and there was no transportation in or out of the village for several days. Mr.

George Burton, a local grocer, to get supplies rode to Cleveland on the first Eastern Ohio Traction Company car that went through. He found the city still digging out, so he purchased a wheel barrow to transport a tub of butter from the commission house to the suburban car waiting at the public square. So with flour from the local grist mill the Chagrin Falls citizens could have their bread and butter. And gradually the snow melted and things were back to normal.

Although this was probably the worst snow storm the village has ever had, it was not the last of the big snows.

Time Capsule
1914

CHAGRIN FALLS EXPONENT

VOL. 41.   CHAGRIN FALLS, CUYAHOGA COUNTY, O., THURSDAY, JUNE 25, 1914.   NO. 26.

News of the cornerstone of New High School Building

Chagrin Falls Village, Cuyahoga ... Ohio, was laid ... Accepted ... 1914, sons of Ohio ... the cornersto...

Council Hall of Chagrin Falls Village

Chagrin Falls, Ohio

MAYORS OF CHAGRIN FALLS VILLAGE.

NAME	Term
G. D. Cameron,	April 9, 1902 to Jany. 1st, 1904
F. P. Shumaker	Jany. 1st, 1904 to Jany. 1st, 1906
S. P. Harris	Jany. 1st, 1906 to Jany. 1st, 1910.
F. O. Gates	Jany. 1st, 1910 to Jany. 1st, 1912.
D. W. McGlenen	Jany. 1st, 1912 to Jany. 1st, 191_
Geo. E. Wait	Jany. 1st, 1914 to

CHAGRIN FALLS
MR. E. C. TEARE, S...

CHAGRIN FAL...

The following is a list of ...
the school year 1913-1914.

High School:
  R. H. Gibson, Principal
  Lila E. Coit, Asst-Prin.

Seniors:
  Mamie Gates
  Treva Hill
  Georgiene Hutchinson
  Catherine Huggleton

BOARD OF EDUCATION
F. P. Shumaker
G. D. Cameron
L. G. Bradley
Mrs. Mary A. Kent
Miss Madge L. Kent

Council Hall of Chagrin Falls Village

MANUAL
Course of Study
CHAGRIN FALLS
PUBLIC SCHOOLS

1912

GRAND LODGE
OF OHIO
F. & A. M.

1913

Chagrin Falls, O., June 22, 1914.

Brother:—
The Master invites you to meet at hall on
Sunday, June 28, 1914 at 2:30 p. m., Eastern
... to assist in laying the corner stone ...

Council Hall of Chagrin Falls Village

Chagrin Falls, Ohio

AN ACT TO INCORPORATE THE TOWN
OF CHAGRIN FALLS, IN THE COUNTY OF CUYAHOGA.

Section 1. Be it enacted by the General Assembly of
the State of Ohio:—That so much of the township of Orange, in ...

BY-LAWS and
DIRECTORY

Golden Gate Lodge
No. 243, F. & A. M.
AND
Chagrin Falls Chapter
No. 152, R. A. M.

CHAGRIN FALLS, OHIO
1911

The Annual renamed Zenith in 1925
1921-1930

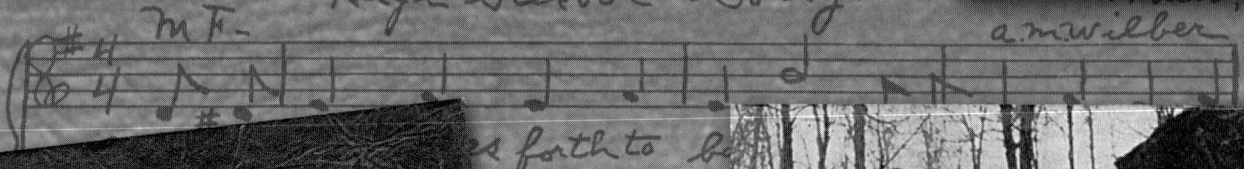

The Early 20th Century Brought New Buildings

The curriculum was broadened - interscholastic athletics were expanded.

The laying of the cornerstone for the new 1914 high school building facing East Washington Street.

The laying of the cornerstone of the new high school building on June 28, 1914 was an impressive event in the community. The ceremonies were conducted by the Grand Lodge of Free and Accepted Masons of Ohio, Past Grand Master Edwin S. Griffiths presiding, assisted by the local Golden Gate Lodge No 245, F.&A.M. The July 12, 1914 <u>Chagrin Falls Exponent</u> had this to say about the event:

One of the most auspicious occasions in the history of Chagrin Falls and one highly interesting and attractive to her citizens, was the public ceremony of laying the corner stone of the new high school building which took place on Sunday afternoon.... The conclusion of the day's events marked a noble purpose fittingly carried out and the ceremonial beginning of a structure dedicated to the intellectual uplift and advancement of the people of this and surrounding territory, not without the influence of the loftier achievements of the spirit.

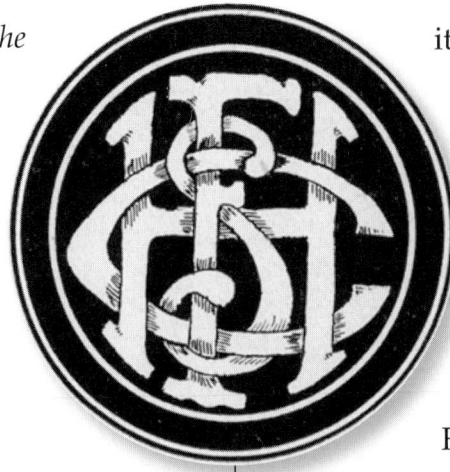

The new brick Colonial Revival/Craftsman high school was built in 1914 and faces East Washington Street. Thus, three separate educational facilities sat on the Philomethian Street and East Washington Street property in 1914. Its completion made the Chagrin Falls School System the envy of surrounding communities. It even had 2 electric lights in each room and a "bubble fountain" (drinking fountain) on every floor. With its four-year high school curriculum and high school building,

In 1914 the students voted to adopt this design by Reveley Beattie '14 as the official Chagrin Falls High School emblem.

it became a favorite tuition school. Most schools in the area were still three-year high schools and remained so into the 1920s.

In 1914 the Cuyahoga County High School Athletic League was formed with Chagrin Falls as a charter member.

Also in 1914, to add spirit to the high school and its athletic teams, the first emblem (logo) was designed by Reveley Beattie '14, senior class president.

One of the highlights for students during the summer of 1915 was a performance by a circus at the corner of Walnut and Center Streets. In later years circuses were held on the vacant land between May Court and the fairgrounds with "real elephants."

"Tom Thumb Wedding" held at the Assembly Hall in the old school building on Philomathian Street in Chagrin Falls. Children from the first three (3) grades were dressed in adult (small sizes) clothes for a mock wedding. This was an event where all the community attended, in 1914 or 1915.

This Tom Thumb Wedding story photo was discovered in the Chagrin Falls Historical Society photo archives.

Carlton E. Lowe graduated from Chagrin Falls High School in the spring of 1915 and became the head football coach in the fall of 1915. His record was 2 wins, 4 losses and a tie. Later he would become the founder of Lowe's Greenhouse which is now located on Chillicothe Road in Bainbridge Township.

The first recorded annexation of land into the Chagrin Falls Village School District was written in the board of education minutes of July 16, 1915. The resolution stated that, "All territory comprising the Rural School District of Chagrin Falls Township be accepted as a part of the Chagrin Falls Village School District."

Two early Chagrin Falls Township schools were located in Bentleyville, one in what was earlier named Griffithsburg, a once-thriving little village in the early to mid-1800s at the corner of Liberty, Solon and River Roads.

The September 9, 1926 <u>Chagrin Falls Exponent</u> contained an article written by Augusta Lane, teacher, titled, "Who Went to School at Griffithsburg?" The article read:

Quarterly report of Augusta Lane, teacher in District No. 1 of Chagrin Falls Township, Cuyahoga County, commencing the 19th day of November, 1849, and ending the 8th day of February, 1850. The whole number of scholars enrolled for the quarter was 22 males and 23 females. The average number in daily attendance as 26. The branches taught were reading, writing, arithmetic,

The 1914 high school Baseball Team. Top Row-Allshouse, Porter (Coach). Second Row-Whims, Rowe, Hine, Dippo, Nichols. Third Row-Ridge, Barnard (Capt.), Lowe, Cochran. Fourth Row-Arthur, Mosher.

grammar, geography, psychology, and philosophy.

The tiny village of Griffithsburg gradually disappeared as Bentleyville and Chagrin Falls grew economically and in population. The other school in the township was located in the area of Miles and River Roads.

That was the first of several annexations made by petition of residents in surrounding areas of the Chagrin Falls Village Schools. The only exception was when the Geauga County

Board of Education requested on July 23, 1957, as stated in the school board minutes, "two tracts of land situated on the southeast side of Russell Road, one parcel owned by E. W. Fries, consisting of 5.20 acres, and a second parcel owned by M. B. Trettin and consisting of 5 acres, be annexed into the Chagrin Falls Village Schools." It was requested for safety reasons after a fatal accident to one of the Trettin family children.

The curriculum in the high school expanded in 1915. A domestic science department was formed with two divisions—sewing and cooking. A manual training department (shop) was organized because "the hands need training." Shop was an important link in the idea that public schools should supply students with skills that would get them a job in the real world. A department of commercial training was inaugurated along with physical training. The physical training was for all grades and boys as well as girls.

The first high school girls' interscholastic basketball team. Miss Brewster (Coach), Elizabeth Rodgers, Marian Brewster, Sylvia Ruch, Mildred Ferris, Lucile Duncan, Katherine MacGlenen, Hilda Ziegler.

54

Domestic Science

Commercial

Physics Lab.

Chemistry Lab.

Manual Training

The high school curriculum was expanded during the 1915-1916 school year to include domestic science, commercial training, manual training as well as physics and chemistry laboratories.

Candid Photos

The START

SOCCER

KICK OFF

BASKETBALL

The first high school operetta, "A Nautical Knot," was presented by the boys' and girls' glee clubs under the direction of Zoe Long Fouts in the spring of 1916. For many years the community of Chagrin Falls looked forward to these performances.

An interesting oddity occurred in the board of education election in 1916. There was a tie vote between Mrs. Adeline Ober and Miss Madge Kent. Mrs. Ober declined the position and asked that Miss Kent be declared the winner. A few years later Mrs. Ober was appointed to the board of education to fill out the unexpired term of Dr. G. D. Cameron who resigned.

The first girls' interscholastic varsity basketball team was organized during the 1916-17 school year. Girls' basketball depended upon the availability of a woman teacher to coach and funding from the school board. During the same school year Elizabeth Rodgers '19 won the girls' county track championship in the baseball throw. Dr. Elizabeth Rodgers is a member of the Chagrin Falls Schools' Achievement Hall of Fame and devoted much of her life's work to the historical preservation of Chagrin Falls. Her writings have detailed the history of the village, including the origin of its name, Chagrin…Whence the Name?

Everett Kline, Jr. '19

The first Chagrin Falls Junior High School commencement occurred on June 4, 1917 in the Philomethian Street School Assembly Hall. The presentation of diplomas was done by Superintendent L. N. Drake, with the benediction given by Reverend Lester L. Wood of the Federated Church. There were 36 members in the graduating class. For many students in the early 1900s, eighth grade was the end of formal education. Several eighth grade diplomas and a 1920 eighth grade graduation program are located in the Chagrin Falls Schools' Historical Preservation Room.

One of the most outstanding athletes in the history of the school, Everett Kline, Jr., graduated in 1919. He is a member of the Chagrin Falls Schools' Athletic Hall of Fame. His athletic abilities earned him a full-page dedication in the 1919 Annual yearbook. "Kliney," as he was affectionately called, excelled in football, basketball and track. A four-year varsity performer in each sport, he captained most of the teams for which he played. In 1917 at the state basketball tournament at Ohio Wesleyan University in Delaware, Ohio, he was selected "third forward" on the All-Ohio basketball team. In track he held several county records which included the running broad (long) jump, the running

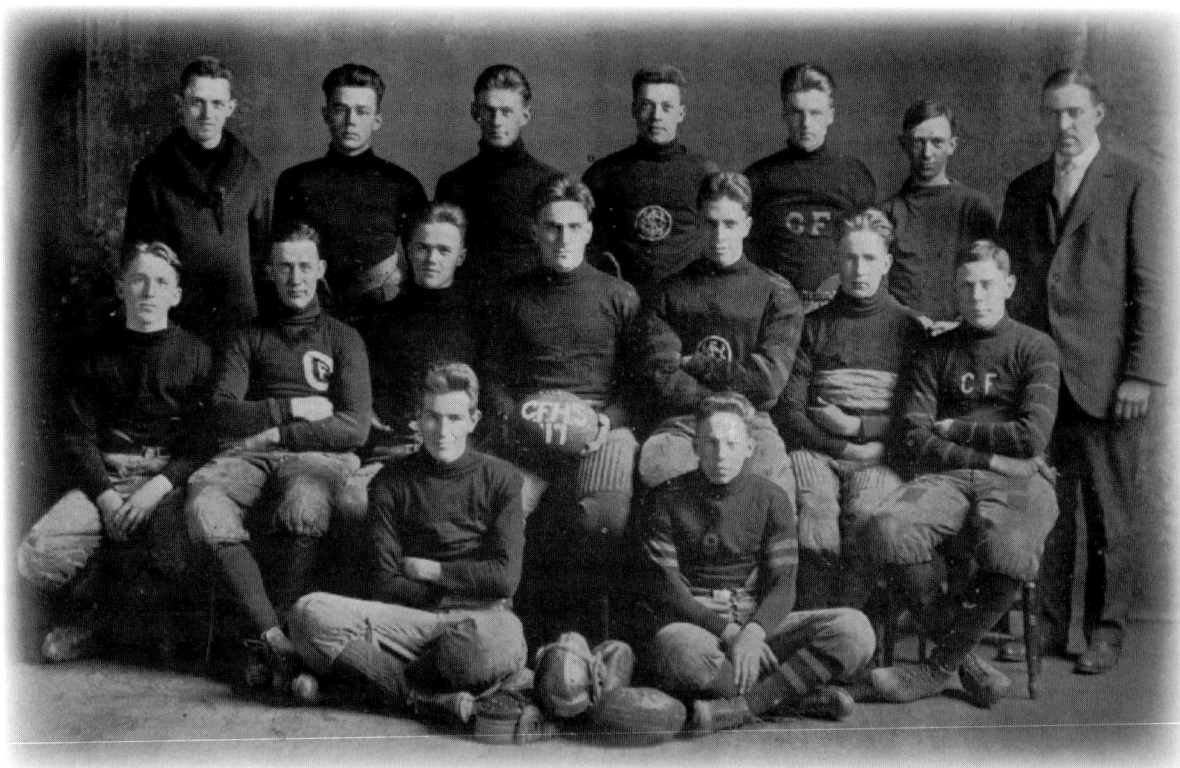

high jump, the shot put and the baseball throw. In 1919 he was presented a silver loving cup by the students and teachers at Chagrin Falls High School for his athletic accomplishments and good sportsmanship. The cup is presently in the Chagrin Falls Schools' Historical Preservation Room.

During the 1917 football season, Chagrin Falls High School defeated Solon High School 74-0, Kent High School 80-0, Ravenna High School 82-0 and lost only to the Baldwin Wallace College freshman team 18-6.

In the spring of 1918, Chagrin Falls High School won the Cuyahoga County track championship.

In 1918 the domestic science department broadened its curriculum to include classes on design and "chemistry of foods." Stereotypes (women's work) were instilled early. Girls were required to take home economics (and typing, too) to prepare the future "little woman" for life at home—to cook, sew, do laundry, and keep the household records.

Required readings in English for seniors, according to the 1918 high school course of study, were <u>Minor Poems</u> (Milton), <u>Essay on Burns</u> (Carlyle), <u>Hamlet</u> (Shakespeare), <u>Democracy Today</u> (Gauss) and <u>The Iliad</u> (Pope).

The following courses of study were found in the 1918 high school course of study:

1. Classical and scientific courses: provided pre-college courses

2. English course: provided general education
3. Commercial course: provided business classes

During the years 1917-1918, the United States was actively engaged in helping to win the First World War. Initially predicted to be "the war to end all wars," World War I ultimately claimed over 15 million lives and set the stage for a century of bloody conflict.

Much hatred and ill will for German-Americans existed during this struggle and was even manifested in Chagrin Falls. On April 2, 1918 a large delegation of citizens presented a petition to the board of education requesting that the teaching of German be abolished immediately from the Chagrin Falls Schools. Some citizens wanted to replace German with French. The board agreed to take the matter under consideration, but maintained that students already in German classes should be allowed to finish the course and obtain their credit. No further action was taken.

The editors of the Annual dedicated the 1918 yearbook "to the alumni of Chagrin Falls High School now in our country's service, fighting to make the world free for democracy." Forty-five Chagrin Falls graduates served in World War I. Many others who had dropped out of school to work also served in the war.

James V. Class '13 wrote the following letter from "somewhere in France" to the alumni editor of the 1918 Annual:

Somewhere in France

To Alumni Editor:

Allow me to send greetings from France to the Annual Board, as well as to congratulate the members for excellency of product, which I am so anxiously awaiting.

It has always been a sort of unwritten law at old Chagrin High

1919 Agricultural Department

that whatever is undertaken must not only equal but excel all such previous undertakings. It has been that spirit which is responsible for the long line of successes in athletics, social, literary and other phases of school life. The most noticeable evidence is the Annual.

I was very glad to learn of the large number of fellow Alumni who have answered the Nation's call. There is no question in my mind but that they will all go out for our Country with the same determination to win that characterized their work back there at Chagrin.

With best wishes, I am

James V. Class

By 1918 the number of students who had graduated from Chagrin Falls High School was 460 (girls 278; boys 182). Tuition in 1918 for attending the high school was six dollars per month. Tuition for attending the first eight years in Chagrin Falls schools was four dollars per month. Approximately 30% of the students paid out-of-district tuition fees. The school system's reputation for excellence continued to grow.

During the late 1800s and the early 1900s, many tuition students and students who lived farther than walking distance came to school in a "school hack" or "kid's hack," drawn by horses or mules. Their seats were boards attached to the wagon. Usually there was a bed of straw on the floor,

The first high school Debate Team. Standing–Harold Wilbur, Carl Zeithamel, Elwin Robinson, Maurice Merryfield, Gordon Nichols, Lawrence Mountjoy. Seated–Norris Class, Miss Weidmann, Arline Dekorte.

but it was still a cold ride in the winter months. The drivers often maintained discipline by making unruly students get off the "school hack" and walk the rest of the distance to school or home. Accidents occurred when horses or mules were startled or slid off slippery curves in the winter.

Some students even rode horses and parked them in "hitch" barns located on May Court and East Washington Street. Sometimes bobsleds were used in the winter. Later, the interurban (streetcar) was used by some, and finally in the late 1920s, the famous later-to-be yellow school bus made its appearance.

An interesting footnote in regard to tuition students: Carl G. Wrentmore, the only graduate in 1883 and the fourth student to receive a diploma from Chagrin Falls High School, was a tuition student from Orange. His graduation took place in the old Opera House at the Town Hall with an admission charge of 10 cents for pupils and 25 cents for all others.

The worldwide flu epidemic in 1918 shut the schools down for several weeks. There were several flu-related deaths in the Chagrin Falls area. Even the 1918 football season was shortened due to the epidemic.

When the 1914 high school building on East Washington Street was built,

Cheerleader Raymond "Pete" Gifford '22 practicing school cheers.

it included an agricultural laboratory for agricultural experiments and classes. In 1919, the board of education, cooperating with the State Vocational Agriculture Board, organized a vocational agriculture department for the Chagrin Falls Schools. It was one of three schools in the state to be designated a state agricultural school; thus, the school board could receive state monies to add more agricultural classes to the curriculum. An interesting result of this new curriculum was that Chagrin Falls student Elmer Zepp '23 won two "state championships" in the potato growing contest. Also in 1919, four students from Chagrin Falls High School were in the "State Corn Tour" to Washington, D.C.

In 1919 a debating club was organized featuring an interscholastic debate team.

During the winter of the 1918-19 school year, the domestic science department began the first school cafeteria. For a nominal price, students and teachers could receive a warm noonday lunch, prepared by the students in the high school cooking classes.

The class motto for the class of 1919 was: "Less than our best is Un-American."

*Superintendents during the early 1900s
were:*

D. W. McGlenen   1901-1908
Ezra C. Teare   1908-1916
L. N. Drake   1916-1920
W. L. Stoneburner 1920-1926
H. E. Michael   1926-1931

Chagrin Falls High School won its first men's Cuyahoga County Class B basketball championship during the 1919-1920 school year. The athletic program was also expanded in the spring of 1920 when baseball once again returned as a spring sport. The very successful 1920 baseball team was coached by Superintendent L. N. Drake. The male students could choose between track and field and baseball.

Track and field remained popular in the spring of 1921 as Britton Tenny, a member of the Chagrin Falls Schools' Athletic Heritage Hall of Fame, won the men's Cuyahoga County Class C track championship. He also won for the second straight year in 1922.

*The first photo of uniformed female cheerleaders
was found in the 1939 Zenith.*

The first mention of cheerleading occurred in the 1922 Annual. Raymond "Pete" Gifford '22 was recognized in the yearbook with the following:

Gifford proved to be one of the most efficient cheerleaders Chagrin Hi has ever had. Quiet and unassuming, yet enthusiastic, he succeeded in swaying the sidelines to the strong support of their men by their hearty cheers.

The 1922 basketball season was a success. Why? A good coach—a strong team—a first-class cheerleader! Gifford rah! Gifford rah! Rah! Ray! Gifford!

In later years, the most popular girls in school were those select few who learned the cheers, mastered the split, shook the pom-poms with vigor and cheered the Tigers on to victory. "Rah, Rah, Sis-Boom-Bah!!"

The Friendship Club at Chagrin Falls High School was formed in 1922 under the leadership of the YWCA (Young Women's Christian Association). The Friendship Club's pledge was to "promote the real spirit of friendship in our high school through sociability and service; to encourage by attitude and examples only those things that are wholesome; to cooperate with other organizations and to train ourselves to Christian citizenship." For some unexplained reason, as the club entered into the 1930s, its name became the Girl Reserve Club, which was the name of the international organization.

The Hi-Y Club was also organized in 1922 under the leadership of the YMCA (Young Men's Christian Association). Its motto was "to create, maintain and extend throughout the school and community high standards of Christian character." An interesting quote from the 1924 Annual regarding religion in the schools stated:

The Friendship and Hi-Y Clubs feeling that religion is an integral part of the life of high school, students are seeking to emphasize that

The first high school Friendship Club 1923. Seated, First Row-Clara Elliott, Gertrude Mountjoy, Catherine Cobbledick, Jean Davidson, Charlotte Dvorak. Seated, Second Row-Odetta Elliott, Lula Bowe, Mary Seibert, Laura Baldwin, Treasurer; Harriet Bowe, Vice President; Irene Murtough, President; Miss Hanna, Adviser; Mary Lynn Trippeer, Secretary; Arline Dekorte, Margaret Tuttle. Standing, First Row-Grace Henry, Mildred Allshouse, Mildred Drake, Mildred Luse, Xenil Burton, Valeda Christian, Isabelle Teckus. Pauline Pealer, Gertrude Smith, Helen Jackson, Viola Esterson. Standing, Second Row-Hilda Murrey, Esther Church, Mary McCann, Fay Barber, Helen Markey, Anna Ziegler, Beatrice Bradley, Irene Lacey, Ethelyn Fischer, Florence Estep, Edna Jones.

The first high school Hi-Y Club 1923. Seated-Britton Tenny, President; Norris Class, Mr. Stoneburner, Adviser; Rev. Pearse, Leader; Bruce ,Schwarze, John Steel,Vice President. Standing-Carl Schwarze, Lawrence Mountjoy Treasurer; Gordon Nichols, Secretary; Harold Wilbur, Charles Kozell.

1924 high school Chess Club. Seated-Clarence Lidlow, Gordon Nichols, Walter Dippo, Milan Wakefeild, Norris Class. Standing-Elwyn Robinson.

endowment. By means of Bible study, worthwhile acts of service and friendly social contacts, they are seeking to accomplish this end.

On February 24, 1926 the Friendship Club and Hi-Y Club began Lenten services at the school.

Another example of its religious influence appeared in the March 24, 1927 Chagrin Falls Exponent:

"Again the Hi-Y Club's gospel team scored a success when it journeyed to Macedonia (Northfield) last Sunday evening to take charge of the church service at Rev. Chase's Disciple Church."

The first Chagrin Falls High School newspaper was published on November 29, 1922. In lieu of a better name, it was called C.F.H.S. In that first issue it asked the students for suggestions for a name. The second issue of the newspaper, dated January 10, 1923, had the name Echo which lasted for many years. The name was selected by the newspaper staff from the two most popular names proposed by the students. Alvin Neuman '24 is credited as the founder of the Echo. An original copy of the first newspaper is in the Chagrin Falls Schools' Historical Preservation Room.

The Parent-Teacher Association of Chagrin Falls was organized in October, 1922. Its purpose was to "bring the school and the home closer together, and thus work for the good of the children." The first meeting attracted 90 people. Membership dues were 35 cents and remained 35 cents a year for the next 30 years.

The 1923 <u>Annual</u> provided the following information about the organization's programs for the first year:

October: Political Issues.
December: Playgrounds and Recreation. Mr. Geo. A. Bellamy.
January: Teachers' Program.
February: Grand Council Fire. Camp Fire Girls.
March: Girls' Problems. Miss Sabina Marshall.
April: Animal Protective League.

The school has shown a very fine spirit of co-operation by furnishing music on several occasions. Several members have shown special interest by attending county meetings, banquets, committee meetings, etc., in Cleveland, thus broadening our field here. At Christmas time this local organization carried on the most successful sale of Red Cross Seals ever held in Chagrin Falls. The Ways and Means Committee, co-operating with the local motion picture house, sponsored a "movie," thus raising the first funds with which this organization hopes to be of help in the needs of the school. In this first short year, we are organized, the membership is good and growing, the interest is aroused and the spirit of co-operation is well on its way.

In 1962 the local P.T.A. dropped out of the national organization and provided a local P.T.O. (Parent Teacher Organization).

An article in the March 1, 1962 edition of the <u>Chagrin Valley Herald</u> gave the following reasons for quitting the national group:

The local organization has neither the funds as a group nor the time as individuals to participate in P.T.A. regional, state and national meetings while recognizing indirect benefits to be gained from such participation, the board concurs that efforts and funds are better spent locally. Also, fathers are more active in this P.T.A. than in most; attendance at afternoon sessions and regional meetings during the week is often impossible.

By 1923 there were 26 teachers employed by the Chagrin Falls Board of Education with a total enrollment of 700. The graduation class of 1923 had 23 students.

World War I brought a renewed interest in physical fitness. In 1923 the gymnasium in the 1914 high school building (the present art room at the intermediate school) was made into a manual training room. The Assembly Hall in the Philomethian Street grade school was altered to make a larger gymnasium for use by the high school. Also added were locker and shower rooms for both boys and girls in the basement of the grade school building. The Assembly Hall continued to be a multi-purpose room for the school and community.

Written in the 1924 <u>Annual</u>:

We boast now of having one of the best gymnasiums in the country. Nor has the hall lost any of its time-honored purposes, for it may be easily transformed again into a comfortable assembling place with fewer obstructions, a raised tier of seats in the rear, and an extra exit.

In 1924 Chagrin's first tennis team was organized, and several matches were played. The following year, matches were played with such schools as Shaker Heights High School,

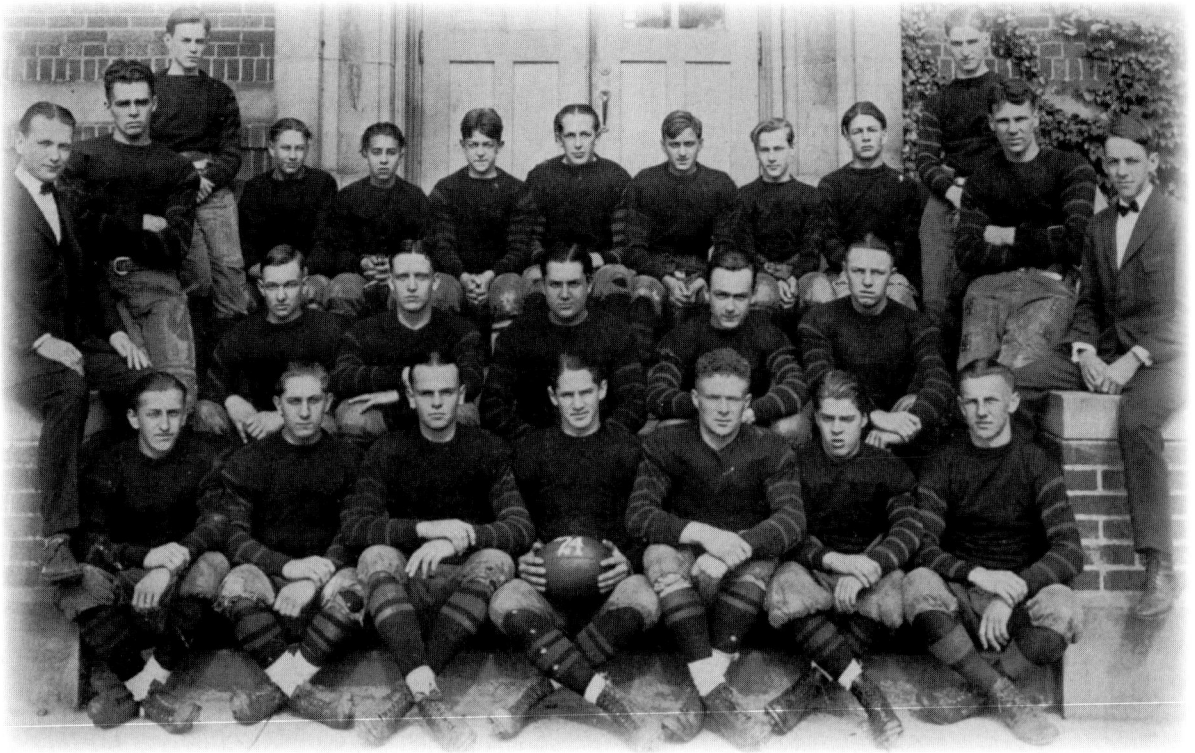

The 1924 Football Team. 1st Row-George Siebert, John Szitar, Louis Hartman, Bruce Schwarze (Capt.), Durwood Nelisse, Robert Hopkins, Russell Fosdick. 2nd Row-Alfred Wilbur, Howard Braund, Charles Rees, Franklyn Payer, Howard Heitch. 3rd Row- Francis Cody (Coach), Elwood Nelisse, Allen Tenny, Robert Zoul, Lawrence Payne, John Honeywell, Robert Bradley, Robert Stern, Robert Milner, Earl Davis, Kendall Fellows, Carl Schwarze, Durwood Gifford (Manager)

University School, Cleveland John Marshall High School, Western Reserve Academy and Cleveland East Tech High School.

The 1924 football team won Chagrin Falls High School's first football championship by becoming Cuyahoga County champions in Class A. The team was led by the Nelisse twins, Durwood and Elwood. Elwood is a member of the Chagrin Falls Schools' Athletic Hall of Fame. Durwood is a member of the Chagrin Falls Schools' Athletic Heritage Hall of Fame.

Also in 1924 Chagrin Falls High School won the Cuyahoga County debate championship.

Class dues remained 75 cents for the Class of 1924.

During the 1923-1924 school year the women's basketball program was reorganized, and once again Chagrin Falls High School won the men's Cuyahoga County Class D track championship through the efforts of Robert Hopkins, a member of the Chagrin Falls Schools' Athletic Heritage Hall of Fame.

The original Chagrin Falls High School "fight song" was written during the 1923-1924 school year by music teacher, Zoe Long Fouts; science teacher, George Behner; Alfred M. Wilber; et al. Et al. (meaning others) will probably always be a mystery.

Zoe Long Fouts was literally "the Music Department" in the Chagrin Falls Schools from 1911-1940 when she retired. She was well known in the Cleveland world of music. George Behner was a very popular high school science teacher during his teaching tenure from 1924-1928. Some sources remember him as a respectable trumpet player. Alfred M. Wilber was a productive musical composer who was born in an area of Russell Township, Ohio in 1880 which is now part of South Russell Village. He taught school in South Russell and later entered the Oberlin Conservatory of Music in 1901, graduating from Oberlin College in 1905. From 1910-1940 he was the organist at what is now The Federated Church in Chagrin Falls. According to the book, Pioneer and General History of Geauga County, published by the Geauga County Historical and Memorial Society in 1953, he composed such songs as "In Ohio" and "Geauga Spring Song." These were used in school concerts in Chagrin Falls, Bratenahl and the Geauga schools. He was also the mayor of South Russell from 1940-1946.

Zoe Long Fouts - music techer 1911-1940.

Thus, the Chagrin Falls High School "Fight Song" was created by three people with outstanding musical credentials. It has changed little over the years. Those graduating in 1924, if alive, would still recognize it today. Cha-grin, Cha-grin, C-H-A-G-R-I-N!

In March 1924 the schools were closed for three weeks as a smallpox scare spread through the community.

The enduring appeal of Chagrin Falls is due, in large part, to the inspired efforts of citizens such as Gordon Nichols '24. He was mayor of Chagrin Falls from 1940 until 1950. He later served as president of the Chagrin Falls Board of Education, and in 1967 the high school library was named for him. He was a founder of the Chagrin Valley Recreation Center and served that organization for 42 years. The recreation building also bears his name. Gordon is a member of the Chagrin Falls Schools' Achievement Hall of Fame.

The editor of the Chagrin Falls Exponent agreed to devote a whole page to news from the high school and other school activities in his weekly newspaper. The name of the page remained the Echo.

In 1925 by a vote of the students, the high school yearbook, Annual, was renamed Zenith. The high school yearbook still remains Zenith.

The Cuyahoga County Oratorical Championship was won by John Honeywell '27 in 1925, and the Cuyahoga County Debating Championship was won by Chagrin Falls High School. Also in the same year, the orange and black won their second consecutive Cuyahoga County football championship in Class A. The only loss was to Niles High School. The team defeated Rocky River, Garfield Hts., Parma, Willoughby, Dover (Westlake), Chardon, Berea and South

Ass't Principal

LEWIS SANDS
Assistant Principal

"Histories make men wise—logic and rhetoric make them able to contend."

M. A.—Western Reserve Unit
" S.—Ed. Ohio U

▲ Chagrin   Falls 1932

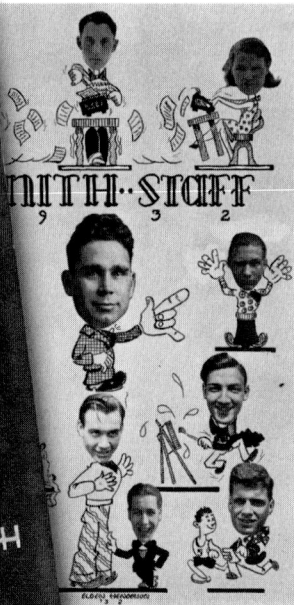

ZENITH·STAFF
9   3   2

The ZENITH 1932

Falls

"Yesterday"   and "Today"

Seniors   1933

HENDERSON
al Course
Staff (4); Z
Art (4).

Academic Course
Friendship Club (4); Dramatic
Club (4); Auburn High School
(1), (2), (3); Glee Club (1),
(2), (3).

Glee Club (2), (3), (4); Friendship Club (2), (3), (4); Cabinet
(3), (4); Echo Staff (3); Debate
(2), (3); Student Council (3);
Zenith Staff, Assistant Editor
(4).

The Annual staff preparing the 1924 yearbook. Harold Wilber-Editor-in-Chief, Gordon C. Nichols-Assistant Editor, Lawrence Mountjoy-Business Manager, Clarence O. Ludlow-Assistant Business Manager, Maurice Merryfield-Editor of Cartoons, Esther Church-Editor of Photography, Alvin Neuman-Editor of Athletics, Irene Murtough-Editor of Alumni, Norris Class-Editor of Jokes, Helen Danielson-Editor of Calendar, Arline de Korte-Senior Reporter, Margaret Tuttle-Typist, Mary Seibert-Typist, Anne M. Weidmann- Faculty Sponsor

Championship cups and plaques, 1917-1925. Top Row: 1924 county debate championship; 1924 county football championship; 1925 county football championship; 1925 county oratorical championship won by John Honeywell. Second Row: 1924 county class B track championship won by Glenn Lippert; 1920 county debate (3rd place) ; 1925 county track championship (Senior division); 1925 county track championship (Junior division} ; 1923 county debate (second place} ; 1924 county class D track championship won by Robert Hopkins. Bottom Row, 1925 class B mile relay championship won at C. A. C. meet; 1918 county half-mile relay championship; 1925 Lakewood class B sprint medley championship; 1920 county class B basketball championship; 1919 county half-mile relay championship; silver loving cup presented by L. F. Harris; 1920 county half-mile relay championship; temporary county oratory cup. Plaques: 1917 county class E track championship won by Everette Kline, Jr.; 1917 girls' county track championship won by Elizabeth Rodgers; 1921 county class C track championship won by Britton Tenny; 1918 county class E track championship won by Everette Kline, Jr.; 1919 county class E track championship won by Everette Kline, Jr.

Euclid High Schools (Brush). Chagrin scored 135 total points to its opponents 34. They held seven opponents scoreless.

In 1925 the high school track team won its first Cuyahoga County team championship. "Bus" Nelisse, a member of the Chagrin Falls Schools' Athletic Hall of Fame, won the Class B mile run in the state track meet in Columbus, Ohio. He brought home the first state championship for the school. His time was 4:46.4.

A new student organization was formed in the high school in 1925. It was named the Student Council and its main object was "to regulate all matters pertaining to the student life of Chagrin Falls High School; to promote in every way the spirit of unity among the students of the school; to increase their sense of responsibility toward each other; and to be a medium by which the social standing of the school can be kept high."

One of the highlights for students at the high school in the spring of 1925 occurred on March 4 when they were permitted to listen to President Coolidge's Inaugural Address on the radio.

At a meeting of the Chagrin Falls Board of Education on September 2, 1926, the board voted to accept the Village of South Russell into the school district. South Russell had incorporated as a village in 1925 for school purposes. The residents did not feel that the new centralized high school in Russell

The first high school Student Council 1925. Top Row: Hartman, Juras, Zeigler. Second Row: Seaborn, Hook, Braund, Trippeer, Teckus. Bottom Row: Haster, Manley.

Township met their educational expectations.

In the 1925-1926 school year Chagrin Falls had 635 children of school age while South Russell had 23. The South Russell students were transported in a Model T Ford school bus driven by Harry Richardson who was also a maintenance man for the school. Today, South Russell provides the highest percentage of students in the school district. Presently included in the school district are students from several communities: Chagrin Falls Village, Chagrin Falls Township, Bentleyville, and parts of Moreland Hills in Cuyahoga County, plus South Russell, parts of Bainbridge, and parts of Russell in Geauga County.

Forty-nine high school girls tried out for the 1925-1926 women's interscholastic basketball team, coached by Elizabeth Jenkins. The team won two games and lost four. Losses were to Orange High School, Euclid Central High School, Parma High School and Orrins (an amateur team in the Orange area). The wins came against the Spencerian Business College of Cleveland and Brooklyn Heights High School. The score of the Spencerian College game was Chagrin Falls 30-Spencerian 0.

Times were good during the 1920s, not only in the nation, but in Chagrin Falls. It was reflected in the 1926 Zenith with the following social activities:

Mother and Daughter Tea – October 3, 1925

Miss Harlow addressed the club members and their guests at the annual Mother and Daughter Tea held October 3, in the successful opening of a new year of activities for our Friendship Club.

Two Penny Dance – October 19, 1925

Mabel Dickerson's Jazz Orchestra furnished the music for the two penny dance on October 19.

Coach Ream was very obliging in excusing the football men from practice, and therefore the dance proved to be a greater success than those of last year.

Football Rally – November 6, 1925

The first football rally of the season was held November 5, under the auspices of the Friendship Club. Brief speeches were given by all football men who found it impossible to escape. Captain Rees and Kendall Fellows cleverly entertained the crowd with an act of vaudeville. Miss Gifford attended as chaperone.

Football Rally – November 25, 1925

'The Farewell Football-Welcome Basketball rally of 1925 was a sure enough knockout,' states the student body.

All speeches were written before hand and were skillfully delivered by the senior boys and Coach Ream. Senior girls gave a one act play entitled, "Wanted Wife," starring Betty Milner.

The sophomores gave an effective stunt involving a serious operation. Of course we know it was just a play.

The freshmen girls' band played some music in a minor key and everyone wept.

The remainder of the evening was spent in dancing. We noticed that Ream does not yet dance the Charleston.

Father and Son Banquet

The Father and Son Banquet was held in the Disciple Church on the

The first high school Athletic Board. Back Row: Andrew Juras, Glenn Lippert, Kathryn Hook, John Honeywell, Donald Church, Harold Jones. Front Row: Helen Manley, Elwyn Van Valkenburg, Marie Spaller.

evening of December 3, sponsored by the senior class. Mr. Teachout, vice-president of the Teachout Lumber Company of Cleveland, was the speaker and delivered a very appropriate address to the gentlemen present.

The senior girls made excellent waitresses and even Mr. Stoneburner, Superintendent, agreed that the banquet was a success.

Senior Sleigh Ride – January 27, 1926

Dorothy Trippeer invited the seniors to her home after the sleigh ride on January 27. On the following morning all the contestants in the New York Charleston contest showed the effect of the previous night to such an extent that Coach Ream remarked about it in history class.

Girls' Basketball Banquet – March 12, 1926

The girls of Chagrin Falls High who played during the basketball season of '25 and '26 celebrated for the last time as a group at a banquet held at the Green Tea Pot tea-room on March 12.

Toasts were given by Wilma Harper, Marie Spaller, Mildred Issac and Mary Thomas. Betty Milner acted as toast mistress.

Yet, not all students enjoyed good economic times in the 1920s. Barney Hoopes '35 remembered several families on the lower half of the economic scale. In an oral history publication done by the Chagrin Falls Schools' Historical Preservation Society, Barney recalled:

The exact year is blurred by the passage of time, but my father dyed a pair of shoes for me to wear to school. My first class was in the northeast room on the second floor, and Ted

Gurney was my teacher. When I walked into the room, all of my classmates covered their noses. I was excused from school for the rest of the day.

Barney's favorite memory was having milk and graham crackers in elementary school.

Allen J. "Pete" Tenny graduated from Chagrin Falls High School in 1926. Newspaper work took him to Illinois and Michigan where he became assistant city editor of the Detroit Free Press. He returned to Chagrin Falls in 1946 and founded the Chagrin Valley Herald and served as its editor for the next 22 years. The newspaper and its reporters earned numerous journalism awards. He, himself, won many awards including the Golden Dozen Award in 1969 for writing one of the 12 best editorials in weekly newspapers throughout the world. After 43 years as a newsman, he retired as "Editor Emeritus" of the Herald Sun in 1973. Alan J. "Pete" Tenny is a member of the Chagrin Falls Schools' Achievement Hall of Fame.

In 1926 an Athletic Board was formed and composed of several students from each class, the high school principal, the school superintendent (who acted as athletic director) and faculty advisor (later, coaches). Its purpose was to manage all financial matters connected with athletics. In the 1950s it became known as the Athletic Council and two student representatives were elected by the student body. The Council had to approve all sports events and athletic awards. It was dismantled in 1959 and replaced on a full-time basis by the schools' athletic director. For many years the high school principal, Theodore Gurney, was athletic director. He was replaced by Ralph L. Quesinberry in 1966.

The 1928 high school Band. Top Row: Law, Wrentmore, Trippeer, Behner (Director), Sherman, Bezdek First Row: Bradley, Kent, Burton, Small, Kent, Blair

The high school's first attempt to establish a band was during the 1923-1924 school year. That attempt was a failure, but in the fall of 1926, a "real" band was organized. It was considered a pep band. It joined the already existing orchestra to form the instrumental music department. They played at a few football games and all the home basketball games.

Encouraged by their success during the previous school year, thirteen members played in the band during the 1927-1928 school year. They played at every football game and most of the basketball games, creating a great deal of pep and enthusiasm. Chagrin Falls had one of the few high school bands in the county in the late 1920s. However, the students soon lost interest, and by the 1930-1931 school year, there was no band. A band did not emerge again until the late 1930s.

Theodore C. Gurney, teacher, coach, athletic director and principal (1926-1966).

In 1927 a central heating plant was built for the Philomethian Street building and ultimately incorporated into the future 1940 addition to the high school (the present intermediate school). The funds came from a $30,000 bond issue approved by the voters in November 1926.

During the 1926-1927 school year, the Chagrin Falls Board of Education received tuition payments for students from the following school districts:

Auburn Township Board of Education, Newbury Township Board of Education, Beachwood Village Board of Education, Orange Township Board of Education, Russell Township Board of Education, Solon Village Board of Education and Bainbridge Township Board of Education.

The Cuyahoga County Fair was moved from Chagrin Falls to Berea in 1924, leaving the Chagrin Falls' 54-acre fairground with a questionable future. In 1927 the Chagrin Falls Board of Education obtained permission from the Cuyahoga County Commissioners to use the fairgrounds for recreational and educational purposes. They obtained a 99-year lease with a fee of one dollar per year. The horserace track was made into a quarter-mile running track and the football field was moved to the center of the track and placed much closer to the grandstand. It is the present 7-12 school campus on East Washington Street, including the Chagrin Valley Recreation Center.

The first additions to the fairgrounds by the board of education were tennis courts and a baseball field in 1932. Baseball was played on the infield of the racetrack.

In 1927 Theodore C. "Ted" Gurney, a member of the Chagrin Falls Schools'

Athletic Hall of Fame, began his head football-coaching career at Chagrin Falls High School with 3 wins, 4 losses and 3 ties. Also in 1927, Cecil Hill '27, a member of the Chagrin Falls Schools' Athletic Heritage Hall of Fame, finished first in the Class B mile run at the state track meet in Columbus with a time of 4:48, while tennis (as an interscholastic sport) reappeared after an absence of three years.

The results of Coach Gurney's first year as head football coach were not greeted with much enthusiasm in the athletic community of Chagrin Falls. Two of the losses were to Garfield Heights High School, 96-0 and Berea High School, 56-0. As the 1927-1928 school year was coming to a close, there was talk of not having him back as the high school coach. However, he was well liked by his players and popular with the students at the high school. Thus, in early April 1928, sixty-three students signed the following petition that was then presented to the school board:

> *We, the pupils of the Chagrin Falls High School, have decided to draw up a petition concerning our coach for the coming year. Our unanimous choice is to have coach Theodore Gurney back again. Although he did not make a championship team in football, you must remember that we played schools much larger than Chagrin. Basketball was very successful and He developed a team that was good enough for the semi-finals. Track is just beginning and the outcome looks very favorable as we have just won the triangular meet. We, the pupils of Chagrin, sign below for having Coach Gurney back next year.*

The students were proven to be correct in their wishes to keep Coach Gurney, for in the fall of 1930 the football team was undefeated and Cuyahoga County League Champions.

Ted Gurney remained as a teacher and coach for many more years. He was named principal of the high school in 1937 and retired from coaching in 1946. He continued as athletic director and principal. After 40 dedicated years at Chagrin Falls High School, he retired in 1966. In 1968 Gurney Elementary School in South Russell was named in his honor.

The first annual homecoming football game was played Thanksgiving Day morning, November 24, 1927. The orange and black played Maple Heights High School with the game ending in a 6-6 tie. A program from that game is in the Chagrin Falls Schools' Historical Preservation Room.

The board of education hired its first art teacher in 1927. Her name was Grace Cook. Teachers soon realized the number of activities they could devise that included scissors, tasty white paste and construction paper. Crayola crayons were a must in any early art class.

Alice Neff was hired in 1927 to teach math and English. She expected much from her students and was very stern but well respected. She substituted after her retirement in 1958. Alice Neff died in an auto accident on Bell Street in 1973.

In the October 28, 1928 Chagrin Falls Exponent, an interesting column appeared:

> *"Extracts from Senior Diaries"*

> *Monday, Sept. 10 – A Senior at last. Now I can walk through the halls without fearing upper classmen. Rushed to school to choose the seat I wanted and in five minutes we were seated alphabetically. How I wish I had slept. Spent part of the morning*

making out schedules. Mother thinks I ought to take domestic science but why should I? I'm going to have several maids when I'm married.

Chapel the latter part of the morning. All the teachers gave addresses. Mr. Dobbs said he was 53 Washington.

Tuesday, Sept. 11 – I awoke this morning fully convinced that the stray kitten I had brought home isn't as cute as I thought it was. It has too great a lung capacity.

In school I recited fairly well but didn't seem to satisfy the teachers. I'm sorry I disappointed them but there is a new girl in every one of my classes who smiles so nicely every time I begin to recite. No wonder that I forgot what I want to say.

Thursday, Sept. 13 – We have a new kind of history class. Mr. Sands calls it "socialized recitation." The pupils have charge of the class. Every time anyone recites, he must say "Mr. Chairman," I didn't know that and being the first one to recite, I omitted saying it. Mr. Sands stopped me and said "you're out of order." I always knew it but I wonder who told him.

In English we are studying American authors and their works. Last year we studied English authors. I can't see why those people didn't stay over in England and so we could have finished studying them last year.

Friday, Sept. 14 – I'm tired of pronouncing French vowels so I'm glad it's the last day of the first week. Wish there were a football game. I've learned that much is expected of a senior concerning behavior and grades. But I'm going to try to be on the honor roll this year. It might help my dad's disposition.

The P.T.A. had a different idea for beginning the school year in 1928. On Friday evening, October 12, they held a dance for parents, teachers and students. It announced:

"This is your chance for a get-together to meet your children's faculty members, and for teachers to meet the students' parents. Weisenberger's orchestra will again play for us. Admission is 50¢ for adults and 35¢ for children."

Chagrin Falls High School was the first school in Cuyahoga County to be accredited by the North Central Association of Colleges and Secondary Schools. The year was 1928.

In preparation for a bond issue to build a new high school at the old fairgrounds, the school board published the following notice:

Notice is hereby given that the board of education of Chagrin Falls Village School District, Cuyahoga County, Ohio, will offer at public sale on the old fairground premises, on the 28th day of April, 1928, at 2:30 o'clock, p.m. and will sell at auction to the highest bidder, therefore, the following described property:

Said property consists of nine (9) wooden frame buildings, designated as (1) agricultural hall, (2) art hall, (3) dance hall, (4) treasurer's office, (5 to 9 inclusive) stables and sheds, which property said board, by resolution, has decided to sell.

The board offers for sale only the frame work and lumber in above buildings, the foundations to remain the property of said board of education.

A condition of such sale is that each building so sold shall be removed within 45 days of the date of sale.

Terms of sale: Cash on day of sale.

The board reserves the right to reject any or all bids.

H.B. Pugsley
Clerk of the Board of Education of Chagrin Falls Village School District, Cuyahoga County, Ohio.

The first parent open house occurred in 1928. School classes were held in the evenings for public visitation.

Tragedy struck the school system during spring break of 1929. The April 2, 1929 Chagrin Falls Exponent headlined:

4 DROWNED WHEN AUTO PLUNGED INTO CREEK; 2 LOCAL TEACHERS

Two Members of High School Faculty and Two Companions Drowned Near Marion Friday

Were on Way to Their Homes to Spend the Easter Vacation Car Goes Into Creek Five Miles from Marion Fog and Rain Blamed For Accident

The young girls with their baggage were pinned in the submerged automobile, but although it was evident that they made a frantic effort to free themselves, the onrushing water trapped them and they drowned before they had a chance to escape.

Miss Ada Michner was a 32-year-old Latin teacher and Miss Hilda Lehman was a 23-year-old French teacher. It was Lehman's first year at Chagrin Falls High School and Michner's second.

The 1929 Zenith wrote "In Memoriam" the following poem:

Vote "YES" On The High School Bond Issue

Good Schools Are a Community's Best Asset

Election, Tuesday, November 6th, 1928

High school bond issue brochure. November 6th. 1928 - Issue lost

True friends are not forgotten and we, of Chagrin High, In honor of those friends, shall let their memories never die.

A bond issue was proposed for $390,000 to build a new high school on a site at the newly acquired fairgrounds (presently the middle school, high school and "Rec" Center campus). A citizens' committee supported the board and helped to present the issue to the voters. Results of the election were: 650 votes for and 772 votes against. It wouldn't be until 1957 that a school building would be built at that site.

The school's excellent musical reputation was featured in the newspaper, Cleveland Press, Thursday,

The high school operetta, "The Belle of Havana."

"Bull-fighters, dusky Cuban beauties, tango dancers and typical Latin soldiers act and sing thru the three acts of the piece." (Photos were included in the article.)

The first Thespian Club, which was named after Thespis, the reputed founder of the Greek drama, was initiated in the fall of 1929 by English teacher, Eleanor Nunvar. Its first president was Eleanor Brown '29. They presented six plays in their first year of existence. For many years the senior class presented a play in December, and the junior class in April. The music department's annual operetta continued to be held in February.

On September 27, 1929, Chagrin students filled the old grandstand for the dedication of the new football field and quarter-mile cinder track. The playing field had been moved closer to the grandstand. The score of the football game that followed was Willoughby High School 45-Chagrin Falls High School 0. The Cleveland Plain Dealer referred to the new facility as "one of the finest in the state of Ohio."

As a result of the new facility, the annual Cuyahoga County Track and Field Meet was held at the Chagrin Falls High School Athletic Field under the direction of the Cuyahoga County Athletic Council on May 31, 1930.

One of the more interesting school activities in the 1920s was the annual all-school sugar bush hikes. Norris Class '24 wrote the following poem in the 1923 Annual:

THE SUGAR HIKE
One Tuesday morn at 'leven twenty
Mr. Stoneburner brought good news

April 11, 1929, with the following article:

*Chagrin Falls High School's
Annual Operetta*

*Chagrin Play
Draws Throngs*

*High School Glee Clubs
Present "The Belle of Havana,"
Dramatic Operetta*

A packed house is expected to see the second performance of "The Belle of Havana," annual operetta of the Chagrin Falls High School Glee Clubs, tonight.
The production was first presented before an enthusiastic audience last night.

aplenty.
He told of the annual meet
In short—of the sugar hike feat.
He said, "Be back at one-ten,
Forget about paper or pen.
But bring your pan and spoon
(But you'll get panned if you spoon)
And be ready to go this afternoon."

The garbs made quite a style show.
And the day was cold enough for
snow.
Yet all started up the big hill,
The pavement sure we did fill.
We crossed both meadows and brooks,
We scaled over barb wire hooks.
At length we espied a camp
(I might say the ground was a bit
damp.)
And now for the fun,--for the syrup is
done!
'Twas a mighty stir and beat,
Till sugar came—delicious to eat.
But now comes the saddest part,--
To home we're forced to start.
In looks a weary sight were we,

And how we felt, ah me, ah me!
(Norris Class '24)

Janet Henry Foote '50 has contributed the following description of some of those early sugar bush hikes (copy undisturbed from original source):

When I was a little girl my dad, Edward Henry, who was graduated from Chagrin High in 1919, used to tell me about the annual Sugar Bush Hike when he went to school in Chagrin. As he told the story, every year on a late winter morning in February or March, the superintendent would announce that that was the day the whole school was going to the sugar bush. Teachers and students would go to the cloakroom to get the coats and galoshes they had just taken off and bundle up again. Then the entire school would trudge together through the mud and snow out Bell Road to a sugar bush. They'd spend the whole day watching the farmers make maple syrup. The men would gather the sap from the tapped maple trees. Big buckets of sap would be hauled back to the sugar bush on

1920's annual all-school Sugar Hike

sleds drawn by workhorses. At the sugar bush, the sap would be boiled for hours in long evaporating pans. It was a never-ending job to saw wood to keep the fires going. The process of making maple syrup went on for days at a time, but the students and teachers would wander back to town by the end of the school day. In my dad's 1919 Annual, there is mention of a Sugar Stir being held by the teachers as well as a picture of a group of students in front of the sugar bush where steam is billowing out of the log building.

My dad's younger sister, Hilda Henry Fosdick, who graduated in 1927, remembers some of the details a little differently. She remembers knowing in advance what day they were going to the sugar bush and she thinks it was only the high school that went. In elementary school she remembers Margaret Leach bringing in molded pieces of maple sugar from the Leach's sugar bush for everyone in the class. As a high schooler, she remembers going to the sugar bush on the Snow Farm out Bainbridge Road. In my Uncle Russ Fosdick's 1925 Zenith, there is a page of snapshots from the Sugar Bush Hike.

By the time I went to Chagrin Falls' schools in the 1930's and 40's, the Sugar Bush Hike was a tradition of the past even though there were still many sugar bushes operating in Geauga County. We did make maple sugar in class, stirring for what seemed an eternity before the hot syrup turned to creamy sugar. Every winter my grandmother would buy several gallons of maple syrup for the family. When the metal gallon can was opened, we would heat the syrup and can it in quart jars. I still remember the year that maple syrup went up to $6.00 a gallon and Grandma refused to buy any more.

It has been many years since I've seen a sugar bush, but every spring when the weather has started to warm and then we get a mild snow, I think "Sugar Snow" and picture happy schoolchildren with a day of freedom heading out of Chagrin.

Schools today are asked to do more and more things that were once done by the home and/or community. There was a time, however, when the Chagrin Falls Schools and a local doctor went beyond the call of duty.

One tidbit from the 1920s dealt with schools and tonsils. Beginning in 1925 and for the next 15 years, a local doctor, Chauncey Wyckoff '00, would arrange to spend a day each year at the old 1885 Philomethian Street School, the one torn down in 1940. He was there to take out students' tonsils at a cost of $7.50 per student in the old building's Assembly Hall. With their parents' permission, students would line up and wait to be called. Once called, they would be given a little ether and have their tonsils removed. The tonsils were then thrown into buckets and the youngsters placed on cots and given ice cream and pieces of ice to chew. Once recovered, the children were sent home. This whole procedure was often observed by other local children through the windows of the building. They did not need television, VCR's, DVD's or computers to be entertained.

1930 Cafeteria & Home Economics Building

What happened to the buckets of tonsils remains a mystery. One probability is that they ended up at the old village dump on Solon Road, which is known as River Run Park.

Dr. Chauncey Witter Wyckoff graduated from what was then Chagrin Falls' three-year high school in 1900 and went on to Ohio Wesleyan University. He took five years of college work in four years to make up for the three-year high school course. Dr. Wyckoff graduated Phi Beta Kappa and went on to medical school, finishing his medical residency at the new Babies and Children's Hospital in Cleveland, Ohio in 1911.

H. E. Michael assumed the superintendency in 1925 and continued in that position until 1931.

In 1930 the need for a kindergarten program was felt, so with financial assistance from the board of education, the Kiwanis Club and the Chamber of Commerce, a room was obtained at the Federated Church for none was available at the school. Mrs. James Brower was hired as the teacher. This endeavor lasted two years and was not resumed until 1939.

In 1930 a small separate wood-frame cafeteria and home economics building was built for the amount of $3,142 northwest of the 1914 high school, near the Federated Church. With students now coming from South Russell and an always increasing number of tuition students, a larger lunch area was needed. However, the kitchen in the cafeteria remained a place of culinary mystery. Also, the domestic science department continued to grow. With the completion of this building the Chagrin Falls Schools consisted of two brick buildings, two wooden-framed buildings and a separate central heating system.

The 1930 football team was undefeated and Cuyahoga County league champions. The team scored 265 points in 9 games to their opponents 34. Included were an 87-0 defeat of Bainbridge High School and a 54-0 defeat of Orange High School.

Brand new jerseys and a bitter rivalry set the stage for Chagrin Falls' homecoming game in 1930. Austin Foster '32 remembered the big game:

The (Chagrin Falls) team had

The 1930 Cuyahoga County League championship undefeated football team. Back Row-Hatcher, L. Robinson, Bates, A. Blair, R. Conant, R. Neldon, Simmons, Lambert, Kermode, Ober, Walling, Waterston, Henry, Law, Foster, Coach Gurney. Front Row-Brondfield, Neldon, Seliga, K. Blair, Kelley, Reitz, R. Robinson, Bjorkstrom, Pealer, G. Conant, Wrentmore, Gilmore, W.Robinson, Bradley, Kent.

played together for three years, starting as sophomores, and was Coach Gurney's county champions. They were undefeated. For that season the school had furnished new helmets, the first to be furnished by the school, and new bright orange jerseys. These were worn for games only. We practiced in old, beat up black jerseys. The game was homecoming against our bitter rival, Orange High School. It was billed as a tough game and could go either way. When the teams took the field, here comes Orange in bright orange jerseys also! The ref took one look and said 'no way!' Chagrin, being the home team, had

William "Bill" Robinson   "None but himself can be his parallel."General Course: Athletic Board (I);Basketball Varsity(I),2),(3),(4); Football(I), Varsity (2), (3),(4); Track (I),(2),(3),(4); Four Square Club (I)

Seniors

1911

1952

1928

1916

Senior Boy (thinking he had been given too much change)
"But i've got a girl with me"
Ticket Seller (looking at the freshman girl)
"Yes but we only charge 5 cents for children"

1911

SUGAR HIKE in THREE GULPS

GOING — THERE MORNING AFTER

Dec. 18 "Ev" Xmas Vacation

No MORE "Miss Goll"

1918

THE FRESH MAN AND HIS MASTER

By— John Szitar. 1922

Saturday Bath.

The Bath this year prints a picture of a dominating person. She can be found in all public schools. She is there to teach and to rule. She is called a ....

Anyone guessing who she is and sending in the correct answer will be shown how to write his name.

C.F.H.S. Waiting For Vacation.

ANDY

1926

2-Penny Dance

Waiting For Football — Season —

Mr. Skyjack From Mars — By John Szitar   1922

While walking down the street — saw two earth beings talking — One handed the other some black object — The person receiving it was well pleased.

Shadow Drawings By John Szitar

I present you this badge for making the ALL-STAR County Basket Ball Team.

1943

CFHS

1950

to change to our old beat-up black practice jerseys. No more incentive was necessary. Final score: Chagrin 54, Orange 0!

The orange and black were led by "Rompin Bill" Robinson '31, a member of the Chagrin Falls Schools' Athletic Hall of Fame who made many spectacular touchdown runs. The final record was 8 wins and 1 tie. It was Coach Gurney's first championship team. Bill Robinson won the state championship in the 100-yard dash in the spring of 1931. He became the third individual state champion in track.

The senior prom was held in late spring of 1931 at the Grantwood Country Club in Solon, Ohio. Approximately seventy couples attended the dance. Mayor and Mrs. Frank W. Stanton of Chagrin Falls were the official chaperones, together with some of the seniors' parents.

Miss Madge L. Kent was born in 1863 in Kansas and less than a year later she and her family moved back to the family's place of birth in Chagrin Falls. She attended schools in the village; however, there is no record of her graduation. Her grandfather was Adamson Bentley, founder of Bentleyville in 1831 and a friend of future president, James A. Garfield. She

Madge L Kent, teacher 1880-1900, and member of the board of education, 1913-1919.

went on to complete a 20-year teaching career in Chagrin Falls and was a member of the board of education from 1913 through 1919.

Miss Kent's father died in 1904 after purchasing the house at 137 East Washington Street. In this house, this amazing woman, after the death of her sister in 1906, raised her sister's two children and cared for her elderly mother who died in 1911. The house was very large, and as a result of its size, she made a home for teachers who taught at the old Philomethian Street School.

It became known as the "teachers' house." The 1931 Zenith was dedicated to her with the following tribute:

To one who has been a pioneer in education in Chagrin Falls, who has done much for the Chagrin Falls Schools, who has maintained an active interest in school life, the senior class of 1931 dedicate this edition of the Zenith.

The 1931 annual football banquet was held in the new home economics building.

A class in public speaking was added to the curriculum in 1932. Several related subjects were added: storytelling, dramatics, recitations, stage-managing and makeup.

The first class at Chagrin Falls High School to wear caps and gowns at graduation was the class of 1932. Graduation still took place at the Assembly Hall in the Philomethian Street Grade School.

Golf became a club sport in the spring of 1932. By the spring of 1935, Chagrin had entered a league for interscholastic golf.

Robert Cathan '33 submitted to the alumni office in 1997, the following memories of the old school buildings on East Washington and Philomethian Streets:

Miss Kent 's "teachers' house."

Some of the outstanding memories to me—going to gym class in the Philomethian auditorium, the locker room where some of the towels were there too long and became 'over ripe.' Going back to class on a very cold winter day and having frozen hair when arriving at the high school building. The 1932 basketball game with Orange that wound up in a free-for-all. Players were fighting, spectators were on the floor fighting and Mr. Sands, Mr. Gurney and the Orange coach trying to quell the crowd. (I believe Chagrin won the championship that year.) A show was presented that year in the auditorium and Bill Murtaugh made a special ticket shelf. When one reached to pick up his ticket, the ticket seller spun a dynamo with his feet and sparks flew and you were shocked when you *touched the shelf. It caused quite a stir. The Junior- Senior banquet and dance. The juniors served the banquet in the cafeteria followed by a dance.*

The class of 1933 had the misfortune of having their class money lost when the Chagrin Falls Banking Company collapsed during the depression year of 1933. Their yearbook, the <u>Zenith</u>, was committed to the printer; thus they scurried to make money with odd jobs and class activities to pay for them. The class worked hard and the yearbooks were paid for and distributed.

The class of 1933 had another problem— whether to wear caps and gowns at graduation or not. Audre Blair, a member of the class of 1933, in an oral history interview for the Alumni Association in 1997, remembered when Superintendent H. E. Zuber came into the senior homeroom shortly before graduation and announced: "I'm ordering your caps and gowns for graduation and they are going to be ten dollars apiece." Our class president got up and he said, "We've decided we're not going to have caps and gowns."

Blair further commented:

You could buy a suit of clothes then for fifteen, or twenty dollars, a complete suit. We couldn't see throwing in ten dollars for that and then hand them back. He (Zuber) went out of there and I think that door was a revolving door the way he shut it and he never came back into our room…at graduation we had our suits, we all had dark suits and the girls chose their dresses.

In 1933 school did not open until October 2 because of a lack of funds. The state legislature was being encouraged to come up with a permanent solution to school funding. According to The Chagrin Falls Exponent, "They seem to be in no hurry to act." Teachers' salaries were cut on several occasions during the 1930s. Even in the early 21st century, a solution to school funding is still being sought in the state of Ohio.

During that fall of 1933 a new weekly newspaper, The Athletic News, began to appear in the village. It was edited by Tom Walling '31 and published by the Falls Publishing Company. It was a shoppers' special which printed news of local sports and advertised weekend specials for the local stores. It appeared on the streets within one-half hour after the Friday afternoon football games were completed. Most high school sporting events were played on Friday afternoons.

The advertising sections and sports features of the paper were completed before game time; all that was needed to complete the paper was a play-by-play description of the game being played at the stadium. Tom's sister, Mary Walling '33, and others would call back the results at the end of each quarter. He would then type in the play-by-play, and when the results of the fourth quarter were finally written, he would print the completed newspaper. Thus, by the time the students and spectators walked back down the hill to the village, the tabloid-sized shopping special was distributed. Saturday night was the time for shopping in the village; thus the customers would be well prepared. Also, they would know all of the details

of the Friday afternoon football game. The Athletic News last appeared at the conclusion of the 1935 football season. It was a free publication.

During the 1935 football season, Tom Walling gave the team the nickname, "Wildcats." He used this name because they fought like wildcats. The nickname lasted only one year.

The Girls' Athletic Association (G.A.A.) was started in 1933 as a group of girls who would organize and manage athletic activities for girls. Its purpose was to bring more interest and participation in sports. Each sport was managed by one girl, and points were kept for the girls who took part in each sport. As soon as a girl received 300 points she was allowed to become a member of the association.

Lewis Sands assumed the superintendency in 1934, replacing H. E. Zuber (1931-1934), and continued in that position until 1958.

The Chagrin Falls High School football team of 1934 holds the record, along with the 1897 and 1900 squads, for the least points scored in a season (0). However, the 1934 team did manage two 0-0 ties for the season.

Paul Foster '37 remembered that season very well. In his Memoir he wrote:

Our coach (Gurney) went right out of his mind—even painted some footballs white—so we could practice by moonlight. We played the two co-championship teams to scoreless ties, and everyone else beat us. Our high school yearbook that year listed only the schedule and nary a word about the outcome.

In the summer of 1935, the school board agreed to pay for the rental of a cement mixer to be used in the construction of a swimming pool at the old fairgrounds on East Washington Street. They rented the mixer for one month with the cost not to exceed seventy-nine dollars. The Cuyahoga county commissioners agreed in turn to pay $8,000 as the county's share on the New Deal's Federal Economic Recovery Act for the project with the labor by the W.P.A. (Works Progress Administration).

In 1935 the P.T.A. bought the first "motion picture machine" for the Chagrin Falls Schools. Also in 1935, the Girls' Glee Club, according to its usual custom, sang Christmas carols for the tubercular invalids at the Warrensville Sanitarium in Warrensville, Ohio.

After a period of a little more than one year the pool was ready for its first season in 1937. It became an immediate success. The school board administered the pool and hired two lifeguards and one attendant for that season. However, both lifeguards were fired in less than three weeks for "questionable" behavior. The attendant was paid three dollars per day while the lifeguards earned five dollars per day. By the end of that first season the pool had closed early because of an infantile paralysis (polio) scare. The pool continued to be administered by the Chagrin Falls Board of Education until the Chagrin Valley Recreation Council was established in 1943.

Pete Clemens '38 remembered in a Chagrin Falls Alumni Association interview in 1998, the excitement and opportunities the new swimming pool offered students. He gave a colorful description of how students plotted to escape capture by Superintendent Lewis Sands while "skinny dipping" at night in the new pool! Sands lived near the pool. Pete explained (copy undisturbed from original source):

With the completion of the

swimming pool, we were offered opportunities for skinning dipping at night. The pool was enclosed with a chain-link fence that had some very sharp, twisted wire points sticking up on top of this fence. Lewis Sands desired to catch us in this act. We accepted his challenge, leaving our clothes (except shoes) outside the fence, carefully laying our towels over the sharp points of the wire. The light switch for the pool lights was in the grandstand. When the lights would go on, we were prepared to make our departure. We hid over the ridge, watching him as he ran to see who was swimming. He could not catch us. After his departure and the lights were off, we returned to our swimming.

Also graduating in 1936 was one of Chagrin Falls Schools' most prolific writers, Will Stanton, a member of the Chagrin Falls Schools' Achievement Hall of Fame and a graduate of Princeton University. One of his books, Golden Evenings of Summer, was based, in part, upon his memories of Chagrin Falls. An episode from the book was made into a Walt Disney movie, "Charlie and the Angel," starring Fred McMurray. Will's humorous stories and poems have been published in many magazines including Life, Look, Reader's Digest, Saturday Evening Post, the New Yorker, McCall's, Redbook and Good Housekeeping."

Because of the possibility of an infantile paralysis (polio) epidemic, school did not open the first scheduled week in 1937. It finally opened on September 13.

In 1935 the board of education applied to the Ohio State Department of Education in Columbus, Ohio for permission to become an "exempted village school district." Permission was granted on condition the district qualify under the Ohio school laws.

This was completed in 1937, and the Ohio State Department of Education declared the Chagrin Falls Public Schools to be exempt from supervision of the Cuyahoga County Board of Education. Thus, the board of education had complete control of all matters pertaining to school affairs in the district without any supervision or dictation from a county superintendent. Being an exempted village school district does not hinder it from receiving state and federal monies.

If the village of Chagrin Falls reaches a population of 5,000 or more, it automatically becomes a city. At that time the Chagrin Falls Exempted Village Schools will not necessarily become a city school district. That decision would be left to the board of education. There would be no change in organization or operation of the school system. There are very few exempted village schools left in Ohio. Since 1954, the state statutes have not permitted the further creation of exempted village school districts. Exempted village districts are permitted to become reclassified as either city or local school districts, but may not later return to exempted village status.

Douglas E. Ruch '36 in an April 1999 letter to the Alumni Office wrote an interesting anecdote as to how the high school chemistry lab received its first Bunsen burners (copied uninterrupted from original source):

> One day in chemistry lab during the 1935-1936 school year, one of the blow torches acted up, shooting flames up 5 or 6 feet. Fred Kendall (chemistry teacher) dashed out and got I think it was Mr. Sands (super.) so he could see the fire works. Well, the results was that we got gas and bunson burners in the lab in a couple weeks. This is how we got bunson burners.

Charles A. Hubay graduated from Chagrin Falls High School in 1936 and became a surgeon, professor and medical researcher of special distinction. He was associated with University Hospitals in Cleveland, Ohio, throughout his career. Dr. Hubay authored more than 150 research papers. His work included studies of organ transplantation and rejection and the treatment of advanced breast cancer. He never forgot the inspiration provided by his music teachers, Albert Freeman and Zoe Long Fouts. Dr. Hubay established the Fouts-Freeman-Hubay Award, which is presented each year at the high school honors banquet to the outstanding senior in the field of music. He is a member of the Chagrin Falls Schools' Achievement Hall of Fame.

During the 1936-1937 school year the high school band was once again reorganized on a grander scale. It was composed mostly of younger students, some of them still in elementary school. During the next school year the band started "complicated marching" and the "formation of figures." In 1938 the band was given uniforms to wear for the first time. Mariam Church Stem '16 helped design and make the uniforms. She was a member of one of Chagrin Falls' earliest families. Members of the Church family continue to reside in the village. Mariam was a noted local historian and authority on her grandfather, Henry Church, Jr.

By 1940, the Chagrin Falls High School band was playing in the charity football game at the new Cleveland Stadium next to Lake Erie, at local football games and in parades. Concerts were even played during the summer months. The band had become an important part of the music curriculum.

Every Veterans' Day, on November 11, the signing of the armistice ending WWI in 1918 is observed. Originally, the day was referred to as Armistice Day. In 1937 there was a special observance shared by the school and community. The Friday, November 5, 1937 Chagrin Falls Exponent announced:

PLAY WILL BE PRESENTED BY H.S. CAST
"Memories of 1918"
With Local Legion Post Participating
PUBLIC INVITED TO ATTEND

Armistice Day, next Thursday, Nov. 11ᵗʰ, will be observed in a very fitting manner by the Chagrin Falls Public Schools.

At 8:40 in the morning of Armistice Day, in the high school auditorium, a play, "Memories of 1918," will be presented by a high school cast, with members of Chagrin Falls Post American Legion participating. An evening performance at 8:15 o'clock will also be given in addition and a prominent speaker will be presented. All parents and patrons of the school are urged to attend both performances. There will be no admission charge for either the morning or evening.

At 11:00 A.M. taps will be sounded on the park and the flag hoisted from half mast by members of the local Legion post.

In 1937 the high school was granted continued membership in the North Central Association of Colleges and Secondary Schools. At that time

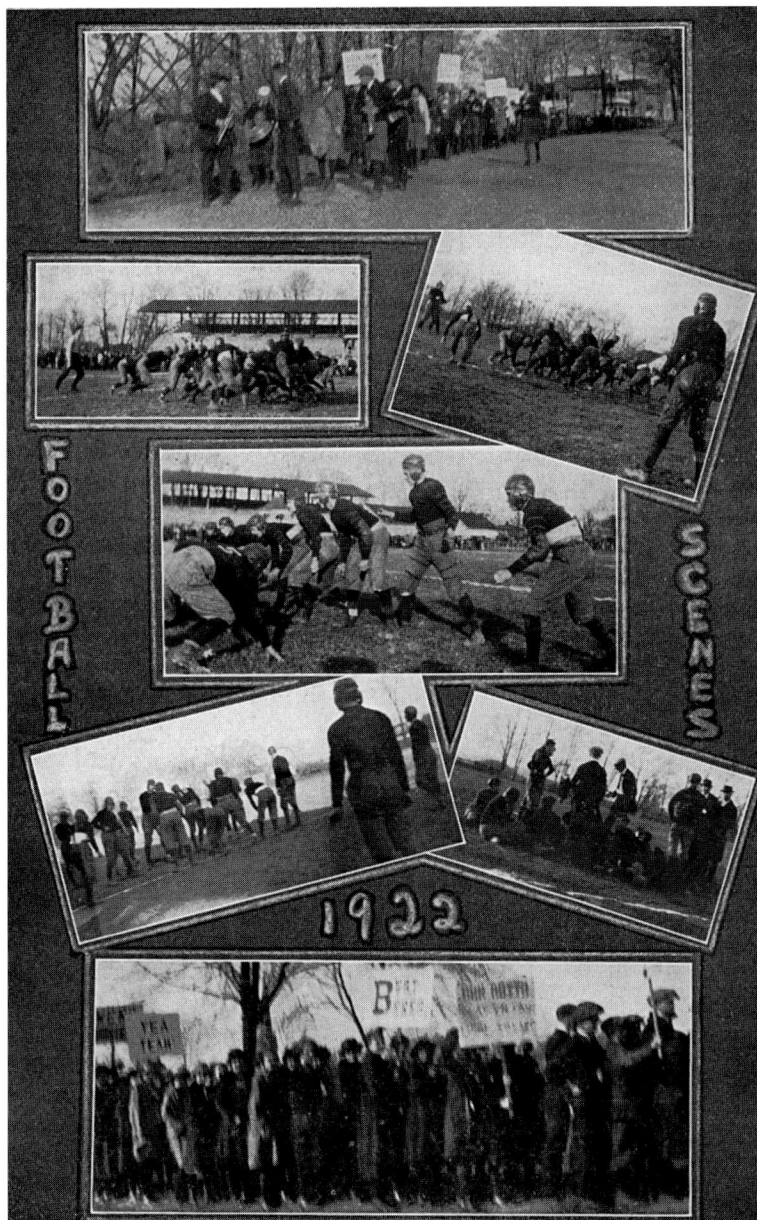

Support for the football team by the band, students and village residents as they walk to the Fairgrounds for a Friday afternoon game.

membership in the North Central Association permitted any graduate of Chagrin Falls to enter any college which was a member of that association without an examination. Also in 1937, the supervisor of physical and health education of the State Department of Education in Columbus informed Superintendent Lewis Sands, "It is with great pleasure and satisfaction that we notify you of the accreditment of your school in physical and health education."

Late in 1937, a $65,000 W.P.A. grant was approved by the federal government for completing renovation work at the old fairgrounds. Work was not completed during the summer of 1937 because of a lack of funds. Later, in cooperation with the Cuyahoga County Commissioners, the school board and the federal government, the W.P.A. finished the project.

Football games were played on Friday afternoons before the installation of lights at the stadium. The team dressed at the old "schoolhouse" in the village and walked to the football field for the game. When there was a high school band, it would lead the team, cheering students and townspeople down into the village around Triangle Park and up East Washington Street to the stadium, creating a lot of excitement. Many merchants closed their stores during the game and followed the procession up the hill. Their sons, daughters and neighbors were participating, and they did not want to miss it. There was much pride in the small village for its school system. Once the games were over, the team walked back to the "schoolhouse" to take their showers.

In 1938, a "bath house" was installed with showers under the grandstand, wells were dug, a few electric lights were installed, plus a pump for operating the swimming pool was added. The bath house was used by the football team and their opponents. During the summer months, the new showers under the grandstand were used as dressing rooms for the new swimming pool. One would receive a tomato basket from Mrs. Sprague, change into a swimming suit in the locker room, put the clothes into the basket and return it to Mrs. Sprague on the way to the pool. It was very

important to remember the number on the basket, and in later years not to lose the tag with the basket number to retrieve your clothes. Until the Rec Center building was built in 1957, one walked across the track and football field to the pool.

It is impossible to talk about Chagrin Falls without mentioning Chagrin Hardware. Ken Shutts, Sr. '38, a member of the Chagrin Falls Schools' Athletic Heritage Hall of Fame, started to work in the hardware business while in high school. In 1964 he and his wife, Jean, purchased Chagrin Hardware & Supply Co. on North Main Street from his uncle, Jim Bannerman. The store was built in 1857 and is the third oldest hardware store in Ohio. It is the oldest retail business in Chagrin Falls and still maintains its original hardware atmosphere almost 150 years later. The Shutts family, Ken, Jr. '63, Jack '66, Sue '67 and Steve '70 continue to work at the store. Bob '64, a member of the Chagrin Falls Schools' Athletic Hall of Fame, is a lawyer in Arizona.

During the summer months, Saturday nights were something special. The village boomed with activity as the stores remained open until 9:00 p.m., and even doctors and dentists had evening office hours. This was the night that farmers from surrounding communities came to town to stock up on supplies and to visit with one another. Local residents walked the friendly streets of the village and every now and then enjoyed a concert by the local Odd Fellows Band. The depression years seemed to bring small villages like Chagrin Falls closer together.

In 1938 the paving of Grove Hill was completed by the W.P.A., thus creating new adventures for the youth of Chagrin Falls. Where there is a hill, youngsters will find objects to roll down it. Bob Mercer '42 wrote the following in the August 1992, alumni newsletter, <u>Tiger Tales</u>:

FORERUNNER TO THE 'GREAT PUMPKIN ROLL'
(An Eyewitness Account)

Back in the late 30's, several irreverent future alumni from the north end of town were wracking their brains for a use for some of the scrap tires piled behind Hern's Texaco Station. (The beginning of recycling?)

The idea of rolling a tire down Grove Hill sounded challenging, exciting and fun. After all, hadn't the WPA spent thousands of dollars to pave the hill and ruin the best bobsled track around?

Could they get a tire to roll straight, and how far would it go down Main? There was only one way to find out. Several were lugged up the hill.

It was decided to wait until quite late (at least 9:30) so that most of the solid citizens would be home and off the streets. No sense attracting attention. People might not understand.

The first test proved inconclusive. Hitting the curb at mid-bridge, the tire bounced over the railing and into the river. The second try, given a greater initial thrust, rolled straight and true, gathered tremendous speed, and followed the centerline all the way through town. It was last seen crossing the intersection of Main and East Washington.

They decided it would take at least 2 out of 3 to prove anything, so a third missile was launched. It, too, rolled straight and true and reached escape velocity. However, as in most scientific experiments, an unforeseen problem arose. A car pulled out of East Orange Street directly into the path of the missile. KABLAAMM!! Broadside, right between the front and rear doors.

No one was hurt and the car suffered only minor damage (they don't make them like that anymore); but needless to say, all those future scientists scattered and the sound of police sirens put an abrupt end to any future thoughts of this nature.

Since the late 1930s, many other objects such as tennis balls, bowling balls, marbles and a stray pumpkin or two have been rolled down Grove Hill. However, it was in the autumn of 1967 that the real "Great Pumpkin Roll" began. Mike Solether '69 wrote the following in the August 2002 alumni newsletter, <u>Tiger Tales</u>:

ORIGIN OF THE 'GREAT PUMPKIN ROLL'
(The Final Word)

Concerning the recent controversy regarding the origin of the 'Great Pumpkin Roll', it is my intention to clarify beyond any doubt that the Class of 1969 unwittingly began this tradition in the fall of 1967. Recently, participants in this Charter event have come forward confirming the above claim, and they wish to be identified for historical purposes as being there. Further, the Class of 1969 did not act alone, a point which insured that the perpetuation of the roll would continue into the future.

Let me again take you back to the fall of 1967. Every year about this time mischief-makers had acted individually or in small groups to gather pumpkins or other rollable items to observe this physics experiment of gravity at work. Not this time. A group of the Class of 1969 had set a goal to collect 69 pumpkins to roll down Grove Hill in

one colossal dump. Unknowingly, Steve and Allen Leach became the leaders of this secret undertaking. With the help of many members of the class, pumpkins were summarily stolen and deposited in the Leach's barn on Falls Road. Watching what was taking place was the Leach twins' younger brother, Richard. Intrigued by what was happening, he and other members of the Class of 1971 began to participate in the gathering of pumpkins. As a result of their efforts, they were allowed to be included in the big event. Their involvement, I believe, caused the perpetuation of the roll.

Finally the time had come. The Leaches and Kim Lapick both had identical blue Country Squire station wagons. The pumpkins were loaded into the back of the vehicles, and they set out for their destiny with history. Along with this group of 69'ers were members of the Class of 1971, Richard Leach, Paul Snavely and Kinney deHammel, Class of 1970. When the coast was clear, they backed to the top

of Grove Hill, opened the tailgates and let loose the pumpkins. When unloaded, they sped away full of the joy of a mission well done. Talk of even bigger and better rolls was already underway.

Because of the nature of this crime, secrecy was paramount. Credit would not be richly deserved until now. Many have memories of their individual efforts, but they were not organized on a Class level until now. This first roll was a Class Act with no one knowing the significances until years later. I use this chronicle as final claim on behalf of the Class of 1969.

The Chagrin Falls High School National Honor Society was chartered in 1938. The original charter is presently displayed in the Chagrin Falls Schools' Historical Preservation Room at the high school.

On September 30, 1938 a special election was held for the purpose of issuing bonds in the amount of $190,000 to improve the junior/senior high school building built in 1914 by enlarging it and making much needed repairs and renovations. Also, the bond issue would include a new fireproof elementary school. The election results for this new Georgian Revival addition was 970 for the bond issue and 397 against. The board of education immediately applied to the New Deal's Federal Emergency Administration of Public Works for help and received a grant totaling $155,409 in federal aid.

Consequently, a large addition to the 1914 high school building was built which consisted of space for 16 rooms for elementary grades, one music room, one auditorium (capacity 700), one gymnasium (seating 950), size 100' by 70' with two shower rooms, a cafeteria (seating 300), a library and two rooms for a commercial department. The architect of the school was Don M. Allison of Chagrin Falls with architects Warner and Mitchell as consultants.

They had designed many schools in this region. The entire school had been built with the purpose of making it a community center.

All grades K-12 were now under one roof. It was referred to as the Philomethian Street School. With its elaborate cupola, it remains a village landmark.

The wood-frame 1st and 2nd grade building built in 1909 was torn down in 1940. The old brick Philomethian Street School built in 1885 was also torn down that year. The new school facilities were occupied by the students when school resumed after Christmas vacation in January 1940. The total cost of the project to the citizens of the Chagrin

CHAGRIN VALLEY HERALD

The 1940-1941 boys' basketball team won the Western Reserve Championship in 1941 and compiled an unbroken string of 17 victories before finally being defeated at Kent by Clearview, 33-30. Bill Edwards(front row, left),Dick Mitchell, Jim Krausaar, George Sindelar and Bob Kulhman; coach Ted C. Gurney (second row, left), Glenn Snider, Tony Rosengreen, Gordon Bradley, Roy Warburton and John Kenning..

Junior Class

One link more and the chain is forged.

Freshman Class

THE FIRST ROUND.

Freshmen

GREEN GOODS

TIME TELLS!

1942

THE END

SENIORS

FEATURES

CHAGRIN FALLS
HIGH SCHOOL —

ELDEN HENDERSON
'32

The first high school Biology Club. First Row: Tuttle, Lowe, Smith, Sindelar, Ettinger, Bagley, Hopkins, Fowler, Selleck, Suter. Back Row: Mr. Casebolt, Allshouse, Kulscar; Peterson, Brooks, Martin, Henderson,Larkworthy, Mercer, Stratton. Second Row: B. White, Danciu, Kolm, Colescott, Babcock,Stanton,Crotty, Kimpel, Bottomy, Kraushaar, L. White.

Falls School District was $190,000 with the federal government (P.W.A. Project No. OH-2117-F) supplying an additional $155,409.

The annual spring concert, held in 1940, was the first public program in the new auditorium. On March 7, 1940 the new gymnasium was dedicated at the Chagrin Falls vs. Mayfield basketball game. The orange and black were victorious, 36 to 24.

The class of 1940 was the first to hold graduation ceremonies in the new auditorium. This tradition continued until the first outdoor graduation at the athletic field in 1959.

The auditorium has continued to serve the school and community well through the years. For many years the Kiwanis Club Minstrel Show and the Chagrin Valley Little Theatre used the facility, just to mention a few of the community groups.

For many years a carnival was held at the high school gymnasium on Halloween night. Various school organizations at one time or another sponsored the event. In the early 1950s the event became a P.T.A. fundraiser.

On August 26, 1940 the Milton Beattie property on the south side of East Washington Street, just east of Savage Road in Bainbridge Township, was annexed. Shortly after, the Frank Matthews property, just east of the Chagrin Falls Village boundary and south of Walters Road, was annexed from Russell Township.

After graduating from Chagrin Falls High School in 1940, George Clemens embarked on a career in education—in particular, special education. In 1965 he was appointed Director of Retarded Children's Program in Geauga County. During that same year Metzenbaum Opportunity School opened its doors and George was named its first superintendent. He was instrumental in beginning the Middlefield Care Center, an Amish birthing center. George is a member of the Chagrin Falls Schools' Achievement Hall of Fame.

In 1939 the Chagrin Falls Schools established the first kindergarten program since the closing of the first class in 1932. That same year baseball reappeared as a spring sport after an eight-year absence. High school baseball was a "sometimes thing." If a male teacher could be found who was willing and able to volunteer as coach and the school board could afford equipment, there was a team. Most years there was not a team until the spring of 1956, when it reappeared under coach Dale Bruce.

Also in 1939 Chagrin Falls High School helped to form the Western Reserve Athletic League which included the schools of Chardon, Kirtland, Perry and Mentor. The sports were men's football, basketball, track and baseball. Chagrin Falls High School won the football championship in its initial year. The team was led by the hard running of Bill Edwards '41. He is a member of the Chagrin Falls Schools' Athletic Hall of Fame.

The 1940-41 basketball season was one of the most successful in the school's history. It recorded 18 wins and 3 losses. The team marched to the championship of the newly formed Western Reserve Athletic League and were the District Tournament champions. Seventeen of the eighteen victories were won in a row. The three teams who beat Chagrin were: Hudson, champion of the Summit County League; Willoughby, a Class A school; and Clearview, the Lorain County titlist at the district finals at Kent State University. The new league gained prestige by virtue of Chagrin's showing against bigger, non-league teams. The

The "Balsa Bugs". Back Row: J. Smith, Kulcsar, Altoff, Selleck; D. Lumme. Second Row: Smith, Chittenden, Anderson, Mr. Fry, Halstrom, Root, Koogler. First Row: Ernie, Sziter, Ryan, Rentz, Banks, Kolm, B. Lumme.

team was led by George Sindelar, a member of the Chagrin Falls Schools' Athletic Heritage Hall of Fame. Sadly, team members, Tony Rosengreen '41 and Roy Warburton '42 were killed in action during World War II.

In 1941, after completing the addition to the 1914 high school building, there was much discussion as to why the addition had still not been dedicated. It seemed that the school board, composed of Republicans, was hesitant to put the plaque from the federal government giving the New Deal and President Franklin D. Roosevelt, a three-term Democrat, credit for helping to build the addition. The November 28, 1941 edition of the Chagrin Falls Exponent stated:

"The money from the government was accepted and the addition completed and has been in use for nearly a year. It would appear that if it is good enough to use, it should be good enough to dedicate. What are we waiting for?"

Without fanfare, the plaque was attached to the front of the ticket booth in the foyer of the auditorium where it still remains. It reads:

*Federal Works Agency
Public Works Administration
John M. Carmody
Federal Works Administrator
Franklin D. Roosevelt
President of the United States
Chagrin Falls Public Schools
1940*

In the fall of 1941, the first Biology Club was begun as an outgrowth of the Science Club. In that same year, the Balsa Bugs, whose main purpose was to encourage the designing and building of model airplanes, was formed under the guidance of Norman Fry.

The new head football coach in the fall of 1941 was Michael J. "A. C." DePaola. Also, a new nickname, the "Skippies," was adopted during that football season. The name came from a tiny toy fox terrier who was the team mascot. The team ended the season with only one win.

In the late 1930s and into the 1940s the senior class had a Kid Day at the end of the school year where the class would dress up as little children and just "act silly." The class of 1942 was informed by the school administration that Kid Day was cancelled due to the seriousness of World War II which had just begun. Disappointed, the class decided to have a different kind of day and to cut school and "play hooky" at the shelter house in Metropolitan Park. With the military draft looming ahead for the senior boys, one last fling seemed appropriate. Margaret Manley Batchelor '42 remembered that the class was punished with three additional days of school. The teachers were not amused. It remains a cherished memory for the class of 1942.

In 1942 Coach Gurney returned as head football coach, but the Skippies finished with the same result as the year before—one win.

On October 7, 1942 Superintendent Lewis Sands sent the following letter to the parents of students in the Chagrin Falls Schools:

The entire school program this school year is geared to the idea of winning the war against the axis. One may well ask, 'What can a public school do to help win the war?'

First, we can brace ourselves against the flood of defeatism that sweeps periodically over our land. Strengthen our spiritual resolves, and gird ourselves for the struggle ahead by determining now the sacrifices we can and will make.

Secondly, we can teach boys and girls that beyond the war lies peace. While we are fighting the war we must prepare for the peace to follow. Our youth must be made to see that the

freedoms we cherish and fight for can be lost if we do not prepare now to defend and preserve them to ourselves. Boys and girls must be indoctrinated in the philosophies of the American Way of Life. Our Republican form of government must be maintained.

His last paragraph included the following:

This year in addition to the usual program in every department, we are developing a pre-aviation course. The class is made up of boys of senior high school age, and is designed to give them training which will be valuable in case of induction into the armed forces of our nation.

The 1943 Zenith listed 169 former Chagrin Falls High School students, graduates and non-graduates serving in World War II.

On the local level, Chief Air Raid Warden Edward J. Schroeder of Report Center 21 reported that senior air raid wardens had been selected for all twelve sectors in Chagrin Falls.

The Friday May 28, 1943 Chagrin Falls Exponent announced:

"The surprise blackout here was a success; one merchant left his night light burning; the post office made tests under the air raid warden to conceal their lights; he will make recommendations. . . ."

Chagrin Falls–An Ohio Village History includes an interesting project in the high school junior and senior classes during World War II. It states:

The Junior and Senior High School classes conducted war bond drives. If the school could sell $70,000 in war bonds, a fighter plane would be named 'Chagrin Hi.' They could sponsor a trainer if they could raise $17,000.

No evidence is available that the war

1941-1950

ZENITH

ZENITH
1945

1
9

bond drive was successful.

In the summer of 1943, a small group of parent volunteers organized the Chagrin Valley Recreation Center. Its purpose was to organize summer recreation in Chagrin Falls for the youth of the Chagrin Falls schools. Its original facilities included the swimming pool, tennis courts, baseball fields and the football field at the old fairgrounds. Also included in its program were the gymnasium and rooms at the Philomethian Street School. The first season was a huge success and the school board began a long-standing plan of cooperation with the Rec Center. The Chagrin Valley Recreation Center still continues a commitment to the youth of the Chagrin Valley area by offering a wide range of educational and recreational programs and activities.

Arline Miller Moore '43, a popular elementary teacher for many years at Lewis Sands Elementary School, retiring in 1995, remembered community dances held during World War II in the school gymnasium for the U.S. Army Air cadets training at the Chagrin Falls Airport, presently Kensington Green in South Russell. The cadets were stationed at Hiram College.

Anne Gumprecht '42 wrote the following description of the dances in her book, Annie's Anecdotes:

Alice Griffith (Mrs. Harry) was chairman of social dancing for the Chagrin Valley Recreation Center program. In the summer of '43 George Stallings of the Recreation Council and Mrs. Griffith instigated an invitation to Lieutenant Fell, Commandant at Hiram for the Cadet Corps, to attend a Recreation Program Dance, called a "Rally" Dance, to be held in the Middle School gym. Admission 25 cents – servicemen and women, free. The program

began at 8:30 p.m. with a concert by the Odd Fellows Band, Truman Hoxter, Director, and was followed by a panorama of Recreation Center Activities, the Blue Star Mother's cake walk (an amazing achievement during this time of sugar rationing), and at 9:30 p.m., regular dancing to Bill Marie's Orchestra. Evidently this was enjoyed because it was repeated the following week with one addition. The Mother's Club served refreshments! The Exponent received a letter in late August, 1943, from Bill Larkworthy '42 who was stationed in San Antonio, stating the dances held in Chagrin were successes according to the cadets from Hiram, who were now in San Antonio too!

In 1943 the Skippies played in their first night football game at Madison, Ohio. They beat Madison High School in a thriller, 14-12.

Student government at the high school was re-established in 1943. The Student Council constitution was revised and then ratified by a student vote at a school assembly.

Elton A. Root '45 submitted the following humorous remembrance to the Chagrin Falls Alumni Association in 1996. The story occurred (circa) 1943:

. . . I'll have to admit to picking up the dead cat by the tail at the corner of Water and Maple on the way to school. It was rigid, but not yet noticeably decomposing.

When I passed Feather Waite's service station I realized that maybe I should make a plan for the cat because the two attendants nearly fell off their chairs laughing. The bell had just rung as I headed up the Washington school walk, but instead of students leisurely moving into the building they evacuated the area with Nancy

103

Gleason, arms in the air, crying.
Coach Gurney faced me at the steps,
arms folded and shaking his head. I
said tentatively 'for the biology lab'?
He shook his head more vigorously.

'What do you want me to do with it'?

'I don't care what you do with it
but you can't bring it in here.'

It was a warm spring and the grass
was high in the fields behind the homes
down from the school. My grasp was
firm on the tail as I flung the carcass
over the fence and it disappeared in the
fieldgrass. That is the last I saw of the
dead cat.

The next morning the cat was on
the floor of Mr. Sands' office. Someone
had retrieved it and made a very
accurate throw through the front office
window. The window had been left
open through the night but there was a
glass panel angled out that prevented
wind from blowing directly in. The
marksman managed to heave it
through that small opening. Everyone
assumed it was me. Who else knew
where the carcass was? Years later I
learned it was an active young man
who was in the class behind named
Tom Read '46.

Social issues such as child labor did
not escape the students and community
of Chagrin Falls. The following is a
letter written by Superintendent Lewis
Sands to the Chief of Police, Alvin
Smith, dated March 15, 1944:

Dear Sir:

I am sending this letter to inform
you of the fact that the local Bowling
and Recreation Parlor has been
working elementary school boys from
4 o'clock in the afternoon to 12 and 1
or 2 o'clock in the morning.

On March 14 Richard Lanesky

was out of school during school time.
He was found setting up pins at the
Recreation room.

I wish to protest vigorously against
the practice of using these boys during
school time. It would seem that laws
regulating child labor would take care
of the late hours.

Very truly yours,
Lewis Sands, Superintendent of
Schools

Earlier school records indicated that
the Adams Bag Co. (Ivex) had been
fined for violations of child labor laws.
It was not uncommon to find some high
school students working at such places
as the Adams Bag Co. at night and
attending high school by day. Falling
asleep in class was obviously quite
common.

The Chagrin Falls Township Hall was
partially consumed by fire on November
30, 1943. Village landmarks such as
the Town Hall were important to the
students growing up in the village.
As the student newspaper, The Echo,
stated, "It was a sad day in Chagrin
history."

A much happier event in 1943 was
the second time the Skippies won the
football championship in the Western
Reserve League's five-year existence.
The team was led by the outstanding
play of Chagrin Falls Schools' Athletic
Heritage Hall of Fame players, Charles
Benbow '44 and Don Lumme '45.

One of the first major improvements
to the old Cuyahoga County Fair
grandstand came in 1944 when Carlyle
S. Harris '14 headed the Chamber of
Commerce fundraising committee
to light the stadium. He was also
president of the board of education.
Under his leadership, funds were raised
and lights were erected one year later.

Also born at that time was the Chagrin Falls Booster Club under the leadership of George Camp, its first president. The organization began at a meeting on October 17, 1945 in the art room at the 1914 high school, which is now Chagrin Falls Intermediate School on Philomethian Street. It was the culmination of a year of hard work on the part of many members of the Chagrin Falls community.

Sports were not the sole interest of the Boosters. At its organizational meeting, it declared the following purpose:

To be of service to our youngsters in school whenever needed, to acquire working equipment within the school and at the athletic field, which at the present time does not come within the scope of the school budget, to increase attendance at all school functions and to bring a closer spirit of relationship in cooperation between the schools, its officials and students and the citizens of Chagrin Falls.

Dues were set at five dollars annually.

Carlyle Harris made many contributions to Chagrin Falls and its schools. In 1936 he was elected to the Chagrin Falls Board of Education, on which he served for 20 years, 16 of them as president. In 1967 the football field and stadium were named in his honor. He is a member of the Chagrin Falls Schools' Achievement Hall of Fame.

Jerald Finch '45 wrote an essay of memories entitled "The Emerald Village" for his 50th class reunion in 1995. In his reminiscence he included a humorous story of his football career at Chagrin Falls High School:

... I got into my first game in October of 1942. Was it against Mentor? 'Finch, go in for Beattie,' Coach Gurney said. I grabbed up my black leather helmet, raced onto the field and jerked a thumb at Ralph Beattie. Harold Stoneman called out the play (88: a punt, which was probably Chagrin's most-used play that year), and I got into my crouch to race down the field under the ball with the intent of tackling the receiver. A whistle blew. Both teams stood up, and I felt a hand on my shoulder. 'Son,' the referee said, 'how about turning your helmet around. You've got it on backwards...'

Jerald Finch ended a long journalism career as senior editor of the Richmond-Times Dispatch, Virginia's largest newspaper. He received many journalistic awards on the local, state, and national level. Jerald is a member of the Chagrin Falls Schools' Achievement Hall of Fame.

The first night football game at the stadium was October 18, 1945. Chagrin Falls beat Chardon under the lights, 13-6. A ticket from that game is in the Chagrin Falls Schools' Historical Preservation Room.

Three weeks later the Boosters sponsored Dad's Day for the game against Orange on November 9, which was described in the next week's Chagrin Falls Exponent as "the most colorful athletic event in Chagrin Falls' history." It was estimated that over 2,000 spectators saw fathers from Orange and Chagrin sit on the benches with their sons. After the game the Boosters provided refreshments under the grandstand for the Orange and Chagrin squads and their dads.

For many years Dad's Night, the last home football game of the year, was the night when the football queen was crowned on the football field. The queen was elected by the Varsity Club from two senior girls nominated by the senior class. A few years later, the homecoming game and the crowning of the homecoming queen became the tradition.

An editorial written by W. R. Bailey in the September 20, 1946 <u>Chagrin Falls Exponent</u> commended the Boosters for attempting to:

"bring in every citizen to encourage the citizens of tomorrow in all activities at school. Truly, the emphasis so far may have been on athletics, but…if athletics is the answer to public interest in our schools, then athletics should be used to create it."

Bailey added that the Boosters "hope of success lies in a large membership in individuals who will show the youngsters in our schools a spirit of 'we're back of you." In conclusion he advised, "You should join in with a program to bring the general public and our schools closer together."

Booster membership has grown steadily over the years. Over the past fifty-nine years, well over one million dollars has been donated to Chagrin Falls Schools for academic, athletic and extra-curricular activities.

One of the favorite Booster Club ads appeared in its fall and winter sports program in 1964:

Good Hunting, Tigers
May the Lion's Share Fall to You Often
--But If you Get Hungry--
Meet You at Dog 'N Suds Drive-In
Breeders of World Famous Coney Dogs--
The Dog That'll Make You Wag your
Tale.

The Dog 'N Suds Drive-In was located on the north side of East Washington Street near the Route 306 intersection.

David Ingraham Draz graduated from Chagrin Falls High School in 1944. He then entered the Navy College Training Program at Northwestern University, graduating as an Ensign in the USN in 1946. He continued on active duty and became one of the few active duty officers to be qualified in submarines and as a naval aviator (i.e., Wings & Dolphins). He spent 14 years operating from aircraft carriers. From 1970-1973 he was the U.S. Naval Attache' in Karachi, Pakistan. He served in three wars and was honored with numerous awards and medals, among them the Order of the Legion of Merit and Navy Commendation Medal. He retired in 1977 after completing 33 years of continuous active duty with the rank of Captain. David is a member of the Chagrin Falls Schools' Achievement Hall of Fame.

As World War II was nearing an end, dollars for education in the state of Ohio were scarce. Superintendent Lewis Sands wrote the following to then Governor, The Honorable Frank J. Lausche, on March 7, 1945:

… However, I would like to let you know that the Chagrin Falls School district is in need of funds to carry on its normal functions. The need is particularly pressing in the matter of salaries for teachers and other employees. The Board finds it extremely difficult to keep help because of competition from the war plants. This is not a complaint, just a statement of fact.

If you can support S.B. 39, you will give Education in Ohio the financial support it deserves and needs.

Governor Lausche responded:

I am glad to have your views regarding Senate Bill No. 39. The sincere civic interest which prompted

you to write is to be commended.
May I assure you that this important
legislation will have my very careful
attention.

Sincerely yours,

Frank J. Lausche, Governor

The bill was never passed as written.

In the spring of 1945, many senior boys were turning 18 years of age and thus eligible to be drafted into the U.S. Armed Forces. As a result, as graduation neared, Superintendent Lewis Sands wrote letters to the parents of the senior boys who were already drafted and serving in the military. The following letter was written to Mr. and Mrs. Edwin Miller, parents of senior Ralph Miller:

April 24, 1945

Mr. and Mrs. Edwin Miller
143 Franklin
Chagrin Falls, Ohio

Dear Folks:

I am writing at this time to give you some information about the commencement activities.

The Junior-Senior Banquet and Dance is to be held at the school May 25th, starting at 6:45 P.M. The Baccalaureate Service will be held in the school auditorium Sunday evening, May 27th, at 8 P.M., Rev. Charles Jack will deliver the Sermon.

Graduation exercises will be held in the school auditorium Tuesday evening, May 29th, starting at 8:15 o'clock. The speaker will be Dr. Charles B. Ketcham, President, of Mount Union College. Ralph as a member of the senior class is entitled to five reserved seats. I shall mail them to you about a week before the graduation date. In the event that Ralph cannot be present for his

graduation, I shall be happy if one of you will be present to come forward to receive his diploma.

I fervently pray that this terrible conflict will end soon, and that your son will be returned unharmed.

Trusting that these statements will satisfy your questions about the closing of school for the year 1944-45, and with the kindest personal regards from all of us at school, I am

Very truly yours,
Supt. Of Schools
LS:dfh

Ten members of the class of 1945 were in the U.S. Armed Forces before graduation, helping to end World War II. Well over 100 Chagrin Falls graduates, men and women, served in World War II. Four gave their lives in the service of their nation: George Rowe '37, Anton Rosengreen '41, Roy Warburton, Jr. '42 and Alvin Smith '44. PFC Roy Warburton was killed in action on August 22, 1944 in France. He had been married less than a year. Many others who had dropped out of school to work also served in the war.

During World War II, John E. Szitar '25 worked for two companies, U.S. Rubber Company and The Weatherhead Company, both of whom had contracts with the War Department in Washington, D.C. They were involved in secret projects for the U.S. government. In 1995, while preparing for his class' 70th class reunion, John wrote to the Alumni Association:

. . . I guess by this time, no branch of National Security is jeopardized, so will explain the statements stated in the preceding article. It entailed (at the time) utmost secrecy for security reasons, entailed much travel and time as the projects unfolded. With U.S. Rubber Company and

The Weatherhead Company, an engineering liaison was established, whereby it was involved in designing couplings to join together fuel cells made by U.S. Rubber Company, in a B-17 bomber's wings, and extra fuel cells were installed in the bomb area. All this to increase the flight range of this bomber. This modification was conducted secretly at Wright Field Air Force Base, Dayton, Ohio. Eventually, this bomber was used in a mission to fly General Douglas MacArthur from Pacific Island to Australia, and finally to the United States. Time was a factor in this program.

. . . Continuing with U.S. Rubber Co., we (Weather and myself) were also involved with supplying couplings for fuel cells, installed in B-25 bomber wings, in a South Bend Airport hanger. A B-25 bomber was always setting outside a hanger there, and was flown occasionally and returned to the same spot. But, actually a B-25 bomber was in this hanger being modified. When completed it exchanged places with the B-25 outside, under cover of night. During the day a crew flew it away, but it seemed in no time it returned to be parked outside the hanger.

Actually, another B-25 bomber (with same paint job and markings) was flown in, until all of 16 were modified. These planes were flown to a secret staging area, and eventually were placed on board a carrier, the U.S.S. Hornet. These sixteen B-25 bombers, commanded and led by Lieutenant Colonel James Doolittle, were launched from the deck of a carrier, April 18, 1942, and flew over 600 miles to Japan and bombed the Toyko area. Then they flew toward the China mainland. Many crew members later died in crash landings in China, some were captured by the

Japanese. Only one plane landed safely in Russia, and were imprisoned, but within a year, they escaped into Iran.

The immediate effects of the bombing were for the most part symbolic, doing little damage to military installations, but did shake the morale and cause concern to the Japanese people. Additionally, the unexpected results was that Japan was provoked into extending its defensive lines in the Pacific arena, a decision which led to an ill-fated Battle at Midway Islands only a few weeks later, a crucial Japanese defeat which turned the tide of War with loss of several Japanese fleet carriers and their irreplaceable pilots and planes.

During World War II, W. R. Bailey, editor of the Chagrin Falls Exponent, sent a free copy of the newspaper to every Chagrin man and woman who was away in wartime service. When many came home, they made a point of stopping to thank him.

While World War II was raging, the Federal Works Agency's Office of Price Administration leased two rooms in the basement of the elementary wing of the Philomethian Street School. As the war came to an end in 1945, the national government cancelled its lease.

Chagrin Falls High School withdrew from the Western Reserve League in 1944 and played one season with an independent schedule. The next year, 1945, the athletic teams began play in the new East Cuyahoga County League. Chagrin Falls was the only school that had lights for nighttime football.

Quoted from the 1945 football banquet program: "First quarter, salad; second quarter, roast beef, mashed potatoes and gravy, corn and peas; third quarter, pie ala mode; fourth quarter, coffee."

For many years the football stadium was considered the most "charming" football facility in northeastern Ohio. According to the <u>Cleveland Plain Dealer</u>, nothing was comparable. The first college football game ever played in the Chagrin Valley was played under the new modern lighting system at the old stadium on September 28, 1946. The night game featured Kent State University vs. Hiram College. A crowd of 5,000 or more saw Kent State beat Hiram 40-0. It was believed to be the first college football game ever played in a non-college town in Ohio. Former Cleveland Browns' head coach, Bill Belichick's father, Steve Belichick, was the head coach at Hiram College.

In the spring of 1946, the newly organized Chagrin Falls Booster Club sponsored an essay contest at the high school to replace the nickname Skippies. The winner was to receive a prize of ten dollars. The class of 1946 had the winner, David Griffith, who wrote his essay naming the new school mascot, "Tiger." He wrote:

A compact and powerful team with plenty of scrap and determination needs a name and colors to match. The tiger provides both the name

Coach Ralph L Quesinberry: teacher, coach, athletic director (1946-1980). "Quiz" is a member of the Chagrin Falls Schools' Athletic Hall of Fame.

and the colors for Chagrin's teams. Our traditional orange and black is displayed proudly by our friend in stripes about his body. With this name for our teams, we can listen with glee to our opponents' shouts of 'Hold that Tiger.'

David Griffith was also a very successful and well-known electrical engineer. He has written and presented hundreds of papers and articles for technical conferences around the world. In his retirement he was an active member and leader in Rotary International. David is a member of the Chagrin Falls Schools' Achievement Hall of Fame.

During the summer of 1946, the old wood-frame cafeteria and home economics building built in 1930 was sold and the space it occupied was used as a playground for the lower grades. The acoustical treatment of the new school cafeteria, built as part of the 1940 addition to the 1914 high school building, was completed.

A new assistant football coach, Ralph L. Quesinberry, was added to the 1946 football staff. The Tigers finished the season with a win over archrival Orange High School, 52-0.

For 22 years (1924-1946) the Chagrin Falls Exponent printed the high school newspaper, the Echo, in its pages. On December 13, 1946 a change occurred when the high school began to publish its own Echo. Students were charged three cents for the first publication. Interestingly, Solon High School helped publish the Echo by running off the newspaper on their new mimeograph machine.

The first driving instruction course was introduced at Chagrin Falls High School in the spring of 1947. A 1947 Ford was provided by the Parmelee-Kent Co. of Chagrin Falls. Well remembered in those early driving instruction classes was the first attempt to drive up and down Grove Hill. Interestingly, it was a much steeper dirt road before it was paved during the depression years by the W.P.A.

More traffic led to a new school organization, Safety Patrol, with terms such as: slow—school crossing, hold hands, walk in line and cross only with the red light. For many years Police Chief Smitty was the popular crossing guard at Main and Washington Streets. He was well liked and respected by the students and the community.

Also in the spring of 1947, Chagrin Falls High School conducted its first boxing tournament under the direction of Coach Ralph Quesinberry.

As school was coming to a close in 1947, the high school cafeteria on May 29 offered the following menu:

Plate Dinner
  Meat Loaf, Green Beans, Potatoes....15 cents
Soup
  Chicken Noodle or Tomato..............5 cents
Sandwiches
  Cheese, Deviled Egg or Jelly............8 cents
Salads
  Tossed, Waldorf or Pineapple..........10 cents
Dessert
  Ice Cream, Cake or Pudding.............5 cents
Milk
  Chocolate or White.......................6 cents

Robert Paul Dye graduated from Chagrin Falls High School in 1947.

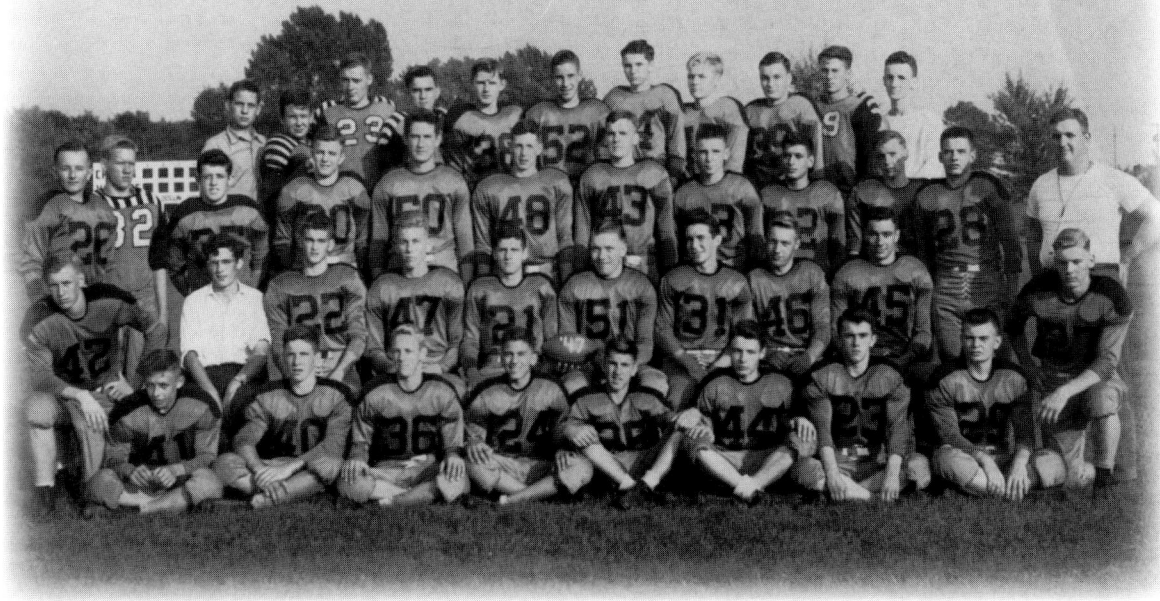

1947 East Cuyahoga County championship undefeated football team .

After earning an M.A. in English from Western Michigan University in 1958, he embarked on a career in communications, earning prestigious awards for his accomplishments. He has written many books and his Hawaii Chronicles: Island History from the Pages of Honolulu Magazine received an award from the Hawaii Book Publishers. His publication was also nominated for the Kamakau Award for the best book of the year. He wrote numerous articles and reviews for various newspapers and magazines. He was a contributing political editor to Honolulu Magazine, and has been a political and election-night commentator for Honolulu television stations. Paul is a member of the Chagrin Falls Schools' Achievement Hall of Fame.

During the mid 1940s, a rift developed between the minister of the Federated Church, Lester L. Wood, and Lewis Sands, the school superintendent. The issue, according to Reverend Wood, was that the members of the local Methodist Church dominated the Chagrin Falls Schools from conducting baccalaureate services, commencements and assemblies to board membership, administrators and teachers. Beginning in 1944 both began to exchange letters dealing with the situation, even to the point where Reverend Wood refused to attend a school assembly to which he had been invited. It reached a climax on May 31, 1947 when Reverend Wood wrote the following letter to Superintendent Sands:

May 31, 1947
Dear Mr. Sands,

I have your good letter of yesterday. Thanks for the tickets. I shall be on hand to help as best I can.

I hesitate to mention this matter again. But my feelings enter so deeply into the picture that I must mention it. One's frame of mind has so much to do with even a prayer or benediction. I have the feeling that I am somewhat insulated when I go to the school for any function. This time it is to be again a Methodist

111

The first Varsity Club. Back Row: T. C. Gurney, Froebe, Briggs, Danciu, Kagy, Doell, Imars, R. L. Quesinberry. Second Row: Talcott, Plazak, Davidson, Cox, Hileman, Green, Sindelar, Hoopes. First Row: Smith, Black, Eggleston, Winship, Dye, Hubbard, Miraglia, Green, Skeel.

team, with the exception of myself, who are to graduate the class. This was the case in every instance, with but one possible exception (Mrs. Cameron presided once), when I was here previously during the six commencements. And as best I can discover, it was true long before I came to Chagrin, and continued to be true all the sixteen years I was away from Chagrin (Rev. Wood served as minister of the Federated Church on three separate occasions: 1918-1921; 1923-1925; and 1941-1947).

Louis, I know you do not appreciate my point of view. I know you think I am inventing some things. But statistics will prove that my suspicions are well founded. Next year, if you desire me to do anything in the schools, I shall try hard to do it. I simply want you to know that it is a real chore when I do try to function, this because of my feeling that the Federated Church has not for forty

years had a good break in the schools. We have not had superintendents, and we have not had high school teachers giving to our church any attention. They have practically all been in your church. This is a discouraging note to make in a commencement. But since it must be in my heart, I venture to put into yours also, this in order that we may soon remedy the wrong.

Most sincerely,
Lester Wood

Several months later the Reverend Lester L. Wood retired as minister of the Federated Church. He served as a member of the Chagrin Falls Board of Education from 1920-1922. He was also the founder and advisor to the Hi-Y Club from 1922-1925.

Under the new head football coach, Ralph L. Quesinberry, a member of the Chagrin Falls Schools' Athletic Hall of Fame, the 1947 Tigers were undefeated, scoring 233 points vs. opponents'

The 1949 Boxing Tournament Champions. 1st Row (Left To Right): Bob Scott, Jack Buchanan, Jim Hubbard, Karl Hoekstra, Ben Miralia. 2nd Row (Left To Right): Rolf Tinge (Assistant), Ray Arnold, Ray Henderson, Bill Adlerfer, Bill Hern (Assistant), Coach Ralph Quesinberry.

22. Emil Danciu '48, a member of the Chagrin Falls Schools' Athletic Heritage Hall of Fame, scored 13 touchdowns while Jack Skeel '48, a member of the Chagrin Falls Schools' Athletic Hall of Fame, scored 7 touchdowns and threw 11 touchdown passes from the single wing formation. Bob Plzak '49, also a member of the Chagrin Falls Schools' Athletic Hall of Fame and a member of the East Cuyahoga County championship team, lost his life while serving his country in the armed forces during the Korean War.

The 1947-48 varsity basketball team was also coached by Ralph Quesinberry. It was the only year that he coached varsity basketball.

An innovation for the Chagrin Falls High School band in the fall of 1947 was the wearing of flashlights on the band hats. Also new that year, head majorette JoAnn Honeywell '48 used a lighted baton.

As the band continued to increase in numbers in the late 1940s and into the 1950s, the need for more and appropriate uniforms emerged. Thus began the annual magazine sales campaign to aid in funding the expanding instrumental music program.

One of the worst storms, possibly the worst in the village's history, occurred Sunday evening, September 21, 1947. After the storm, in the next issue of the <u>Chagrin Falls Exponent</u>, the

113

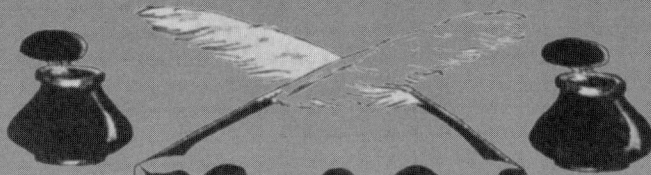

Teachers

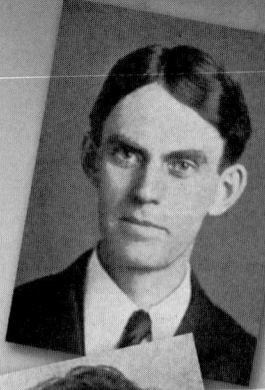

FACULTY

E N

Z L F

J C G

H E J

W M S

M R

L N

newspaper described the storm in its front page headline, "THE BIG BLOW! or Nature in the Rough." Many village residents referred to the storm as the "Tornado of 47." The damage was very significant—enough to close school the day following the vicious storm. Fortunately, it has been the only time that school was closed due to a possible tornado.

In 1947 the Standard Drug Store was replaced by the new roller skating rink as the local student hangout. However, many students remained loyal to Standard Drug because of their famous "cherry cokes."

In 1947 the first Varsity Club was organized. It was composed entirely of Chagrin Falls High School lettermen. Its purpose was the promotion and betterment of all school sports. A dream of many elementary school boys was earning a varsity letter in athletics, along with a personalized varsity jacket and letter sweater. At present, there is no Varsity Club at the high school.

Once again, under the direction of Coach Quesinberry, the 2nd annual boxing tournament was held in March, 1948, with 102 boys participating. It was sponsored by the Varsity Club. The purpose of the boxing tournament was to learn the art of self-defense and develop good muscle coordination.

The contestants in the boxing tournaments were divided into weight classes and used 16-ounce gloves. Each match was three one-minute rounds. The first-round matches were fought in the boys' physical education classes and at noonday tournaments. The final matches took place in the evening. These boxing shows lasted for four years, 1947-1950, and were discontinued because of concerns for the participants' safety.

One of the highlights of the 1947-1948 school year was the writing of the Chagrin Falls High School Alma Mater to the tune of "Far Above Cayuga's Waters" which is also the Cornell University Alma Mater. It was written by Archibold Croswell Weeks in 1872, and the tune was composed by Wilmot Moses Smith in 1874. The melody of the Alma Mater has been copied over the years by dozens of other universities, colleges and high schools. Chagrin Falls was one of those high schools.

The Alma Mater was written due to the need for a more refined school song than the fight song. Also, the fight song was very difficult to play with musical instruments during half-time shows performed by the band at football games. Many other school bands at that time were playing more sophisticated alma maters.

During the research of several school and alumni projects dealing with the 1940s, a single sheet of notebook paper was discovered with four student names written next to four verses under the title, Chagrin Falls High School Alma Mater, "Far Above Cayuga's Waters."

During the school year of 1947-1948 the high school students were confronted with a voluntary assignment to write verses for the Cornell tune. The challenge came from the school administrators, Lewis Sands, superintendent, and Theodore Gurney, high school principal, along with the schools' music department. The music department consisted of Albert Freeman, instructor of instrumental music and an accomplished violin player and William Freeland and Jane Voelker, vocal music teachers. Entries were to be turned in from each grade level, 9-12. The students wrote four line verses and turned them into the school officials with one verse being chosen from each high school class. There seems to have been some collaborating among classmates. Memories are beginning to fade in regard to how much and by whom. However, according to the preserved single sheet of notebook paper, Helen Spielhaupter '48, Betsy Schroeder '49, Russell Peterson '50 and Alan Kewish '51 wrote the words for the Chagrin Falls Schools' Alma Mater. Except for five minor changes of words, it remains the same 55 years later: "Praise to thee, our Alma Mater, praise to thee, Chagrin."

In 1948 Ed Kagy graduated from Chagrin Falls High School with a class prophecy: "Will some day own his own advertising agency." In 1967 he became co-owner of Liggett-Stashower Advertising Agency in Cleveland, Ohio. He won numerous awards including Best of Show from the Art Directors' Club of Cleveland and two Best of Cleveland Advertising Awards from the Cleveland Advertising Club. He was a founder of the Cleveland Society of Communicating Arts. Ed is a member of the Chagrin Falls Schools' Achievement Hall of Fame.

Janet Johnson joined the teaching staff at Chagrin Falls High School as a music teacher in the fall of 1948. Before leaving in 1954, she married fellow teacher, Neal Wheatcraft. Their first date was at the 1951 Y-Teen Formal. It was truly a "high school romance." The 1954 yearbook was dedicated to them.

For many years, beginning in April 1949, continuing into the early 1960s, Coach Quesinberry and later Barbara Brown, women's physical education teacher, would have their physical education classes perform a gym show for the community, usually in the month of March. It included tumbling, rope climbing and gymnastic stunts with the springboard. At the conclusion of the event the senior boys performed a silent marching routine, a close-order

drill. It required strict concentration and memorization since all of the precision turns and "about faces" were given without any commands. Even after the gym shows came to an end, Coach continued his silent marching routine in the high school for men and women.

Coach Quesinberry was selected National Athletic Director of the Year by the American Association of Health and Physical Education and Recreation Teachers in 1972. Upon his retirement in 1980, after thirty-five years of dedicated service to the school system, the high school gymnasium was named in his honor: the Ralph L. Quesinberry Gymnasium.

Valedictorian of his class and president of the Honor Society in 1949 at Chagrin Falls High School was Peter T. Cubberley. He has been the Medical Director of the Free Clinic of Greater Cleveland, where he volunteered as a physician for over 25 years. Dr. Cubberley was instrumental in setting up the HIV / AIDS CARE program at Kaiser / Permanente and continues to devote much of his professional time to the care of persons with this disease. He has received many awards for his humanitarian work in the Greater Cleveland area. Peter is a member of the Chagrin Falls Schools' Achievement Hall of Fame.

Bill Darlin graduated from Chagrin Falls High School in 1949. He has dedicated much of his life to humanitarian efforts. He has served as deck officer for Spirit of Grace, a 2000-ton humanitarian freighter which carries food and medicine to third world countries. He has also volunteered as an English teacher in China. Bill is a member of the Chagrin Falls Schools' Achievement Hall of Fame.

1951-1960

ZENITH

1953

1960 ZENITH

The 1950's Brought Progressive Changes In Curriculum

New schools were built at the old fairgrounds - teachers were encouraged to improve their proficiency – the schools remained committed to excellence.

The end of World War II did not bring to an end the turmoil in the United States and the world. Competition between the world's two superpowers resulted in a tension-filled "Cold War." The Soviet leader, Nikita Khrushchev, warned, "We will bury you."

The Korean War in the early 1950s demonstrated the struggle between the two superpowers.

From information supplied for the recently published book by the Chagrin Falls Historical Society, <u>Chagrin Falls - An Ohio Village History,</u> Ed Kagy '48 described experiences of eight members of his class during the Korean conflict (reprinted with permission of the Chagrin Falls Historical Society):

Minute Men of 1950

World War II was not the last war that would find Chagrin Falls men and women serving their country. The Korean War (1950-1953) also called upon young men and women to serve. One cadre of soldiers mustered in Chagrin Falls and stayed together as a unit throughout their tours of duty.

The <u>Chagrin Valley Herald</u> labeled them "The Minute Men." The 3641ˢᵗ Medium Automotive Maintenance Company was a locally based unit of the Ohio National Guard. Formed in 1948 in Chagrin Falls, the Company

The First High School Key Club. First Row: J. Hubbard, Hine, T. Hubbard, J. Rodgers, Kennedy, Boone, Hawn.Second Row: Stevenson, W. Barber, Evans, Babcock, Luckay, Wiley, McCabe, D. Evans, Stanton, Gibson, Worstell. Third Row: Mr. Gurney, Bullock, Moyse, B. Barber, Anderson, Miraglia, Kewish, Ebel, Hoekstra, T. Rodgers, Conway.

was charged with maintaining and servicing military vehicles.

The Company enjoyed the leadership of a number of World War II veterans, most of whom were Chagrin Falls residents and Chagrin Falls High School graduates. The majority were young men who were college students or recent high school graduates living and working in the Chagrin and southwestern Geauga County area. Among the young men were eight from the Chagrin Falls Class of 1948 (Bob Farrar, Don Smith, Joe Miraglia, Ed Kagy, Dave Hoopes, Willard Felger, Marshall Jennison and Lester Green) as well as a number of young men from Orange and Newbury schools and nearby Cleveland suburbs.

When the call-up came in September 1950, the Company was well prepared and became a cadre (training) unit for the draftees coming in from Michigan to fill out the ranks of the Company. The *Chagrin Valley*

Herald reported the community send-off given the unit in September 1950 as it left for Camp Atterbury. Nearly 5,000 residents of the Chagrin Valley turned out in Triangle Park in Chagrin Falls to send off the 3641st. The patriotic crowd heard Mayor Robert W. Gresham say, 'We have the best in both Cuyahoga and Geauga Counties here tonight. This is the first time since the Civil War that a group of soldiers has left Chagrin Falls as a unit, and I want you to know we're proud of you.'

The Company was part of Operation Blue Jay, the most closely guarded secret of the Korean War. Their mission was to build over one summer a Strategic Air Command base at Thule, Greenland which would ultimately have facilities carved into the mountainside under the ice cap capable of storing supplies for 10 divisions (about 50,000 men) for one year.

Upon completion of their job,

The First Choral Club, "A Cappella Choir", Was Formed By Combining The Boys' And Girls' Glee Clubs.
Back Row: Simons, Burke, Behlen, Dunton, Don Evans, Cobbledick, Dick Evans,Luckay, Ryan, McCabe, Hill,
Van Gorder, Mason, Kaserman, Stevenson, Richards, Lambert,Fram. Second Row: Mr. Freeland, Myers, Ebel,
Henry, Shatford, Stoneman, Root,Hubbard, Miraglia, Draz, Barber, Bullock, J. Ebel, Smith, Pearch, Bradley,
Weeks, Curtiss, Babcock. First Row: Collier, Schaaf, Green, Shurmer, Rogers, Worstell, O'kane, D. Ebel,R.
Crowe, Stroud, B. Crowe, Bullock, Carleton, Keary, D. Richards, Bowe.

the unit was sent back to Camp Atterbury. The men who had joined back in 1948 for a 4-year enlistment were discharged. The draftees of 1950 who had joined the 3641st were not as fortunate and many were reassigned to the Far East Command to fight the ground war in Korea.

Highlights of the "Fabulous 50s" were not always fabulous:

Senator Kefauver of Tennessee exposed the Mafia on television.

H-bombs were tested by the Soviets and Americans, resulting in home bomb shelters.

Students practiced "duck and cover" in school.

President Eisenhower sent federal troops to help integrate Little Rock, Arkansas' schools.

The Korean War dominated the struggle between Communism and the Western World.

President Truman fired popular General Douglas MacArthur.

Popular television quiz shows were found to be rigged.

The Communist-hunting McCarthy hearings were televised, creating "blacklists" of various kinds.

Rosa Parks and "freedom marchers" demonstrated for integration.

The move to "suburbia" increased, resulting in urban sprawl.

The 1953-1954 student handbook for Chagrin Falls High School had a separate page designated to Civilian Defense. It read:

If there is sufficient time after an alarm, all pupils will be evacuated home; but in the event time is short provisions have been made to care for

In 1950 the Student Council became the first Student Activities Council. Standing: C. Cramer, Van Nort, Lambert, P. Stoneman, Waller, M. Anderson, Dunton, Schaaf, Myers, Ebel, McNally. Seated: Mr. Swagler, T. Rodgers, Hine, Bailey, Crowe, J. Stoneman, Shurmer, Draz, Hawn.

them in the school auditorium and the lower inside corridor where the pupils and teachers can be made comfortable.

The Chagrin Falls Exempted Village School has been designated as a hospital center by the Civilian Defense Organization and an $8000 allotment has been assigned for equipment and supplies.

However, through the decade of the 50s, the Chagrin Falls Schools continued on their course of excellence and its students reveled in the good times of the "Fabulous 50s."

The 1950s were "kinder, gentler times" for many. Ruth Barriball Weber '55 remembered those times in material she provided for the Chagrin Falls Historical Society for an oral history project in 1998. Ruth explained:

We spent our summers at the rec swimming, tennis lessons and attending the canteen dances on Fridays. Frequently all the girls in class enjoyed slumber parties at various homes. Staying up telling stories, talking about boys, teachers, etc., and making home made fudge comes to mind when I think of our bonding with our classmates. Classes pretty much stayed with their own classmates on socializing and dating. It was unusual if someone dated an upper or lower classmate. Sports and dances were the few ways the classes mingled. And it was almost unheard of to date or socialize with kids from other schools. Perhaps the lack of having cars early was a reason.

The High School Key Club was organized in May 1950 under the sponsorship of the local Kiwanis Club and the guidance of the high school administration. The club was formed by selecting boys in grades 10-12 on the basis of scholarship and participation in extracurricular activities. Its purpose was to perform services for the Chagrin Falls Schools and community.

In 1950 the Theodore Thoren property, just east of the Chagrin Falls Village boundary and north of Walters Road, was annexed from Russell

1950 Ukulele Club. First Row: Richards, Fram, Evans, Dunton, Worstell, Schaaf, Luckay, Behlen, Crowe, Second Row: Curtis, Hoekstra, Cubberley, McFarland, Wince, Lawyer, Mr. Harper, Short, Toth, P. Hoekstra, Hawersaat.

Township. Several years later, the Lopatt property south of Walters Road was annexed from Russell Township, and the James Lewis development north of Russell Road in the Cardinal Lane area was annexed.

The first year for an A Cappella Choir was 1950. Also, a new type of student government was formed, the Student Activities Council. It was in charge of all student-sponsored social events and activities and became the "voice of the students."

Stuart D. Root, a 1950 graduate from Chagrin Falls High School and Columbia Law School graduate, was actively involved in designing the legal structure for the largest real estate acquisition in Manhattan since Rockefeller Center. His client was the Bowery Savings Bank, one of the largest savings institutions in the world at that time. In 1970 he became the legal architect for a new federal agency known as Freddie Mac (the Federal Home Loan Mortgage Corporation). From 1981 through 1983

he was President and Vice-Chairman of the Bowery Savings Bank in New York City and was Executive Director of the Federal Savings and Loan Insurance Corporation from 1987-1989. Stuart is a member of the Chagrin Falls Schools' Achievement Hall of Fame.

Also graduating in 1950 was Richard Draz. He went on to excel in a teaching and coaching career paralleled by few. He has been referred to as "a living legend" in the swimming and water polo circles of southern California. He has received numerous awards. In 1986 the National High School Athletic Association presented him the National Coach of the Year Award for being the top swimming coach in the United States for that year. In 1990 the National Interscholastic Swimming Coaches Association honored him with the National Outstanding Service Award. He is listed in the book, America's Greatest Coaches, by Michael Koehler. Dick is a member of the Chagrin Falls Schools' Achievement Hall of Fame.

The First High School Junior Red Cross. First Row: Mrs. Hensley, Behlen, Ryan, Hubbard. Second Row: Rodgers, Nichols, Birkin, Griffith, Bell, Ebel, Fisher. Third Row: Polk, Curtis, Moyse, Wiant.

In the fall of 1950 co-captains and Chagrin Falls Schools' Athletic Hall of Famers, Ken Wiley '51 and Don Evans '51, led the Tigers to 6 wins and 2 losses. Evans was the East County League's Most Valuable Player.

Because of a revival of interest in the ukulele, a Ukulele Club was formed during the 1950-1951 school year. It met once a week to learn new songs and receive chording instructions.

The Junior Red Cross Council was also organized during the 1950-1951 school year. It was dedicated to public service in the school, community, nation and the world. It assisted with blood drives and even promoted civil defense in the schools. The club conducted the first United Fund Drive in the school district in 1958.

John B. Rodgers was valedictorian of the class of 1951. He continued his practice of excellence in the field of medicine. Dr. Rodgers is a recognized expert in lipid research and has been published widely in medical journals. The Albany Medical Center honored him by establishing the Dr. John B. Rodgers Endowment Fund for Continuing Education in Gastroenterology. He is a member of the Chagrin Falls Schools' Achievement Hall of Fame.

Also graduating in 1951 was Joanne Griffith (Root) who later became the founder of a suburban newspaper, Holden Landmark in Holden, Massachusetts. As editor and publisher, her staff earned many awards from the New England Press Association and the Massachusetts Press Association. Included were a second-place award for General Excellence in 1989 and first place awards for Editorial Writing in 1985, 1988 and 1992. In 1994 she was a finalist for the Business Person of the Year Award from the New England Women Business Owners. She was a member of the Board of Directors of

Chagrin Falls Schools' administration, faculty, staff and spouses at the class of 1951 graduation party at the Chagrin Valley Country Club. 1st Row (Left to Right): Tom Spencer, Paul Devore, Peg Quesinberry, Barbara Brown, Charlotte Legge, Janet Johnson, Ralph Quesinberry, Bill Freeland. 2nd Row (Left to Right): Dorothy Heck, Frieda Hensley, May Matthews, Mrs. Schaaf, Mrs. Sands, Elsa Jane Carroll, Mrs. Gurney, Mrs. Harper, Elizabeth Routt. 3rd Row (Left to Right): Esther Howarth, Unknown, Faye Armstrong, Mrs. Lopatt, Dan Lopatt, Mrs. Lewandowski, Joseph Lewandowski, Norm Fry, Mrs. Fry, Mr. Schaaf, Mrs. Freeland, Mr. Hensley, Unknown, Lewis Sands, Jim Harper, Ted Gurney.

the New England Press Association. Joanne is a member of the Chagrin Falls Schools' Achievement Hall of Fame.

Another successful graduate from the class of 1951 was Richard W. Evans. His distinguished career included a very successful printing business and a dedication to service for his alma mater and community. In 1968 he received the Chagrin Valley Jaycees' Distinguished Service Award. Sun Newspapers selected him as Citizen of the Year in 1992, the same year he was named to the Solon Chamber of Commerce's Hall of Fame. He received many awards for excellence in printed communication. He was president of the Chagrin Valley Chamber of Commerce in 1967 and 1994 and life member in the Chagrin Valley

Little Theatre, Valley Art Center and Chagrin Falls Historical Society. Dick is a member of the Chagrin Falls Schools' Achievement Hall of Fame.

Neal Wheatcraft was a much respected high school science teacher and was known for his "unknowns" in chemistry class. He began to teach in Chagrin Falls in 1951 and remained there until his retirement in 1986. He was chairman of the National Honor Society from 1960 to 1980 and chairman of the High School Science Department on several occasions. The Neal Wheatcraft Senior Science Award is still awarded at the high school.

Apartments for teachers were still very scarce in Chagrin Falls during the

1940s and 1950s. Many single teachers lived in furnished rooms even in the homes of their students which, at times, led to awkward situations. Neal Wheatcraft remembered:

We had to eat dinner out each night and ate together at Frizzell's Restaurant (corner of drive to village parking by the falls on North Main). We had a double table located by the window. We were in the fish bowl.

By 1951 the schools were cramped for classroom space. According to school board minutes, on August 23, 1951, the board of education employed the architectural firm of Small, Smith, Reels and Draz to prepare plans for modernizing and renovating existing school buildings. A bond issue in the amount of $250,000 was put before the voters on November 6, 1951 and passed with the following vote: 893 for; 356 against. On June 23, 1952 the board signed a contract with the Harbor Construction Company of Willoughby, Ohio, to make the alterations and additions. Five classrooms, a clinic and boys' and girls' restrooms were added to the third floor of the 1940 building over the cafeteria. New glass block windows and better electric lighting and thermostatic heating controls were added to the 1914 high school building.

It was hoped that this addition of classrooms and remodeling would see the Chagrin Falls Schools through the year 1960. However, in the spring of

Class clown, Tim Conway '52

1953, all of the new classrooms were occupied entirely by elementary classes with the exception of one small room used for foreign language classes.

In 1952 the famous Cleveland radio disc jockey, Bill Randall, and the Four Lads appeared at an assembly at the high school auditorium, now the present intermediate school. A few years later Pat Boone made an appearance on the auditorium stage.

One of the most famous, if not the most famous, Chagrin Falls graduate was the "class clown," Tim Conway '52. He was Tom Conway until he got to Hollywood where there was already a celebrity named Tom Conway; thus Tom became Tim. He has achieved monumental success in motion pictures, television and on stage. Tim is a member of the Chagrin Falls Schools' Achievement Hall of Fame.

John B. Hurst '52 began coaching boys' cross country at Chagrin Falls High School in 1963. His first three teams went undefeated in dual meet competition. In 1970 his team finished second in the state meet and in 1971, won the state crown. It was the first ever in any sport by a Chagrin team. John is a member of the Chagrin Falls Schools' Athletic Hall of Fame.

Also graduating in 1952 was another coach, Jack Stanton. He served a long tenure as head track coach. As varsity track coach his teams won two

The first high school Future Teachers of America. Sitting: Hawthorne, Birkin, Smith, Tilton, Mattern, Wilson, Engelhardt, Rodgers.Standing: Robinson, Mr. Wheatcraft, Schwerzler, Worley, Otis, McClanahan, Hawn,Givens, Miller, Ulrich, Fitzpatrick, Hunt, McNally, Turner.

conference championships. His track athletes qualified for the state meet in eighteen consecutive seasons. Three were state champions. Jack is a member of the Chagrin Falls Schools' Athletic Hall of Fame.

Graduating from Chagrin Falls High School in 1953 was David J. Farris, who went on to graduate from the Advanced Management Program of the Harvard Graduate School of Business. During his business career he has served as Chief Operating Officer of Beneficial Corporation and President and Chief Executive Officer of Beneficial Management Corporation, a subsidiary. He has been Director and Past President of the National Home Equity Mortgage Association. David is a member of the Chagrin Falls Schools' Achievement Hall of Fame.

Don Bullock was also a member of the Chagrin Falls High School Class of 1953. Before retiring from TRW, Inc., he was Chief Scientist for Lasers and Optics in the space and defense sector. His innovative, technical accomplishments have served to advance our country's defense and space programs. In 1989 Don was awarded the TRW Chairman's Award for Innovation, recognizing his performance-enhancing contributions and laser weapon systems. In 1990 he was elected to TRW's Space and Defense Technical Fellows Program. Don is a member of the Chagrin Falls Schools' Achievement Hall of Fame.

In the fall of 1953, led by most valuable player and Chagrin Falls Schools' Athletic Hall of Famer, Jon Fitzpatrick, the 1953 football squad finished with 6 wins and 2 losses.

The following poem was written by Jon Fitzpatrick '54 and read by him in his acceptance speech into the Chagrin Falls Schools' Athletic Hall of Fame banquet on September 25, 1997:

We Were Young Tigers...

The reorganized high school Student Council replaced the Student Activities Council. Sitting: Otis, Van Nort, Lauterer, Hunt. Standing: Davis, Blair, Mills, Smith, Rodgers, Parker, Kewish, Barriball, Rowe, Tenny, Lewis.

Young women of the fifties
We did it all for you;

But we were young tigers,
And truth be known, we did it,
For a bit of glory, too;

There was no war to fight,
We had just ended one;
And the next war had
Not yet begun;

You, with your page boys and bobby sox,
You were all so fair;
And we, in jeans, t-shirts and white bucks—
We all had hair;

Patti Page, the Four Lads,
Slow dancing and football—
What else matters?
Bill Randall spun the platters;

But our coach was tough
Like a drill sergeant he worked us hard;

He made us fight for every extra yard;

But coach was a psychologist, too;
He got the ultimate effort from us—
And from many of you;

Yes, we knew mud, sweat, and blood
And today our knees can foretell the weather;
But that doesn't matter
When old teammates get together;

We were young tigers,
Women of the fifties,
We did it all for you;
And for our Moms and Dads.
Coach – our teammates,
And for our school, too.

We were young tigers…

Innovative social studies teacher, Dale Richmond, arrived at Chagrin Falls High School in the fall of 1953. His fiancé, Marylyn, was his date for

128

the Christmas formal that year. After their marriage she taught at the high school from 1954-1957. His years as a classroom civics teacher included progressive programs such as mock Senate debates and elections, field trips to the Cuyahoga County Court House and United Nations programs. Dale was also Dean of Students from 1972 until his retirement in 1985.

The school system remained small with just 44 graduates in the class of 1954. The Board of Education owned three school buses during the 1953-1954 school year.

A newly chartered club, the Frank W. Stanton Club, appeared in the fall of 1954. It was composed of high school students in the three upper grades and was directly associated with the local, state and national Future Teachers of America Association. Its purpose was to interest students in the teaching profession. The club was named for local educator, Frank W. Stanton.

Dale Bruce, head basketball, baseball and assistant football and track coach (1954-1956).

One of the largest annexations to the school district after South Russell was the Chagrin Heights Subdivision (Stanton Allotment) in 1954, just east of Hazelwood Drive. It included the areas of Blackford, Birchmont, Clarion and Sylvan Drives. It is located in Russell Township.

During the 1954 football season the first electrical scoreboard was used at C.S. Harris Stadium. Seniors Jim Van Gorder, Larry Wiley and Pete Van Nort were three of the many standouts on the 1954 team that won six games in the rugged East Cuyahoga County League. Pete Van Nort went on to attend the U.S. Naval Academy and Larry Wiley attended West Point. Early in Pete Van Nort's career, he worked with Admiral H. G. Rickover, managing the application of nuclear power in ships. Pete is a member of the Chagrin Falls Schools' Achievement Hall of Fame, while Larry is a member of the Chagrin Falls Schools' Athletic Hall of Fame.

Also in 1954, the present intermediate school stage and auditorium were remodeled with improved lighting.

On February 19, 1954 in the auditorium of the Chagrin Valley Little Theatre, the Chagrin Valley Junior Chamber of Commerce was born. It was better known simply as the Jaycees. "Their common bond in Jaycee work is a desire to give their time to the civic improvement of their community," the February 26, 1954 Chagrin Falls Exponent stated.

The first Jaycee festival was staged two years later in 1956 and was named Blossom Time. It was a resurrection of the old Chagrin Valley Home Days celebration which was begun in 1935. A precursor to the festival's present name came about in 1937 when the event was advertised as "Chagrin Valley Week When It's Blossom Time in the Valley." The celebration was discontinued in 1942 because of World War II.

129

The 1954-1955 Basketball Team Left To Right: Charles Jenkins, Tom Mattern, Dennis Bradley, Alvin Flynn, Larry Wiley, Joel Jones, John Engstrom, Ken Lauterer, Dave Sekeres, Pete Van Nort.

The new Chagrin Valley Jaycees was up and running by the late 50s with the school providing queens and lots of carnival participants. As they say—the rest is history!

Joel M. Jones graduated from Chagrin Falls High School in 1955. He went on to earn his B.A. from Yale University in 1960, his M.A. from Miami of Ohio in 1962 and his Ph.D. from the University of New Mexico in 1966. For 19 years he had been a professor of American Studies at the University of New Mexico. He later became President of Fort Lewis College in Colorado and Salisbury University in Maryland. He has published more than 50 scholarly articles, chapters of books and reviews covering such topics as American social and intellectual history, environmental studies and cultural diversity. Joel is a member of the Chagrin Falls Schools' Achievement Hall of Fame.

The 1954-1955 and 1955-1956 basketball teams, coached by Dale Bruce, were among the most outstanding in Chagrin Falls basketball history, winning 37 games during that two-year period. The 1954-1955 team won 16 games and were Cuyahoga County tournament, Orange sectional tournament and Burton Christmas Invitational tournament champions. The 1955-1956 team won 21 games, the most victories ever up to that time by a Cleveland area Class B school. The team, en route to the state semi-finals, won the county, sectional, district and regional tournaments. The team set the school scoring record of 106 points against Independence High School and most points in one season, 1,861. Team captain, Ken Lauterer '56, a member of the Chagrin Falls Schools' Athletic Hall of Fame, scored 618 points in the season, still the boys' single season scoring record. He set the single game record of 36 points against Strongsville High School. Bill Cordes '59 also scored 36 points against Kent State High School during the 1958-1959 season.

One of Chagrin's finest all-around athletes, Dave Banning '57, led the football team to an 8 wins and 1 loss season. John Thomas '57 gained over 900 yards rushing while Banning scored 85 points including a 95-yard

1955-1956 Basketball. Left to Right: Kam Mayner, Dave Banning, Corky Solether, Dennis Bradley, Dave Robbins, Jim Fletcher, Tom Keal, Ken Lauterer, Bob Williams, Parks Odenweller, Gary Curtiss, John Thomas, Tom Carlson, Dicke Behnke, Coach Bruce.

punt return for a touchdown. Dave is a member of the Chagrin Falls Schools' Athletic Hall of Fame.

John Thomas had a 34-year career of distinction with J.P. Morgan Investment Management, Inc., including twelve years as a member of the board of directors, five years as president of J.P. Morgan Trust Bank, the group's operating company in Japan and nine years as head of marketing. He was also a superb athlete at Chagrin Falls High School and at Ohio Wesleyan University. John is a member of the Chagrin Falls Schools' Achievement Hall of Fame.

The 1956-1957 boys' basketball team, coached by Bil Gallagher, won the county and sectional championships and the first East Cuyahoga County title in fourteen years. It also set the Philomethian Street School gymnasium scoring record with a 103 to 39 win over Cuyahoga Heights High School. The team was cheered on by a newly organized pep band.

For those interested in photography, the Camera Club was formed in 1954, under the leadership of Norm Fry. Pictures were taken at school functions and sold to students who were interested in obtaining their own photos. They also took photos for the yearbook. One of Mr. Fry's students, Harold Short '57, later did some developing of the first moon shots.

Norm Fry came to Chagrin Falls in 1937 to teach industrial arts (shop). Through the years he had many "firsts" to his credit. For example, during World War II, he worked evenings in the school with a group of juniors and seniors who built, to specification, model airplanes—replicas of the fighter planes and bombers that were being used in the war. These models were then used by the United States government to teach soldiers identification of planes. What he was most remembered for was the use of his famous paddle. Norm retired in 1977 after "forty years of fun!" In an oral history project conducted by the Chagrin Falls Schools' Historical Preservation Society in 1989, he explained how he handled discipline problems:

131

The first high school Camera Club. First Row: Mr. Fry, Woodworth, Searcy, Rowe, Crawford, Short. Second Row: Stoneman, Stoney, Chapman, Barriball, McCormick. Third Row: Steele, Bateson, Hart, Behnke, Thoren, Neff, Criswell.

You handled them with a paddle, and you didn't call home and ask pop for permission to whale him one; you just hauled off and fired him one and that was it. And usually he didn't go home and tell, but if he did, in many instances, he got another one. It simplified things so much. You see, now you have to get permission from the parents and you have to see a lawyer to see if it's all right and you have to see a judge to see when you can have a trial so when you get around to it the kid forgot what he did wrong. The other way you could wham him one and that was it.

In 1955 the Chagrin Falls School Board purchased the old Cuyahoga County Fairgrounds, the present 7-12 school campus, from the Cuyahoga County Commissioners for $5,000. The purchase of land was settled before Judge Joseph A. Artl in the Cuyahoga Common Pleas Court in a "friendly suit." The school board had held a 99-year lease for the property since 1927.

Cheerleading remained a popular activity for girls in the 1950s, especially since there were no interscholastic athletics. Tryouts were before the present cheerleaders and members of the faculty who voted for three of the candidates. They were under the supervision of the women's physical education teacher. At the end of the first year of service each cheerleader received a letter. In her senior year she received a miniature megaphone on a chain.

Several popular cheers were:

Strawberry shortcake, huckleberry pie, V-I-C-T-O-R-Y.

Are we in it? Well I guess!
Chagrin Falls High School
      Yes, Yes, Yes!

The team got in a huddle,
The captain bowed his head.
They all got together,
     And this is what they said—
     Our team is red hot.
     Our team is red hot.
     Our team is red hot
     We've got a team that's red hot!

A reorganized Science Club was formed in the fall of 1955, under the guidance of science teacher, Neal Wheatcraft. Its purpose was to increase students' knowledge of science and understand its importance in society.

The 1950-1951 high school cheerleaders. 1st Row (Left to Right): Barbara Schaaf, Barbara Bullock 2nd Row (Left to Right): Nancy Dunton, Rhea Collier, Peg Carlton, Pat Stoneman

On November 8, 1955 the board of education submitted to the voters of the school district a bond issue in the amount of $630,000. Its purpose was to build either an elementary school or high school at the old fairgrounds on East Washington Street. A debate ensued as to which to build—an elementary or high school. Thus, the board of education hired two consultants, one from Kent State University and the other from the Ohio State Department of Education. The two met with the board, reviewed the facts and ultimately came to a split decision. One argued for the building of an elementary school, and the other

strongly for a high school building.

The problem was resolved by the board of education at a meeting on February 25, 1956, when it authorized the architects to proceed with plans for an elementary school building consisting of two kindergarten classrooms, twelve other classrooms, and an all purpose room and other necessary facilities to be erected near the tennis courts and swimming pool. At the same meeting the board decided to put before the voters another bond issue of $500,000, to which any funds remaining from the $630,000 issue were to be added for the purpose of erecting a high school building just east of the elementary building.

A special election was held on June 26, 1956 with the following results: for the bond issue – 604; against the bond issue – 306. Ground breaking occurred for the new elementary school in the fall of 1956. However, the building was not ready for occupancy until December 2, 1957.

In December 1958 a new school bus was added to aid in the transportation of students to the new Lewis Sands Elementary School. It was purchased from Collier Oldsmobile Company in Chagrin Falls for $7,275.

The August 24, 1956 <u>Chagrin Falls Exponent</u> proclaimed the following

Sports

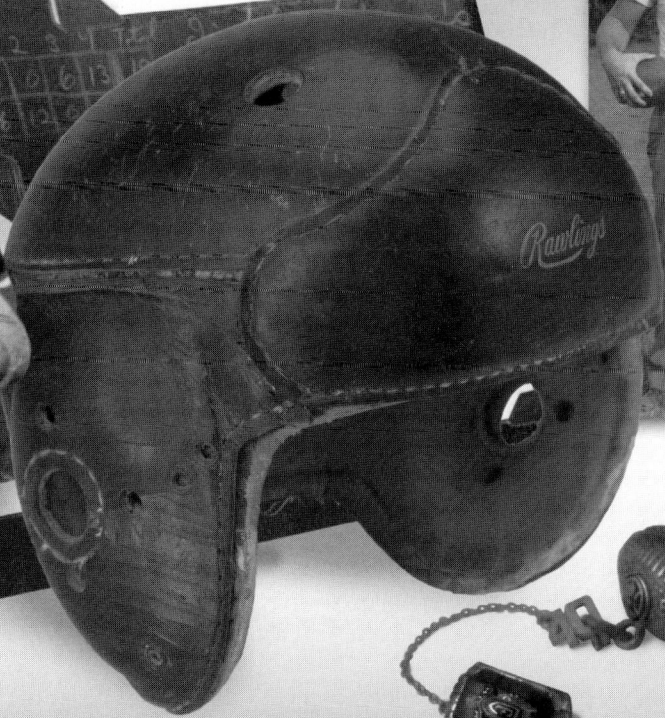

The reorganized high school Science Club. Sitting: Fitz, Southmayd, Groth, Henry. Standing: Mayner, Van Nort, Fish, Rice, Cleaveland, Thoren, Loan, Baker, Mr. Wheatcraft.

in regard to the dedication of the new school:

> *The Chagrin School Board of Education passed a motion to name the new elementary school in honor of the superintendent Lewis Sands. The school will be called 'Sands Elementary School.'*

The article continued:

> *After the Board's action, Mr. Sands was quite overcome and it was a few moments before he could express his appreciation. He said that he deemed it a very great honor and that 'it makes me feel very humble.'*

In September of 1927 Lewis Sands accepted the position of principal at Chagrin Falls High School. The position also required him to teach several classes a day. In 1934, when he was appointed superintendent of schools, his new contract still required him to teach Civics classes. He was well remembered for his kindly face and bushy eyebrows. Many earlier principals and superintendents preferred to teach

and did so voluntarily. Lewis Sands resigned in 1958 to take the position of clerk-treasurer of the school board. He served in that office until his retirement on August 31, 1959.

Dr. Robert M. Finley was appointed superintendent of the Chagrin Falls Schools in 1958.

In the mid-fifties, rock 'n' roll with the help of Elvis Presley found its way into student consciousness through songs on the radio or in the movies about high school life and love. While some high schools prohibited this rock and roll music, Chagrin Falls permitted it at school dances and social events.

The senior prom in the spring of 1956 became famous for its "tree cutting caper." Two days before the prom several junior boys took it upon themselves to "liberate" some trees from private property to use for decorating the high school gymnasium for the prom. Justice was swift, and several girls did not get to go to the prom because their dates were not allowed to go. For many years the junior-senior prom was held in the gymnasium on Philomethian Street..

Sock hops remained popular after Friday night athletic events. The only problem was making sure one found the right shoes at the end of the dance.

The Guidance Department became an integral part of the high school program in the mid 1950s. Joseph Lewandowski was the first part-time counselor. He was followed by Regis Mourier during the 1956-1957 school year. The school mourned his sudden death on December 13, 1958. A page was dedicated to him in the 1958 Zenith. The first full-time guidance counselor was Richard Palermo in the fall of 1959.

Lewis Sands, teacher, principal and superintendent (1927-1959).

A Drama Club was also formed in the fall of 1955 and by 1957 it was presenting two annual plays, one in the fall and one in the spring. The club became known as the Falls Footlighters.

The Leaders Club was organized in the 1956-1957 school years as an addition to the girls' physical education department. It helped teach skills in volleyball, basketball and tumbling. Weekly practices were held to prepare for games with nearby schools. Another purpose of this new club was to assist the physical education teacher in her classes. A sometimes not-so-fond memory of the Leaders Club was the "tortures of initiation."

The high school newspaper, The Echo, was reorganized in the fall of 1956 and renamed Tiger Rag. It was published bi-weekly. A new mimeograph machine, the first in the school, made the work much easier.

The first Honors Banquet was held in the spring of 1957. National Honor Society advisor, Elsa Jane Carroll, organized the banquet and it has remained an important yearly event at Chagrin Falls High School. Science teacher, Neal Wheatcraft, was advisor for many years beginning in the late 1960s until his retirement in 1986. Its purpose is to recognize achievement not related to interscholastic athletics. A program from that first banquet is in the Chagrin Falls Schools' Historical Preservation Room.

Elsa Jane Carroll was a beloved Chagrin Falls High School English teacher who taught at the high school from 1942 until 1961, when she joined the faculty at Orange High School. She retired in 1969. No one will forget her green ink as she continuously inspired and motivated hundreds of students to become the best that they could be.

Ruth Maus arrived at the high school in 1957 as a home economics teacher. Some of her very early classroom memories were: students putting salt in a sugar bowl for a principal's dinner and grade books being stolen throughout the school. Ruth still asks, "Who did this?" The result was that the teachers gave grades of what they

The Lewis Sands Elementary School was named in honor of former superintendent, Lewis Sands. It was located near the Recreation Center swimming pool and tennis courts. It consisted of two kindergarten classrooms, twelve other classrooms and an all-purpose room. The school opened its doors for classes in December 1957 and was demolished in 1998-1999 to make room for a new Chagrin Falls Middle School.

thought the students' grades might have been rather than extending the grading period. Another remembrance was when turkeys were not cooked for a faculty Christmas party because some student turned off the ovens.

Two very well respected and successful coaches joined the teaching staff in the fall of 1957: John Piai, football, and Glenn Wyville, basketball. Both became head coaches and are members of the Chagrin Falls Schools' Athletic Hall of Fame.

John Piai's teams won 175 games, including eight conference championships and had two 29-game undefeated streaks in 29 seasons as head coach.

Glenn Wyville's teams won 352 games, including seven conference titles with three of his teams reaching regional competition in 28 seasons as head coach. He is a member of the Ohio High School Basketball Coaches' Hall of Fame, inducted in 1999.

Several new clubs were established in the fall of 1957. The Spanish Club was organized and composed of students interested in Spanish and the study of Spanish culture. Also, a new addition to extra-curricular activities was the Art Club, formed to promote knowledge and interest in art.

Football team captain, Steve Van Nort '58, led the Tigers with 110 points and played in the Ohio Jaycees All-Ohio game. The 1957 team finished with 6

The high school Drama Club later became known as the Falls Footlighters. Seated: McPeak, Spielhaupter, Mr. Frebault, Nichols, Otis. First Row: Gilson, Rufener, Banning, Terry, Strick, Class, Stoa, Wagner, Gurney, Barriball, Neidhardt, Campbell, Brooks,Mogg. Second Row: Rood, Grose, Hegerty, Schuster, Kaserman, Stone, Daggett, Burke, Matthews, Day, Hurtt, Bullen, Brown, Rock, Foster. Third Row: Bowers, Guilbert, Steele, Kermeen, Picking, Jamieson, Hoekstra, Heaps, Hudson, Quillan, Crittenden, Baehr, Vercoe, Smith,Foster, Spanagel, Searcy. Fourth Row: Simon, Dodson, Burns, Clark, Shelton, Harr, Baker, Anderson, Barriball, Nix, Banning, D. Barrilball, Thoren,Rice, Cummins, Newstead, Simmons, Johanisson.

The first high school girls Leaders Club. Seated: Hoekstra, Stone, Crittenden, Guarnieri, Kermeen. First Row: Rufener, Shelton, Rock, Day, Hegerty, Kascrman, Scott, Hurtt, Robins.Second Row: Herbell, Smith, Hudson, Gurney, Thoren, Wagner, Otis, Picking, Miss Dornback.

The first high school Art Club. Seated: Vincent, Morse, Schwerzler. First Row: Mrs. Schwerzler, Otis, Strick, Yerke, Hurst, Modica. Second Row: Wade, Brown, Wilson, Bayless, Cahill, Mr.Gray, K. Petersen. Third Row: Barriball, Wilbur, P. Petersen.

The first high school German Club. Officers At Table, (Left To Right): Clark, Maves, Mrs. Hensley, Warner. First Row--Rigoutat, Tenny, Brown, Bayless, Hope, Kroening, Greenway, Hill, Dewell,Wade, Mullen, Steele. Second Row-- Davis, Petersen, Pettibone.

The first high school Latin Club. Officers At Table, (Left To Right): Lovell, Salisbury, Hastings, Frew, Miller. First Row: Miss Fisher, Alcorn, Knutsen, Cook, Hellekson, Church, Davis, Lackey, Jones, Kaji. Second Row: McFarland, Gift, Van Doren, Moss, Robinson, Murley.

wins and 2 losses. Steve is a member of the Chagrin Falls Schools' Athletic Hall of Fame.

The fifth annual festival of instrumental music occurred on April 25, 1958 under the schools' music director, E. A. Schear, in the auditorium on Philomethian Street. There were 54 musicians in the elementary band program and 74 musicians in the high school band program. It was the largest instrumental music performance since instrumental music was introduced in the curriculum in 1891.

In the fall of 1958, the Falls Footlighters became a chapter of the National Thespian Society, a national association for drama groups. In the

The first high school Radio Club, nicknamed the "Audio Aces". First Row, Left To Right-Bauman, Swaye, Price, Jefferson, Woodrich. Second Row: Meyers, Biel, Wilbur, Alcorn, Mitchell, Rochet, Petersen, Mr. Fry.

The first high school Junior Council on World Affairs. Officers At Table, Left To Right-Knutsen, Rusch, Pettibone, Miller. First Row: Barriball, Mayner, Brown, Jones, Odenweller, Hurst, Cook, Alcorn, Lackey, Kaji, Bowers, Lowe. Second Row: Mr. Richmond, Nakagawa, Moorhead, Stillman, Rice, Hallstrom, Petersen, Hastings, Kiel, Robinson, Davis, Kuhn, Buus.

spring of 1959, they sponsored "Mardi Gras," the first costume dance in the schools' history.

The German Club was initiated in the fall of 1958. Its first activities included holding a dance, visiting a German movie and having a German potluck dinner. These social activities helped to increase the club membership and spark interest in German as a language and cultural study.

Also organized in the fall of 1958 was the Latin Club. Its purpose was to further the knowledge of ancient Roman culture and civilization.

The Radio Club, nicknamed the Audio Aces, was organized in the winter of 1958. It dealt with interested students of radio, hi-fi's and anything else dealing with electronics.

The Junior Council on World Affairs was initiated at the high school in the fall of 1958 to observe and discuss world affairs. The club participated in the Cleveland area mock United Nations Assembly in Lakewood, Ohio. It represented Japan and chose Ned Nakagawa, Chagrin's first American Field Service exchange student from Japan, in 1958 to help prepare the 12

elected representatives from the high school. Chagrin's other exchange student, Annie Rigoutat, from France arrived in the winter of 1959.

The Chagrin Falls Chapter of the A.F.S. was founded in 1958 with the help of the Chagrin Valley Rotary Club. With its twentieth anniversary in 1978, forty-two Winter Program students from twenty-nine countries had been hosted by the Chagrin Falls chapter. Thirty Chagrin Falls High School students had gone to twenty foreign countries in the Summer Program, Americans Abroad. Presently, Chagrin Falls students are involved in foreign exchanges through Rotary International.

Since the National Merit Scholarship program began in 1957, Chagrin Falls High School as of 2003, has had 104 National Merit finalists. The first three in 1957 were Richard Anderson, Judith Baker and George Rice.

A new winter sport was added during the 1958-1959 school year to the interscholastic athletic program. The high school's first wrestling program was under the tutelage of Ray Tarnowski. By the beginning of the 1959-1960 school year, five sports were

The first high school wrestling program. First Row: Noble, Cowlin, Engstrom, Biel, Gilson, Buus. Second Row: Rice, Adler, Swan, Nakagawa, Alcorn, Carpenter. Third Row: Coach Tarnowski, McNally, Robinson, Haldeman.

offered to high school boys: football, basketball, wrestling, track and field and baseball. Girls' interscholastic athletics still remained a dream. However, that would change dramatically in the 1970s.

A new and very progressive superintendent, Robert Finley, wanted to see the school year for teachers extended six weeks to make it a 42-week professional year. The extension of the school year for students was not an option.

Better teaching abilities, Dr. Finley advocated, would do more for pupils than would year-round school. Better teaching abilities stemming from teachers' summer studies would result in extra pay.

In the spring of 1958, the Chagrin Falls Board of Education approved two ways for teachers to improve their teaching proficiency and, therefore, their earnings. A program named PACT (Parents' Action for Career Teachers) was organized by a group of interested parents and community leaders in the Chagrin Falls School District to help finance the careers of professional teachers.

In-service training was one of these methods. Teachers would be paid to put in two to six extra weeks each summer in workshops and conferences to keep up with the latest teaching techniques, to review and update curriculum and to plan for the upcoming school year. The other method offered pay to teachers who chose to take summer college courses.

This program was funded by voluntary contributions. It was suggested that parents subscribe at a rate of five dollars per semester for each child in school. Since the program for improvement of teachers benefited the entire community, all contributions were welcomed.

The program reached its peak in the next two school years. However, the concept of in-service days before the start of a new school year remained for many years.

In 1957 the Russians launched

Sputnik, the first artificial satellite, then followed that feat by launching a satellite with a dog aboard. One consequence was a national outcry that we had dropped behind the Russians in the technology department. A very common question throughout the United States, including within Chagrin Falls Schools, was "Why aren't our children and teachers more interested in science?" President Eisenhower stated, "Our national survival is at stake." Science education became a matter of urgency as the 50s decade came to an end. Educational changes were on the way.

The 1958-1959 school year brought a tougher classroom regimen under Superintendent Robert M. Finley. Until 1959 commencement week was also "senior week" at the high school with social activities dominating the calendar and occupying most of the graduates' time and attention. Dr. Finley stated at the May 15, 1959 school board meeting: "There will be no senior week this year. Seniors will attend classes 180 full school days as required by state law." The board also gave its approval to the superintendent's plan for final examinations. Senior high students would have two-hour examinations. Junior high exams would be 1-1/2 hours long. Dr. Finley went on to say: "Final examinations will be given in every subject except shop, art and music." Board president, James W. Hine, believed the longer examination periods would be helpful in preparing senior students for college exam procedures.

During the 1958-1959 school year the junior high school (grades 7-8) had a 45-minute class period. It encompassed a nine-period day from 8:05 to 3:34. The high school had a 60-minute class period, encompassing one seven-period day from 8:05 to 3:45.

A study by the board of education in 1959 revealed that 41 out of 63 teachers were married and 42 lived in the Chagrin Falls School District. Five teachers had no degrees, 43 had Bachelor Degrees and 15 had Master Degrees. Among administrators there were five Master Degrees and one Ph.D. Median age of all Chagrin teachers was 32 and ages ranged from 21 to 63.

Art Davidson '59 won the state championship in the 100-yard dash in the spring of 1959. He became the fourth individual state champion in track. Art is a member of the Chagrin Falls Schools' Athelic Hall of Fame.

The first outdoor graduation ceremony was held at the high school athletic field with the class of 1959 receiving their diplomas. The tradition of outdoor graduations still continues. Including students of this class, 2,178 students had received diplomas from Chagrin Falls High School since the first diploma was given in 1879.

In 1959 A. Lee Crawford graduated from Chagrin Falls High School. After graduating from college, he began his long career with General Motors. He ultimately was in charge of Delphi Components Group of General Motors in Mexico which included 48 manufacturing facilities, employing more than 65,000 people. In 1994 Lee was awarded the Mexico Order of the Aztec Eagle, the highest honor that the Mexican Federal Government bestows upon foreign individuals. He was on the board of directors for the United Way of Mexico and in 1994 was named "International Man of the Year" by United Way. Lee is a member of the Chagrin Falls Schools' Achievement Hall of Fame.

Also graduating in 1959 was Claudia Mayner (Greenwood). She went on to become Associate Professor of English, Emeritus, at Kent State University,

In October 1959, the new high school opened its doors to the classes at the former fairgrounds. It was just east of Lewis Sands Elementary School and its main entrance was at the northwest corner of the building. The original master plan for the high school included a gymnasium building and language arts building (1961) and library & industrial arts additions (1965). Many additions and revocations have since been made at the high school, but they were not envisioned in the original late 1950's planning.

Ashtabula Campus, where she taught for more than 30 years. She was a finalist for the Distinguished Teacher Award at Kent State in 1994 and for the Outstanding Teacher Award in 1993. Among her many publications is "Go For It! A Handbook for Women Returning to College." Claudia is a member of the Chagrin Falls Schools' Achievement Hall of Fame.

In the spring of 1959, a number of people in the school district wanted an opportunity to take adult education courses. As a result, the board of education created an adult education committee. A plan was developed, courses were selected and instructors were chosen. The Adult Education Committee was able to offer a series of interesting subjects for the fall of 1959. School facilities were used for the classes. Through the years, community education was an on-again, off-again program. Community interest determined whether adult education

continued or was dropped by the board of education.

The next step in the schools' building program began in 1957 when the school board entered into a contract on September 2 with the W. H. Dick Construction Company in Cleveland, Ohio to build a new senior high school. It was to be located just east of the Lewis Sands Elementary School. On October 25, 1959 the new high school building was dedicated, even though many additions to the building were already on the architectural drawing board.

The first class to graduate from the new high school was the class of 1960. The original Tiger mascot, Mortimer, was a gift from that class. Mortimer has been helping in "Keeping Tiger Pride Alive" for many years.

Since the earliest days of Chagrin Falls High School, a long-standing tradition has remained. It is the

The key, symbolizing leadership, is then given to class officers and Student Council representatives of the freshmen, sophomore and junior classes.

Gar Heintzelman, class of 2004 president, on his "passing of the key" to Jeff McClurg, class of 2005 president, stated: "I present you with the key of Chagrin Falls High School. Lead in the traditions of all those who have gone before you including those of us from the class of 2004. Good luck and best wishes."

The key was then placed in its honored location in the Chagrin Falls Schools' Historical Preservation Room until the next class is ready to continue the tradition of "passing of the key."

As each graduating class departs, let them, like those who have gone before them since 1879, remember these words:

> *We shall soon part . . . soon I shall leave this town, perhaps for a long time, so we shall part. Let us make a compact here, that we will never forget . . . one another. And whatever happens to us later in life, even if we don't meet for twenty years, let us always remember . . . and even if we are occupied with important things, even if we attain honor or fall into misfortune—still let us remember how good it was once here, when we were all together, united by a good and kind feeling which made us better perhaps than we are . . . you must know that there is nothing higher and stronger and good for life in the future than some good memory, especially a memory of childhood, of home. People talk to you a great deal about your education, but some good memory, preserved from childhood, is perhaps the best education. If a man carries many such memories with him into life, he is safe to the end of his days.*

From: The Brothers Karamazov
By Fyedor Destoyevsky (1821-1881)

CONCLUSION
"To Teach is to Touch a Life Forever"

The days we spent in the Chagrin Falls' schools are impressed upon all of us. Our lives were greatly shaped by the formal and informal learning processes, the fun time of sports, dances, school musicals, concerts and other extra-curricular activities. Lasting bonds were made with fellow students, teachers, coaches and the community.

The memories of those brief years continue to be a rich source of inspiration and enjoyment, both in memory and in the contacts made with the people and the places we knew back then.

Lighting those lessons learned for a lifetime were our teachers. At one time or another, we came under the spell of one special teacher. To be touched by such an unforgettable individual is a life-changing experience. That teacher was, in our minds, not just a good teacher, but a great teacher. Meeting whatever standards that individual set for us, it paid off in a lifetime of dividends.

In 1956, while finishing his senior year at Bowling Green State University, a young Tom Conway, later to be named Tim Conway, wrote a message to the Chagrin Falls High School graduating class of 1956. It was dedicated to their teachers.

TO THE TEACHERS . . .

As Mordecai Gorelik states in his book, <u>New Theatres For Old</u>:

"It is by no means certain that a single one of their works will continue to be regarded as having permanent value. But the question will be decided on the basis of their excellence in their kind, and if they fail to survive it will be exclusively because they were not good enough, because they did not succeed well enough in what they tried to do, not because their ideas have grown stale".

****

As the Grand Drape is slowly drawn to a close on the <u>Senior Class of 1956</u>, after its successful twelve-year run in the Chagrin Falls Little Theatre, there is a mad scramble back-stage as the audience struggles impatiently to congratulate the actors. The performance becomes merely a vague generality of memories, but in the confusion and rush to Life's cast party, perhaps some of the actors' educational make-up will be forever imbedded behind their ears.

However, it is not with the actors I am concerned—they have received their well-deserved applause and will go on to bigger and better production. But as the dust on the stage settles in vague patterns under the piercing beams of the spots and the dimmed house lights create a serene atmosphere, there is a group of persons who remain seated and look with wonderment at the empty stage. They are the holders of the prompt books, the interpreters of the cultural works, the masters of creating the characters—the directors.

For twelve trying years they have rehearsed the actors for this performance. I imagine, as they sit in the vacant auditorium they wonder if the performance was a success, and how the critics will treat the show, and, above all, the actors. And what of the actors themselves? Will they continue to employ themselves as craftsmen, or will they fall without a struggle? I imagine they wonder if they have interpreted the masters' works to their fullest degree . . .

There is no encore for the directors— they merely flip off the lobby lights and walk slowly home. Perhaps it is time the houselights are brought up to full strength and the audience and cast remain long enough to turn and applaud the outstanding works of their directors. I am sure there are many past graduates that would like to be part of the audience when they bring on the teachers for a curtain call.

Good luck with your play, <u>Senior Class of 1957</u>, which you have chosen for next year's bill. I'm sure it will be another outstanding success.

Tom Conway, Bowling Green State U.

"I graduated from Chagrin Falls"

...has a nice ring to it, doesn't it?

147

Van Gorder Nails
Four for Chagrin

Chagrin Falls walloped Painesville Riverside, 52-6, in an independent game last night on the Riverside field. Jim Van Gorder, veteran 170-pound halfback, ran wild for the Tigers, scoring four touchdowns in the rout.

Chagrin Falls—52
ENDS—Jones, Flynn, Stretten.
TACKLES—Cleveland, Hill.
GUARDS—Stoney, Butler, Thomas, Otis.
CENTERS—Curtiss, Fletcher.
BACKS—Van Nort, Moyse, Van Gorder, Lauterer, Bradley, Soleher, Banning, Parker.

Painesville Riverside—6
ENDS—Lovka, Esterhay.
TACKLES—Hanpe, Stray.
GUARDS — Blakely, Reeves, Ball, Schrauff.
CENTERS—Thrasher, Wyman.
BACKS—Major, Whitehair, Mayse, Finlin, Morris, Neylon, Yager.
Chagrin Falls .... 20 18 2 7—52
Painesville Riverside 0 0 0 6— 6
TOUCHDOWNS: Chagrin Falls — Van Gorder 4, Van Nort, Lauterer, Jones, Stoney. Painesville Riverside—Mayse.
POINT AFTER TOUCHDOWN — Chagrin Falls—Curtiss, 4 (placements).

Small but Rugged Butler Named "Tiger-of-Week"

A converted quarterback who, at 155 pounds, is the smallest boy on the line, is this week's "Tiger of the Week".

... ler, a scrappy ... se work at offensive ...

Flynn, All-County Grid Picks

Co-champions Mayfield and Brecksville dominated the selections for the All-County football team, chosen at the annual coaches' banquet at Brecksville Monday night.

The Wildcats and the Bees each placed three boys on the first team, while Brecksville players gained two second team berths and Mayfield one.

Improving Moyse Named Chagrin's "Tiger-of-Week"

A year ago, Bill Moyse was the starting center for Chagrin Falls.

A month ago, Moyse seemed to be on the verge of becoming a bench warmer for the Tigers. Converted to a halfback this season Moyse was slow to pick up the fine points of backfield play. Coach Ralph Quesinberry was about ready to give up on ...

Van Gorder Scores 4 TD's as Chagrin Rolls to 2nd Victory

Chagrin Spills Solon; Mayfield Ties for Lead

Chagrin Falls and Mayfield registered shutout victories as they moved into a tie for first place in the County League football race last night.

Chagrin knocked Solon ... the top rung by handing Comets their first league defeat, ... 0, on the losers' field.

Jim Van Gorder made ... game's only touchdown ... the first period on a two ... tween around right end ...

Pillar of Tiger Line, Stoney Honored as Star of Week

... standout, even in defeat, ... ior Guard Stan Stoney has ... voted "Tiger-of-the-Week".

Cleaveland Named "Tiger-of-Week"

A bulwark on defense all year, Tackle Phil Cleaveland was selected as "Tiger-of-the-Week" this week for his work in a losing cause against Orange.

"This may sound strange", Assistant Coach Dale Bruce said in announcing the selection, "bu...

Wiley Chosen Tiger "Star-of-the-Week"

Larry Wiley, 175-pound senior fullback, has been picked as the first "Tiger of the Week" for his outstanding play in Chagrin Falls' 39-6 romp over Kenston last Friday.

Coach Ralph Quesinberry, in announcing Wiley's selection, re...

CF Football Banquet Draws Large Crowd

Approximately 250 persons enjoyed the Chagrin Falls High ...

"Best QB" Named Tiger-of-Week

Labeled "the best quarterback I've ever coached" by Chagrin Falls Coach Ralph Quesinberry, rangy Pete Van Nort put on a brilliant show against Independence last Friday night to win this week's "Tiger-of-the Week" award.

The six-foot four-inch Van Nort, an All-East County League basketball choice last winter, ...

Tigers Crush

Dave Hill Chosen "Tiger-of-Week"

Outstanding on a night when all linemen stood out, Tackle Dave Hill has been named "Tiger-of-the-Week" for his play in Chagrin's 7-0 win over Brooklyn.

Hill, a 190-pound senior, was described by Assistant Coach Dale Bruce as "terrific on defense and excellent on offense" in Monday night's battle on the soggy Brooklyn gridiron.

Banning Sinks 32 for New JV Record

Banning's scoring spree added six points to the old record of 26 set by Tom Mattern only last season. Mattern, now a member of the Chagrin varsity, set his record against Mayfield.

UNDEFEATED Chagrin Falls defending its Burton Tourney championship against a lineup which also includes Perry, Kirtland and Burton.

Chagrin Cagers Gain Tie for East County Lead

Pete Van Nort, Larry Wiley and Ken Lauterer combined offensive talents last night to give Chagrin Falls High School's basketball team a ...

... finishing with 16 points, Wiley 15 and Lauterer 14. Warren Smith and Al Hoover had 16 apiece for Brecksville.

Chagrin now has won two in a row. Orange was idle last night.

Nort to La... from Chag... yard line ...

Chagrin Splashes Past Brooklyn Mudders, 7-0

Tigers Meet Perry Tuesday; Kenston, Solon

Christmas tournaments, with Santa Claus and plum pu... rin Valley's three East County representatives next week to what promises to be the most exciting local holiday cage activity in years.

For a wonderful change this year's tourney's promise keen competition for the shiny gold trophies that will decorate winners' showcases when school reopens next month.

The tournament lineup finds ...

Chagrin Racks Up 3d in Row With 13-0 Win Over Heights

Van Nort Hero

Chagrin Meets Mayfield

CHAGRIN, after three straight losses, snapped back Friday with a solid 67-36 thumping of Strongsville here.

...am's overtime points. Potter, a 6-ft., 4½-in. center ... on hooks, rebounds and one ...

Chagrin Falls' football ... ault on watery Brook... ed to get up enough ... g Brooklyn, 7-0. ... on a field that was ... with as much as two inches of water in spots, the flashy Tiger backs, who had rolled past four previous opponents with little trouble, found themselves enmeshed in difficulties against their winless hosts.

Falls' Rally Gives Tigers Burton Title

Chagrin Falls literally knocked out the scoring punch of Burton High last night to seize honors in the Burton basketball tournament, 58-43.

Perry bested Kirtland, 65-55 in the consolation opener.

The Tigers were down, 30-2... as the third period open... when Burton Center Bob Pott... only five points in the fir... session while Chagrin Falls ra...

Chagrin Five Tournaments Next

Appendices:

Appendix I

A Chronicled History of the Chagrin Falls Schools

1834 - One-room schoolhouses emerged throughout the village.

1842/1843 - The Asbury Seminary School was built on the west side of Philomethian Street. This school was conducted in the interest of the Methodist Episcopal Church but under private ownership. There is some thought that the Seminary acted as a preparatory school for Allegheny College in Meadville, PA.; however, that fact still cannot be proven.

1849 - The first board of education was established in Chagrin Falls.

1858 - The Asbury Seminary was closed and purchased by the board of education which began to consolidate village schoolhouses into a Union School. Board minutes first named it Chagrin Falls High School but the use of that name did not last.

1879 – By completing the entire required curriculum, Hugh Christian received the first Chagrin Falls High School diploma. He was the only member of the graduating class.

1885/1886 - The brick Philomethian Street School was built. It was also referred to as the Chagrin Falls Union School.

1892 - A 750 seat assembly hall and schoolrooms were added to the Philomethian Street School.

1893 - The Asbury Seminary was sold for salvage.

1895 - Electric lights were installed in the Philomethian Street School.

1907 - The Chagrin Falls Schools were granted a charter from the State Department of Education entitled, "First Grade High School," meaning a four-year high school.

1909 - A separate wood-frame two classroom building (1st & 2nd grade) was built on the southeast corner of the Philomethian Street property.

1913 - The grandstand was built at the old Cuyahoga County Fairgrounds on East Washington Street, the present football stadium.

1914 - A brick high school building was built facing East Washington Street.

1923 - Alterations were made to the Philomethian Street School including a gymnasium for use by the high school.

1927 - A central heating plant was built for the Philomethian Street building and ultimately incorporated into the 1940 addition to the 1914 high school.

1927 - The board of education acquired the use of 54 acres of land at the site of the old Cuyahoga County Fairgrounds on East Washington Street for educational and recreational purposes.

1930 - A separate wood-frame cafeteria and home economics building was built at the site of the teachers' parking lot on Philomethian Street next to the Federated Church.

1937 - The Chagrin Falls Schools became the Chagrin Falls Exempted Village Schools, "exempt" from county control.

1939/1940 - A large addition to the 1914 high school building was built which consisted of space for an elementary school program, library, auditorium, gymnasium, cafeteria, and industrial arts wing. The 1914 high school/elementary school building was often referred to as the Philomethian Street School.

1940 - The wood-frame 1st and 2nd grade 1904 building was torn down.
The brick 1885 Union School / Philomethian Street School was torn down.

1945 - The first night football game was held at the high school football field.

1946 - The old wood-frame cafeteria and home economics building was sold and the space it occupied was used as a playground for the lower grades.

1952 - A third floor was added above the cafeteria at the 1914 high school/elementary school building.

1954 - The 1914 high school stage and auditorium were remodeled with improved lighting.

1957 - The Lewis Sands Elementary School was built on the site of the old Cuyahoga County Fairgrounds on East Washington Street.

1959 - The first outdoor graduation ceremony was held at the athelitic field on East Washington Street.
A new high school was built at the site of the old Cuyahoga County Fairgrounds.

1960 - The Class of 1960 was the first to graduate from the new high school building.

1961 - A separate "little red schoolhouse" was built next to the Lewis Sands School.
A new high school gymnasium building was built.
A new high school language arts building (now used as the cafeteria and commons)was built.

1963 - The Chagrin Valley Conference was organized.

1965 - An addition to the high school, consisting of a library and industrial arts wing, was built.

1966 - The T.C. Gurney Elementary School was built in South Russell.

1968 - Additional classrooms were added to Gurney School.
New classrooms and a separate music building were added at the high school.
A press box was added to the visitor's bleachers at the high school athletic field.

1971 - The bus garage was built at Gurney School.
An additional gymnasium and a second industrial arts wing were built at the high school.
The "little red schoolhouse" was connected with the original Lewis Sands building and new classrooms built.
The library was expanded at the middle school on Philomethian Street along with miscellaneous remodeling.

1972 - Miscellaneous renovations were continued at the middle school.
Additional classrooms were added to Gurney School.

1983 - Gurney School was closed due to declining enrollment.
Dr. Arlene Rieger became the first female superintendent of schools.

1984 - Renovations were made to the 1913 grandstand.

A new all-weather track was installed at the high school athletic field.

1988 - Gurney School was reopened due to increasing enrollment.
Major renovations were made at Gurney School.

1989 - Major renovations were made at the middle school.
Interior renovations were made at Lewis Sands School.
The high school science labs were renovated and a new entranceway was built at the high school gymnasium.
The 1913 grandstand was renovated at the high school athletic field.

1991 - Track repairs, resurfacing, and striping were done at the high school athletic field.

1993 - Computer modifications were done at all Chagrin Falls Schools.

1994 - A sanctuary trail was constructed at Lewis Sands School.
Computer modifications were continued at all schools.

1996 - The Chagrin Valley Conference was realigned.

1998 - Four new classrooms were built at the high school.
Additions and renovations were made at Gurney School, a classroom wing and gymnasium.

1998/1999 - Most of the 1957 Lewis Sands School was torn down.
A new Chagrin Falls Middle School containing grades 7-8 was built at the Lewis Sands School location with shared-use facilities connecting it with the high school.

The former Chagrin Falls Middle School on Philomethian Street was renovated and renamed the Chagrin Falls Intermediate School containing grades 4-6.
Classroom additions were made at the high school.
Athletic fields were added at Gurney School.

2000 - The high school gymnasium floor was replaced and the walls painted by the Booster Club.
A photography lab was added to the high school.

2001 - Stadium lights were replaced.
Scoreboards and a comfort station were added to the Gurney School playing fields by the Dad's Club.

2003 - Distance Learning Lab was added to the high school library.
Boilers were replaced at the intermediate school.

Appendix II

Superintendents of the Chagrin Fall Schools

Superintendents and the dates of their tenure

Royal Taylor	May, 1852 – 1855
L. D. Mix	May, 1855 – Nov., 1855
A. T. Allen	Nov., 1855 – 1857
Dr. A. H. Harlow	1857 – Jan., 1860
Jas. Vincent	1860 – 1864
W. S. Hayden	1864 – 1871
Geo. F. Wright	1871 – 1876
C. C. Hubbell	1876 – 1878
C. F. Stokey	1878 – 1879
W. S. Hayden	1879 – 1883
C. W. Randall	1883 – 1887
R. M. Collins	1887 – 1888
F. P. Shumaker	1888 – 1901
D. W. McGlenen	1901 – 1908
E. C. Teare	1908 – 1916
L. N. Drake	1916 – 1920
W. L. Stoneburner	1920 – 1926
H. E. Michael	1926 – 1931
H. E. Zuber	1931 – 1934
Lewis Sands	1934 – 1958
Dr. Robert M. Finley	1958 – 1961
Dr. Robert C. Cawrse	1961 – 1964
Dr. Warren F. Thomas	1964 – 1972
Loyal Cornelius	1972 – Dec., 1982
Dr. Bernard Mudrock	Jan., 1983 – June, 1983
Dr. Arlene Rieger	1983 – 1990
Dr. Jake Hudson	1990 – 1996
Dr. Ruth Ann Plate	1996 – 2000
Dr. David Axner	2000 –

Retired Teachers
of the
Chagrin Falls Schools

*Approximately Twenty or More
Years of Dedicated Service -
Retirement Year.*

Madge Laura Kent-1900
Alice J. Russell-1925
Emily Collacott-1926
Cora Sanders-1929
Zoe Long Fouts-1940
Anna Tornquist-1952
Alice E. Neff-1958
Lewis Sands-1958
Edna M. Gifford-1959
Ida Smith-1960
May Matthews-1962
Fay E. Armstrong-1963
Margaret H. Johnson-1964
Frieda K. Hensley-1965
Theodore C. Gurney-1966
Lillian Maiden-1966
Elsa Jane Carroll-1969
Kathryn Warner-1971
Marian S. Wilson Bennett-1972
Dorothy Fisher-1973
Enid Strick-1974
Norman Fry-1977
Betty Slaybaugh-1977

Roland B. Gray-1978
Lois Place-1979
Walt Jay-1980
Ralph L. Quesinberry-1980
Harold Loesch-1981
Sally Stiller-1981
William B. Shields-1982
Carol Davis-1983
Barbara Greenhill-1983
Elinor (Susie) Miles-1983
Jess Rankin-1983
Ruth Lehman-1984
Mollie Macknin-1984
Barbara E. Smith-1984
Virginia Colignon-1985
Marion Larson-1985
Myron H. "Skip" Riegel-1985
Martha Barton Voorhees-1985
Doris Bennett-1986
Alyce Duncan-1986
Jack Glaser-1986
Frances Jenkins-1986
Bill Morgan-1986
Gloria Powell-1986
Dale Richmond-1986
M. Neal Wheatcraft-1986
Laura H. Wilkens-1986
Ann Barker-1988
Ramon V. Battles-1989
John Ginatos-1989

Robert Hensel-1989
Lois Klingensmith-1989
Dorothy McConnell-1989
Katherine Nelson-1989
Jack Stanton-1989
Don Ferguson-1990
Doris L. Knight-1990
Thomas G. Mattern-1990
Donna Rentz-1990
Lynn Bamberger-1991
Pat Brush-1991
Robert J. Dean-1991
Bill Foley-1991
John Hurst-1991
George Kaschak-1991
J. Thomas Lerch-1991
Gayle Nemeth-1991
John Piai-1991
Barbara Reiss-1991
Grace Shields-1991
Glenn Wyville-1991
Janette Padolik 1992
Jack A. Smith-1992
Barbara A. Haluska-1993
Carolyn Hanson-1994
Ed Gardner-1995
Ruth Maus-1995
Arline Miller Moore-1995
Jane E. Morris-1995

Phyllis E. Patton-1995
Mitzi Furlong-1996
Diane Morgan-1996
Frank McWhorter-1996
Don Wem-1996
Pat Belanger-1997
DeeAnne Davenport-1997
Faith Degen-1997
Bill Fordyce-1997
Jim Howell-1997
Joyce Buck-1999
Kaye Oker-1999
Helen Samstag-1999
Judy Schneider-1999
Al Sekerek-1999
Ann Burns-2000
Greg Gamm-2000
Judy Kramer-2000
Bobbi Lineweaver-2000
Mo McGarvey-2000
Lorna Muzevich-2000
Robert Ohlrich-2000
Pete Olah-2000
Mario Gerhardt-2001
Lenny Balk-2002
Jim Bucar-2003
Lenny May-2004
Wade Tolleson-2004
Claudette Whitelaw-2004

Appendix IV

Graduates of the Chagrin Falls Schools 1879-1960

The Chagrin Falls Alumni Association compiled this list of high school graduates. It was not an easy task. Early names were found in the records of the original 1890 Alumni Association. Many of these included a woman's maiden and married name. Other sources include yearbooks (first published in 1911) and commencement programs when advailable.

1879
Christian, Hugh

1881
Modroo, Theodore
Short, James

1882
Dudley, Ella Whitlock

1883
Wrentmore, Carl G.

1887
Haggart, George

1888
Cleverdon, H.L.
Gates, F.C.
Richards, Lewis
Shackson, Lucy Foster

1889
Bailey, Sarah Stoneman
Bassett, Chatta I.
Fenkell, George
Johnson, Edward T.
Little, Fred A.

Mountjoy, Pearl
Niece, Stella Marble
Overton, Florence M.
Pratt, Lena J.

1890
Bailey, Edward I.
Bartlett, Clara
Carlton, Frank T.
Gifford, Helen E.
Hunkin, Hattie Parker
Hutton, Anna Baster
Sanders, Cora M.
Smith, John A.
Taylor, Lillian Frazer
Wyckoff, Bertha 0

1891
Gates, Florien Tambling
Gleason, Fred H.
Henderson, Fred
Henderson, Myra Pelton
McBane, Gussie Coleman
Stone, Frank
Strick, Henry G.
VanValkenburg, A.H.

1892
Brewster, Grace Stoneman
Clay, Cassius M.
Gurney, Nellie
Hunt, Wilson W.
Larkworthy, Walter M.
Thorpe, Henry G.
Turner, Blanche Kent
Upham, Edward A.
VanValkenburg, Hattie Henderson
Walters, Wilson H.

1893
Church, Ama Burnett
Church, John A.
Douglass, Florence Russell
Gates, Althea L.
Gates, Clement L.
Hastings, Lillian Matthews
Hubbell, Walter H.
Larkworthy, Gertrude M.
Laughlin, Kathryn Hale
Lowe, Wilhelmina Carlton
Thayer, Eva Harris
Waters, Eva Hardy
White, Martha Bull
Williams, Catherine Church
Wyckoff, Grace Pelton

1894
Baldwin, Blanche Savage
Dean, Bert
Hageman, Nettie Burton
Huggett, Irving
LaRue, Hattie Walters
Murfett, Charles
Sheffield, Guy L.

1895
Baldwin, E. H.
Bishop, Gertrude
Burnett, Zila
Cole, Adaline
Fenton, Donna Frazer
Fuller, Vernie L.
Hutchinson, Helen R.
McVeigh, J. Belle
Mountjoy, Olive Dewey
Patterson, Carrie Britton
Sargent, Norma Stoneman
Woodworth, Caroline Rodgers

1896
Arnold, Mattie Wooley
Balke, Clarence W.
Canfield, Katherine Gardner
Cole, Myrtle C.
Myers, Ella Miller
Pettibone, Earl W.
Pratt, Bruce
White, Carrie Stevens
Williams, Ralph L.

1897
Bramley, Mabel Thayer
Browne, Maude Sheffield
Burnett, Guy
Church, Anna
Dube, Louie Henderson
Ely, Leila Allshouse

Kingsbury, Lucy
McClintock, Lloyd
Murfett, Mary
Reeder, Anna Church
Sprague, Roy
VanWinkle, Mattie Hall
Watson, Harry
Wilson, Florence McVeigh
Wilson, Irene Bailey

1898
Beck, Mary Hutchinson
Bramley, Wright H.
Brewster, Carl M.
Brewster, Liela Carlton
Brewster, W. Roy
Carl, Frank M.
Davis, Cora H.
Dippo, George Dippo
Fenkell, Neal C.
Fowler, Mabelle Godfrey
Graham, Agnes H.
Hickox, Bessie Cole
Hill, Claude
Kaske, Anna H.
Leach, Raymond H.
Lewis, Adelia Chittle
Perkins, Archie V.
Luse, J Raymond
McKee, Pearl Losher
Phelps, Roscoe G.
Porter, James R.
Pugsley, Blanche L.
Samson, Adella Pelton
Shepard, Mary B.
Tenny, Lewie A.
Walls, Edna E.
Walters, Franklin H.
Whitman, Carl H.
Woodard, Theresa Emery

1899
Bradley, Lloyd G.
Gore, Lulu Devoe
March, Forrest O
Morrison, Nellie A.
Niece, Lynn A.
Sherman, Maude Bradley
Thayer, Alice Murfett
Treash, Bernice Pugsley

1900
Bayard, George
Bramley, Paul R.
Brewster, Leon B.
Fuller, Elsie T.
Harris, Isabelle Dripps
Hill, Claude S.

Hoffman, Olive Murfett
Honeywell, Raymond W.
Kent, Ella Calkins
Pelton, Forrest B.
Phillips, Mary Niece
Wyckoff, Chauncey W.

1901
Arnold, Ethlyn M.
Bradley, Lillian Archer
Burnett, Maude M.
Carlton, Gail A.
Cunningham, Lura Childs
Lacey, Grace Wyckoff
Lacey, Jessie Phillips
McKee, Pearl Losher
Luse, J. Raymond
Phelps, Roscoe G.
Porter, James R.
Pugsley, Blanche L.
Samson, AdelIa Pelton
Shilts, Edna Robens
Stroud, Minnie Brewster
Teare, Sadie Foster
VanValkenburg, Horace V.
Weimer, Maude Gates

1902
Burton, Phoebe Robens
Corlett, Jessie Eggleston
Dalton, Dora Judd
Davis, Clarence
Gluvna, Eva Dalton
Greenaway, John
Hollis, Mary Warren
Lines, Clifton H.
Lippert, Kate Isaac
McClain, Howard
Muggleton, Bessie Ward
Muggleton, G. Dean
Muggleton, Gertrude

1903
Barrows, Florence
Barrows, Howard H.
Bradley, Bertha M.
Brewster, Anna G.
Brown, Phoebe Tooker
Carlton, Emma A.
Gifford, Clayton H.
Henderson, Lougardia
Holbrook, Abbie Leach
Kent, Paul G.
Landen, Caroline Arnold
Leisk, Viola Hutchinson
March, Harold W.
Miller, Adam J.
Nycamp, Maude G.

Page, Frank B.
Page, Mabel Phillips
Phillips, Dewey C.
Pugsley, Howard B.
Pugsley, Lottie Gnford
Rodgers, Blanche Parkins
Rorabeck, Calvin M.
Rose, Chispa Lempson
Schuman, Vira Hulbert
Squire, Frank A.
Stoneman, Ila
Stroud, Harry W.
Williams, Forrest A.

1904
Arthur, Helen B.
Brown, F. Marion
Campbell, Leslie G.
Cathan, Floyd
Cathan, Helen Campbell
Clark, Florus W.
Cooke, Edna Huggett
Dalton, Blanche Eggleston
Dalton, Harry M.
Davidson, Freda Reno'
Drake, Lura Rorabeck'
Hickox, J.G.
Hintz, George T.
Huggett, Edna M.
Kock, May Patterson
Lines, Lorene Hinckley
Ober, Gale R.
Oldham, Maude Chambers
Payne, Jessie Hissett
Porter, Grace Gifford
Wait, Frank D.

1905
Braund, Lynde
Carlton,Anna
Dripps, Helene
Forsyth,Harry
Gates, Corrine
Gifford, Ethel
Henry, Leila Payne
Hintz, Nina Hinckley
Judd, Forrest
Kent, Zeno
LeRoy, Verne
Matthews, Aleatha Hickox
McClintock, Howard
Mclaughlin, Edward
Murfett, John
Pelton, Gladys
Pope, Jessie Tooker
Robens, Ruby
Rorabeck, Mamie Wilber
Wilmot,Virgil

1906

Arnold, Beulah Lampson
Barber, Jay
Braund, Frank
Bruessow, Emma
Crary, Margaret
Gifford, Edith
Hall,Peter
Henderson, Grace Bradley
Hoopes, Laura
Hutchins, Anna McLaughlin
LeRoy, June
Luse, Ethel
McLaughlin, Ann
Miller, Forrest
Page, Clarence
Simpson, Lucy Walker
Stolph, Bertha
Wilber, J. Edmund
Wooley, Bessie

1907

Authur, Isabelle
Braund, Veda
Carter, Ethel
Clarkson, Agnes
Coulter, Blanche Whitlock
Davis, Alvin
DeKort, Morris
Frayn, Bertha L.
Gifford, Ernest
Greed, William
Green, Minnie Clarkson
Hardy, Minnie Tuttle
Harris, Madeline
Holiday, Lizzie Corlett
Huggett, Bertha Frayne
Huggett, Tryon Virgil
Kline, Clarence
Sargent, Lottie Stonemen
Treat, Glayds Woodard
White, Martha Mae
Whitlock, Cora Holbrook
Wilber, Cornelia Kent
Williams, Eveln Judd

1908

No Graduates
Transition to four year curriculum

1909

Arthur, Georgiana
Bradley, Thomas
Braund, Lyle K.
Burnett, Harry
Foster, Annette McFarland
Giles, Lille

Halsey, Florence
Hoopes, Elmer
Kitchen, Lillie McLaughlin
Matthews, Milton
Modroo, Lucy
Ober, Dean
Ober, Maude
Parsons, Edna Hickox
Pugsley, Lilon

1910

Blackford, Jemima
Blair, Everett F.
Carter, Florence
Coombes, Frank
Fosdick, Arthur
Fosdick, Hazel Jackson
Fuller, Hazel
Gastemire, Elsie
Greed, Gertrude
Kent, Hazel Tambling
Kent, James
Stoneman, Marie
Wilson, Lois

1911

Burnett, Ethel M.
Cibulak, Mamie
Eggleston, John L.
Frayne, Laverne Huggett
Gates, Lawrence
Goldbach, Robert
Henderson, Lloyd F.
Hoopes, William D.
Hutchinson, Gertrude D.
Shumaker, Grace M.
Stoneman, Edith K.
Wilson, Gertrude

1912

Bezdick, Laura McLaughlin
Brewster, Helen
Carlton, Owen L.
Coombes, Harley A.
Elliott, Horace
Goldbach, Ruth
Kline, Turner B.
Modroo, Ruth H.
Ober, Ruth H.
Page, Fred G.
Page, Orrell Rood
Parker, Warren B.
Robens, Olive
Sanderson, Mona
Shepard, Sim J.
Vincent, Alta Warren

1913

Classrooms

1919

1919

1919

1940

1940

1931

1940

Cafeteria

1940

Ayers, Lloyd F.
Bradley, Walter G.
Brewster, Louise
Burr, Edna Shackson
Burton, Frank L.
Class, J. Vernon
Davis, Irene
DeKort, Edna
Gates, Olive Curtiss
Giford, Edna
Halsey, Harry W.
Huggett, Charles W.
Iredale, Mary
Johns, Aleata
May, Howard
Messenger, Cleon E.
Nichols, Muriel
Ober, Hilda
Richardson, Robert
Selleck, Mildred Herndderson
Shumaker, Maurice M.
Shutts, Joyce Sheffield
Stoneman, Lucile
Walters, Roscoe C.
Winchell, Ethel
Wrentmore, Edna

1914
Baker, Harold W.
Beattie, Reveley G.
Davis, Howard H.
Gates, Mamie H.
Goldbach, Mirion
Goodwin, Orvin A.
Harris, Carlyle S.
Hoopes, Harry T.
Humphrey, Treva Hill
Muggleton, Catherine
Nycamp, George W.
Ridge, Sam
Wait, Clarence B.
Wrentmore, Georgiene Hutchinson
Ziegler, Frieda K.

1915
Allshouse, Corinne
Arthur, George B.
Barnard, James K.
Fleming, Bernice
Fosdick, Bertha
Gifford, Elsie
Goldbach, Marion
Kent, Aveline
Kent, Mary
Lowe, Carlton E.
Mattus, Joseph J.
McNish, Gertrude
Ober, Bernice

Ridge, Martha
Stoneman, Ruby
Taber, Dann O.
Thompson, Lucy
Warren, Lucy E.

1916
Brewster, Louise C.
Carzoo, Raymond A.
Church, Miriam R.
Crary, Beatrice M.
Didham, Pauline B.
Gore, Warren H.
Halsey, Dorothea Cope
Hill, Myrl S.
Hine, Ralph C.
Jaros, Anna J.
Johns, Lester A.
Kent, Genevieve M.
Langstaff, Willliam M.
Menges, Iva L.
Nycamp, Henry
O'Malley, Thelma
Richardson, Gertrude Burnett
Rodgers, Margaret D.
Rowe, Francis J.
Schmitt, Florence G.
Timmons, Winifred J.
Whims, Vera A.
Williams, Ernest D.
Williams, Marie McGlenen

1917
Beattie, Mitton
Brewster, Marian E.
Crago, Joseph V.
Dean, Eugenie O.
Dippo, Gordon J.
Gifford, Rhena M.
Isaac, Elmer B.
Pelton, Alice K.
Ridge, Fred
Root, Elton A.
Schwintosky, Elsie E.
VanValkenburg, Dorothy E.

1918
Atwater, Emma
Carzoo, Celia S.
Class, Edwin A.
Dippo, Florence E.
Duncan, Lucile H.
Dutton, Ruby V.
Fenton, Verneita
Fischer, Mildred I.
Gates, Emerson H.
Huggett, Lyman B.
Johns, Merle A.

Maclaughlin, Ruth
Mapes, Glenn H.
Mattus, Mary E.
McGlenen, Wesley
Mosher, Robert E.
Nichols, Eugene P.
Niman, Howard
Rowe, Eva M.
Stevens, Chalmer C.
Van Valkenburg, Marjoie
Warren, Marie G.

1919
Blackford, Sarah J.
Blackler, Mamie M.
Clay, Dorothy E.
Ferris, Mildred H.
Fosdick, Edna 0.
Gifford, Florence J.
Henry, Charles E.
Hoffman, Marie R.
Hoopes, C. Oliver
Hubbell, Margaret M.
Kent, Lewis Z.
Kline, Everett W.
Larkworthy, William J.
Pedler, Flora L.
Robinson, Harold W.
Rodgers, Elizabeth
Ruch, Sylvia A.
Sanders, Earl.
Schmitt, Hilda H.
Sechler, Edith C.
Steel, Paul C.
Truman, Harry V.

1920
Barber, Alman
Bartholomew, Everett
Bartholomew, Merrill
Bowe, Wilbur P
Burch, Rose M
Cline, Arlie
Cope, Edith'
Didham, Philip
Dippo, Ida
Edwards, Leona
Edwards, Marian
Fonten, Mildred
Giles, Dorothy
Gilmore, Lucile
Gore, Helen
Gore, Lois
Harris, Cassius
Huggett, Frances
Hunkin, Gertrude
Jackson, Everett
Johnson, Glayda

Johnson, Glenn
Johnson, Margaret
Johnston, Robert
Mapes, Eugene
May, Norman
Miller, Edwin
Mosher, Frank
Payer, Lillian
Root, Robert
Scott, Ruth
Spielhaupter, Emma
Steever, Leota
Sutter, Marinus
Van Valkenburg, Marguerite
Vesey, Esther
Vodraska, Helen
Zeman, Clara
Zepp, Erwin

1921
Bannerman, John
Blackford, Ada
Braund, Donald
Browne, Florence
Burnett, Cecil
Chambers, Mildred
Class, Ruth
Dean, Hazel
Drake, Claribel
Green, Lester
Henry, Marguerite
Hoffman, Helen
Jencick, Marian
Johnston, Glayds
Keck, Gadys
Kent, Malcolm
Kinsey, Esther
Lambert, Elmer
Miller, Vernon H.
Murphey, Leonard
Nelisse, Leona
Pealer, Kathleen
Radcliffe, George
Rowe, Margaret
Short, Dorothy
Smith, Lois
Trippear, Richard
Wakefield, Elizabeth
Werstat, Barbara
Winchel, Lawrence

1922
Ackland, Kenneth E.
Beeman, Thelma
Bieger, Eleanor
Burnett, Howard
Church, Ruth M.
Clift, Gladys

Croskey, Lenore
Daugherty, **Ila**
Dietz, Edward
Eykyn, Maxine
Fosdick, Leonard
Gifford, Raymond
Giles, Helen H.
Green, Jessie
Greuloch, Emil
Heck, Lester R.
Holmes, Ida
Lauter, Ernest
McCabe, Donald E.
McFarland, Forrestine
Patterson, Howard
Pecsok, Alfred W.
Raikula, William R.
Ricker, Edward D.
Rodgers, Ruth
Seibert, Paul
Smith, Lawrence
Stearns, Dorothy
Street, Herschel L.
Suter, George
Teckus, Isabelle
Tuttle, Paul R.
Whitock, Edith
Wilson, Arthur
Zeman, Charles J.

1923
Allhouse, Mildred
Bowe, Harriet L.
Burnett, Richard
Crago, Charles
Drake, Mildrend M.
Elliot, Odetta
Fellows, Alden
Fenton, Harley
Fischer, Ethelyn Frances
Fowler, Joe
Gore, Leland H.
Henry, Grace
Jackson, Viette Enid
Jones, Edna
Kent, Lucile H.
Franks, Elmer
Franks, Ivan
Kozell, Charles E.
Markey, Helen
Patch, Paul
Taylor, Olive
Teckus, Isabelle
Tenny, Britton
Trippeer, Mary Lynn
Sell, Elmer
Sheer, Willard
Shippy, Thelma

Smith, Gertrude
Steel, John
Zeithamel, Carl
Zepp, Elmer
Ziegler, Anna

1924
Barber, Fay
Bradley, Beatrice
Chapman, June
Christian, Valeda
Church, Esther
Class, Norris
Clift, Harold
Cobbledick, Catherine
Danielson, Helen
Dippo, Walter
deKorta, Arlene M.
Drake, Mary
Edic, Marjorie
Elliott, Elsie
Estep, Florence
Esterson, Viola
Fencl, James
Gilmore, Lowell
Green, Ward
Green, Carl
Jackson, Helen
Juras, Ethel
Kidd, Rollo
Lacey, Bruce W.
Lacey, Irene
Ludlow, Clarence
Matthews, Roy
Matthews, Sidney
Merryfield, Maurice
Milam, Virginia
Mountjoy, Lawrence
Murrey, Helen
Murtough, Irene
Neuman, Alvin
Nichols, Gordon
Pealer, Pauline
Robinson, Elwyn B.
Seibert, Mary
Sell, Bernard
Shackson, Lee
Shatford, John H.
Smith, Ida
Sutton, Harry W.
Tuttle, Margaret
Wilber, Harold

1925
Baldwin, Laura
Bowe, Lulu
Braund, Howard
Braund, Lois

Browne, Bertine
Burton, Xenil
Crago, Daisy
Davidson, Jean
Dean, Olive A.
Eames, Marcia L.
Edic, Kathryn
Elliott, Clara E.
Franks, Herman
Gali, Esther
Goins, Mary Louise
Heitch, Howard
Hippler, Rosemary
Hippler, Verna Marie
Jones, Ernest
Juras, Irene M.
Kutnat, Ethel Anna
Lave, Martha
Lillich, Cameron L.
Luse, Erwin
Luse, Helene J.
Luse, Mildred
Markey, Kathleen
Marks, Beatrice
McCabe, Bernard
McCann, Elizabeth
Menges, Gordon
Messenger, Lewis
Mountjoy, Gertrude
Murrey, Hilda
Ober, Hilda
Ober, Howard C.
Pfouts, Paul H.
Rettig, Louise G.
Rosner, Robert S
Rosner, Samuel
Russell, Ruth
Sacha, Lillian
Schwarze, Bruce H.
Sheefer, Ethei A.
Silsby, Dorothy M.
Stoneman, Harry
Szitar, John Edward
Tomlinson, Ruth
Wakefield, Milan S.
Waller, Gordon
Wilber, Alfred M.
Zeman, Lewis R.
Ziegler, Mary
Zoul, Robert H.

1926
Bailey, Mildred
Burnett, Edna
Church, Annette
Church, Henry
Cliff, Ada
Cline, Lorraine

Coates, Laura
Collins, Sylvia
Davis, Martha
Davis, Richard
DeVoe, Carl
Dickerson, Mabel
Didham, Beatrice
Dvorak, Charlotte
Fellows, Kendall
Foster, Christine
Gharky, Irving
Gharky, Reba
Gore, Elwyn
Gorham, Thelma
Gunning, Samuel D.
Harper, Wilma
Hartman, Louis
Haster, Florence
Hopkins, Robert
Jackson, Bernice
Kent, Eloise
Kermode, Margaret
Kinsey, Lucille
Kittelson, George
Lippert, Ruth
Mapes, Margaret
Milam, Bob
Milam, Sam
Miles, Edith
Milner, Betty
Milner, Robert
Nelisse, Durwood
Nelisse, Elwood
Payer, Franklin R.
Plohr, Elizabeth
Ramsey, Florence
Rees, Charles
Russell, Mabel
Sawyer, Wilford D.
Seibert, George
Smith, Hazel
Smith, Myrtle
Stern, Robert
Stoneman, Joseph
Tenny, Allen
Thomas, Winnifred
Trippeet, Dorothy
Venchiarutti, Teresa

1927
Bradley, Bob
Brewster, William
Teckus, Dorothy
Bolmeyer, Jane
Cambell, William
Cavanagh, Doris
Danforth, William
Davis, Earl C.

Davis, Bertha
Esterson, Sylvia
Finch, Evelyn
Finch, Roy
Gastermire, Ardith
Gates, Elizabeth
Gharky, Irene
Greenaway, Cora
Green, Dorthy
Harris, Martha
Hill, Cecil
Hill, Edward
Henry, Hida
Hobbs, Frank
Honeywell, John
Hook, Kathryn
Isaac, Mildred
Jaite, Muriel
Jenks, Iona
Jones, Harold
Juras, Andrew
Kehres, Dorothy
Kent, Ernest A.
Kimmel, Mike
Lansgstaff, Mildred
Leach, Margaret
Lewis, Pauline
Lippert, Glenn
Manley, Helen
Marks, Harvey J.
Mathews, Myrtle
McFarland, Beatrice
Miller, Myrtle
Payne, Laurence A.
Patterson, J. Wilber
Rees, Dorothy
Rowe, Jessie
Tuttle, Glen E.
Sawyer, Laura M.
Smith, Margeret
Spaller, Marie
Sutton, Louise E.
Sutton, Lucille M.
Van Valkenburg Elwyn E.
Walton, Thomas A.
Wilmont, Arlene

1928
Baird, Jeanette
Bayard, Jeanette
Bennett, Claude
Bjorkstrom, Elsie
Bolmeyer, Harriet
Campbell, Jack
Cavanagh, Max
Christian, Lenore
Church, Donald
Clarkson, Mable

Davidson, Lyle
Edwards, Dorothy
Eykyn, Margaret
Frost, Marie
Gaither, Paul
Gifford, Kathryn
Green, Priscilla
Hern, Charles
Hoopes, Muriel
Hubay, Edlth
Hunt, James
Johnson, Helen
Kent, Thelma
Kermode, Ellen
Kesco, Alex
Kupfer, Irene
Manley, Virginia
McCann, Sarah
McFarland, George
Patterson, Willard
Robinson, Clark
Stroud, John M.
Szitar, Bert
Thomas, Lincoln
Ziegler, Paul

1929
Blair, Virgil G.
Braund, William B.
Briskey, Goldie
Brown, Duane
Bursby, Margaret M.
Chapin, Lewrence S.
Cole, Cathryn
Dean, Frances
Fosdick, M.
Gilmore, Victor D.
Gunning, Wilbert A.
Haster, Winifred M.
Herrington, Fern I.
Koivisto, Helen S.
Lewis, Urmston H.
Mares, William
Mattson, Hilia
Mault, Harlen
McCabe, Harold B.
Menges, Howard H.
Nelisse, Dorthy
Pealer, Vivian
Plohr, Nancy
Pugsley, Marcel
Raki, Anna E.
Ramsey, Raymond
Rees, Lucille
Root, Marion
Seibert, Edward
Thomas, Mary A.
Venchiarutti, Amelia M.

Venchiarutti, Mollie M.

1930
Bradley, Helen
Brondfield, Armand
Brown, Eleanor
Bundy, Dorothy
Childs, Gladys
Church, John A.
Dean, Ruth
Dormish, Harriet
Drake, Charles
Franks, Irene
Gaither, Rebecca
Harper, Elizabeth
Henry, Laurence
Hill, Gordon C.
Hoopes, Ruth
Hubay, Olga
Johnson, Melburn
Judd, Margaret
Kent, Nella
Kermode, Edwin
Kilby, Neil
Kroeger, Betty
Law, Alice
Maki, Irene
Maki, Oscar
McCaa, Claribel M.
Neldon, Nellie
Rodgers, Ellen
Rood, Helen
Russell, Nellie
Sargent, Eloise
Sheperd, Margarert
Small, Herbert
Stroud, Carol
Szitar, Ernest P.
Thayer, Grace
Thoren, Eloise
Tuttle, Lois
Wilbur, Margarert
Yates, Rebecca

1931
Allison, Claudia
Bjorkstom, Ralph
Blair, Kenneth
Burton, Wendell
Cavanaugh, Richard
Cunningham, Grace
Davidson, Agnes
Fehr, Norma
Fellows, Jeannette
Getten, Fred
Gilmore, Robert
Henry, Melvin
Kent, Roger

Liles, Genevieve
Mathews, Robert
Mattson, Ellen
March, Margaret
Pealer, Delbert
Porter, Christine
Ramsey, Elmer
Robinson, William
Rodgers, Laverne
Sawyer, Ruth
Seibert, Margaret
Sherman, Donald
Simmons, Frank W.
Trippeer, John
Venchiarutti, Ann Marie
Walling, Thomas
Watertson, Erwin
Wrentmore, Howard

1932
Bell, George
Bezdek, Durwood
Bradley, Gordon
Brooks, Edward
Brown, Ruth
Conant, George
Foster, Austin
Gore, Burnadine
Greenaway, Spencer
Gunning, Ella
Henderson, Eldon
Huggett, William
Hoffman, Ina
Johnson, Gradon
Kent, Gerald
Kilby, Florence
Kimmel, Mary
Kolm, Elsie
Lambert, Eldred L.
Law, Francis
Mackey, Irene
Manley, Eleanor
Martin, Elizabeth
Neldon, Perry
Oldham, Dorothy E.
Reitz, Walter K.
Robinson, Ula
Scott, Doris
Sheffield, Charlotte
Sindelar, Ruth
Stroud, Harriett
Walling, Robert
White, Cora
Wince, Ruth
Zuber, Earl C. J.

1933
Adams, Betty

Allison, Claude
Arnold, June
Arnold, Leonard
Bates, Fred
Bates, Meta
Bjorkstrom, Sylvia
Blair, Audre
Boswell, Betty
Cathan, Robert E.
Cohn, Ruth
Fehr, Carmita
Conant, Richard
Gaither, Hellen G.
Gilmore, Marian
Hammon, Marshall G.
Henderson, Kathleen R.
Hubay, Cornelia
Hunt, Clarence C.
Jackson, Mildred
Johnson, Elda
Kelly, Melvin
Kramer, Rose M.
Lacey, Pauline
Maroush, Eleanor
McCann, Anna J.
McIlrath, David
Murtough, William L.
Palmer, Stanley C.
Payer, Evelyn
Pugsley, Mary L.
Reitz, Robert S.
Riehl, Mildred
Robins, Mary
Robinson, Leroy
Seliga, George
Shutts, Gordon
Shutts, Janet
Small, Yvetta
Stauffer, Richard
Stroud, Jean
Thayer, Lois
Van Valkenburg, Elizabeth
Venchiarutti, Henry
Walling, Mary
Warterston, Rosalind
Wass, Eleanor
Williams, Eileen
Wilson, Winifred
Zuber, Richard N.

1934
Baird, Dorothy
Baldwin, Howard
Bezdek, Hubert
Boswell, Beatrice
Browne, Harriet
Blair, Helen B.
Bradley, Martha

Crotty, Richard
Edic, Norman
Greenaway, Dorothy
Greed, Martha
Green, Laurene
Gunning, Melvin
Homewood, Velma
Huggett, Nellie
Hunt, Robert
Malinowski, Leonard
Moody, Betty
Quackenbush, Dorothy
Robinson, Richard
Rood, Elinor
Sargent, Norman
Smith, Ruby
Stolph, Lulu
Satava, Charles
Sawyer, David
Shippey, Winifred
Sprague, Edward
Stevenson, Dorothy
Stroud, Frances
Veltmon, Richard
Vincent, Chalmer W.
Wells, Arthur
Wilson, Ross
Wrentmore, James

1935
Black, Carrie
Cathan, James
Cobbledick, Percy
Davidson, Evelyn
Dellner, Raymond
Duffey, Bemard
Fosdick, Francis
Gifford, Vernon
Gore, Marion
Green, William M.
Gunning, Gladys
Helberg, Helen
Hoopes, Byron
Jackson, Jeannette
Johnson, Marcella
Johnson, Stanley
Johnson, Vernon D.
Kent, Janet
Kermode, Glenn
Koteles, William
Langstaff, Marjorie
Mathews, Marian
Mathews, Ruth
McOmish, Elizabeth
Ober, George
Pealer, Cloyd
Prince, Maxine
Ramsey, Charles

Reitz, Wilbert
Ricker, Richard
Richardson, Oliver
Schultz, Esther
Scott, Douglas
Scott, Harry
Seibert, Florence
Simmons, Howard
Venchiarutti, Regina
Wait, Nelson
Walker, Betty
Wilbur, John
Wilson, Evalyn
Wince, Dorothy
Wright, Wilburt

1936
Barr, Kaltlerine
Benbow, William
Black, Roy, Jr.
Bottomy, C. Paul
Brondfield, Sanford S.
Brooks, Margaret
Brown, Ray
Church, Rachael
Cunningham, Martha
Edic, Lola E.
Ettinger, Betty
Fast, Kay
Green, Robert E.
Heene, Chase
Hill, Norvel
Hill, Vivian
Hodgson, Robert
Homewood, Melvin
Hubay, Charles
Hunt, Ruth
Jones, Alfred
Kuhlman, Lucille
Kulcsar, Elizabeth (Nellie)
Kytta, Eleanor
Mattson, Lillian R.
McCaa, Norman
McDermott, Thomas
McFarland, Dan C.
Noble, Eldon
Noble, Fowler
Norman, Lilan
Parmelee, Frederick
Richardson, Eleanor
Riddle, Jane
Ruch, Douglas
Shaw, Barbara
Sheer, Norma
Shippey, Lucrettia
Shutts, Ronald
Squire, Harris A.
Stanton, William

Stenman, Lillian M.
Stoneman, Franklin
Wallace, Jean
Wilmot, David

1937
Arthur, Elizabeth
Behlen, Jane
Black, Marjorie
Burkhardt, Robert
Cathan, Mary
Cathan, Thomas
Chamberlin, Derwood
Christenson, Nellie
Clark, Richard
Davis, Helen
Davidson, Jean
Davis, Richard
Foster, Paul E.
Frank, Charles
Gore, Ralph
Green, Ward
Hammon, Edward
Heene, Janet
Herrick, Martha
Hileman, Margaret
Kimmel, Frances
Mackey, Eleanore
Marty, Hubert H.
Niece, Ruth
Noble, Jennie
Porter, Roger
Rosengreen, Harvey
Rowe, George
Siebert, Genevieve
Smith, Devane
Stolph, Milton
Young, Jane B.
Wrentmore, Donald

1938
Benbow, Margaret
Black, Louis
Carson, Ellzebeth Vivian
Cathan, Hilda J.
Class, James Vernon, Jr.
Clemens, Peter, Jr.
Coffman, Ann W.
Cohn, Phillip
Corlett, Lois
Davis, Perry H. ,III
Elott, Andrew
Ettinger, Walter
Fisher, John
Forsyth, William
Gifford, Melvin C.
Jones, Donald E.
Jefferson, Margaret

Kent, Miriam Audrey
McDermott, Francis A.
Miller, Marian R.
Richardson, Itha Mae
Richardson, Marian
Rufener, Ernest L.
Scott, Robert
Scott, Thelma
Shanower, Harold
Short, Ethel
Shutts, Kenneth
Springer, Yvonne
Wrentmore, Ann Channing
Young, William Hazard

1939
Bagley, Robert J.
Batchelor, Donald
Benbow, John"
Brown, Pauline
Chambers, Virginia
Ditmer, Viola
Duffey, Mary Ellen
Fosdick, Marion
Fox, Howard
Harris, Maxine
Heberlein, Betty
Helberg, Stanley
Hern, James
Hileman, Wallace
Hodgson, Betty
Hopkins, Mary E.
Jackson, Robert
Kraushaar, Donald L.
Langstaff, Donald E.
Law, Stanley
Marriott, Betty J.
Martin, Violette
McFarland, Elaine
McOmish, Kathryn
Muggleton, Eugene
Patterson, Doris
Richards, Olive
Rosengreen, Raymond
Sawyer, Warren J.
Schwind, Dorothea
Sheer, Donald
Smith, Henry
Stoneman, Jay
Stoneman, Margie
Stroud, Harry
Taylor, Bertha
White, Laurene

1940
Anderson, Edward
Banks, Leslie
Burnett, Joel M.

Carson, Jean
Childs, Jean E.
Christiansen, Robert
Clemens, George D.
Fast, Harold
Forsyth, Margaret
Foster, Genevieve
Franks, Ethel
Gordon, Violet
Hahn, Phyllis
Hallstrom, Kenneth
Hill, Ruth
Himler, Alex M.
Hutchings, Eva Jean
Hutchings, Mary
Johnson, Joseph
Kivisto, Margaret
Langstaff, Ralph
Lumme, Bruno
MacRichie, Maxine
Manlove, Kendall
Mapes, Bernard Clell
Nokes, Doris
Oberlin, Betty Jane
Reed, Elizabeth
Rentz, Clifford G.
Ryall, Robert W.
Ryan, Robert
Shelton, Vivian
Shelton, William M.
Solether, David
Stoneman, Ruth
Trible, Jeanne
Vencharette, Josephine G.
Wallace, Anne
Wass, Carol
Yunkes, Helen

1941
Arnold, Nan
Batchelor, Catherine M.
Benbow, Miriam
Bradley, John G.
Brondfield, Sylvia
Burkhardt, Marjorie J.
Dawley, Irene
Ditto, Beth
Edwards, William R.
Eldridge, Mary
Enslen, Eleanor
Fosdick, Theron
Gepfert, Gahl F.
Greed, Janet
Heberlein, Dorothy
Hein, Geraldine
Helberg, Lila
Hissett, Betty A.
Kuhlman, Robert L.

Kulscar, Margaret
Lowe, Robert
Mercer, Mary Lou
Pugsley, Robert H.
Quinn, Arthur
Rosengreen, Anton
Russell, Dorothy
Sargent, William E.
Schwind, Robert J.
Sheer, Roger C.
Sindelar, George W.
Stanton, Thomas
Stoneman, Gladys
Trible, Jeanne
Wilmot, John P.
Wilson, Ethel
Wilson, Carol
Yunkes, Betty

1942
Anderson, William
Bagley, Mary
Beattie, Anita
Benawit, William F.
Bottomy, Margaretta
Burgess, Alice
Carzoo, Jean Alice
Class, Allyn
Crotty, Robert
Davis, Louise
Ettinger, Frank W.
Felhl, Margaret A.
Fowler, Arline
Gaines, Bob R.
Greene, Al
Haskins, Helen L.
Hensley, Evan
Hissett, Earl
Hissett, Elmer D.
Huggett, Reva Ann
Kenning, John J.
Kimpel, Jack
King, Marcia
Kivisto, Mildred
Kolm, Herbert
Kraushaar, James E.
Lambert, Maxine
Larkworthy, William
Maiden, Helen
Manley, Margaret
Marti, Leonard Francis
Martin, William
Mercer, Robert
Mitchell, Richard W.
Naymik, Doris M.
Peterson, Charles E.
Rake, Floyd
Richardson, Margaret

Ricker, Vivian
Rood, Mary
Rosier, Mary
Shelton, Eloise
Smith, Eleanor
Smith, Robert H.
Snider, Glenn E.
Stoneman, Betty
Suter, Beverly
Tinge, Mary
Venchiarutti, Dorothy
Warburton, Roy
White, Loren
White, Patrica
Wilson, Mildred E.
Wright, June

1943
Batchelor, John E.
Beattie, Gertrude E.
Beattie, Ralph
Black, Mildred C.
Brooks, Harry Francis
Cohn, Robert
Crowel, Margaret
Dellner, Norman
Dobson, Peggy M.
Enslen, George
Fairweather, Elanor
Farrar, Irene
Feihl, Marie
Greed, Richard Allen
Hahn, Chester W.
Harvey, John
Hodgson, Jean Alice
Hopkins, Elsinor
Kerns, James R
Kofsky, Elliot B.
Kovisto, J. Karen
Krebs, Nella M.
Lane, Irene
Lewis, Eleanor
Martell, Frances H.
Miller, Arline
Newton, David
Nichols, Donn M.
Pekarek, Pearl
Rood, Doris
Sargent, Batty
Scheffler, Winnie
Schultz, Harold D.
Scott, Glen
Shelton, Anita
Shelton, Oakley
Sindelar, Dorothy J.
Sindelar, Irene Louise
Smith, Ruth
Stewart, Ruth

Stoneman, Harold
Szitar, Robert
Taylor, Clint
Truman, Kay
Wilson, Leonard
Woodward, James A.

1944
Benbow, Charles E.
Burnett, Walter
Clemens, Richard
Clemens, Robert A.
Colvin, Patricia
Danciu, George F.
De Long, David R.
Draz, David I.
Dunton, Winifred A.
Fast, Howard H.
Gleason, Nancy
Henderson, Herbert G.
Hensley, Jeanne
Hine, Frances
Hoopes, Aibert C.
Imars, Betty L.
Jones, Curtis H.
Kachele, William P.
Kennedy, Betty B.
Kolm, Elmer
Kulcsar, Louis A.
Lambert, Jean
Lowe, Geraldine
Schanck, Jeanne
Selleck, Robert E.
Shelton, Wanda D.
Smith, Joel B.
Sprague, Lynn
Stanton, James H.
Stephens, Lucille
Stone, Douglas M.
Stratton, Jim, Jr.
Sturges, Bill R.
White, Quentin E.
Wilson, Wayne
Wing, Louise

1945
Beattie, Gretchen
Beattie, Hugh V.
Bowe, Shirley
Briggs, Virginia
Carleton, Richard D.
Crain, Patricia
Crotty, Jean
Crowel, Robert
Ensign, Jean
Farrar, Betty
Felger, Forest F.
Fellers, Cleo

Finch, Jerald A.
Gresham, Lyndall
Hein, Helen
Kachele, Alice
Kagy, Martha
Kaserman, Ann
Lander, Roberta
Lewis, Mary
Lowe, Fred W.
Lumme, Don
Maiden, Ann
Marriott, Arthur
Martell, Fred H.
McBride, Edith J.
Miller, Ralph
Newton, Milton J.
Peterson, Donald L.
Reece, Nancy
Reed, Wanda
Richardson, Phyllis
Roeder, Mae Louise
Root, Elton A.
Schrock, Robert R.
Sindelar, Beatrice
Stem, Fredrick
Taylor, Nancy
Tuttle, Betty
Whitlam, Doris

1946
Black, Lois
Bond, Annette
Brower, Jim F.
Danciu, Comel J.
Doner, Tom
Duffey, Carol
Esry, George
Ettinger, Richard S.,Jr.
Evans, Barbara
Felger, Norma J.
Griffith, David C.
Jefferson, Xenil
Kelley, Phyllis
Kramer, Barbara
Lambert, Ethelyn
Larkworthy, Marilyn
Laughlin, Jackie
MacRitcie, Jack L.
Miralia, Charles T.
O'Kane, Richard
Rentz, Gene
Roeder, Robert J.
Rood, Harry L.
Sasak, Dorothy
Sauer, Joanne S.
Shelton, Bev S.
Silvernail, Evelyn
Smith, Keith

Spangler, Gloria
Spielhaupter, JoAnn
Stephan, Mary
Stoneman, Marian R.
Stratton, Shirley
Tuttle, Charles
Vencharetti, Phillis J.
Werder, Alice
Wittig, Anna May

1947
Arthur, Cynthia
Beattie, Lucy L.
Bond, Dick
Bowers, Betty
Briggs, Edward
Briskey, Charlotte
Cohn, Bettie
Cox, Gordon
Davis, James
Doell, Donald R.
Dye, Robert P.
Edwards, Jo Ann
Eggleston, Neil
Finn, Jay
Fischer, Joan
Fisher, Wilson
Frihauf, Ethel
Green, Donald
Gygle, Ramona J.
Heaps, Jack
Hileman, David M.
Horn, Nancy
Hubbard, Joseph
Imars, Edward
Kerns, Miriam
Kimpel, George
Lindberg, Larry
Matthews, Don R.
Myers, Joan
Myers, Romi
O'Kane, Sally
Rood, Carolyn
Root, Nancy
Shelton, Betty Lou
Simons, Joyce
Sindelar, Martha
Sindelar, Richard S.
Snider, Marian
Squire, Donn
Stone, John P.
Swan, Joyce
Wass, Martha
White, Olive
Williamson, David
Wilson, Mary J.
Winship, William B.
Wood, Molly

1948
Albrecht, Ellsworth R.
Ayers, Carol
Barriball, Joan
Batchelor, Barbara
Beattie, Beth
Beattie, Carolyn J.
Behlen, Mary
Black, Robert
Carson, Corwin, Jr.
Chambers, Laverne
Cuddy, Nan
Danciu, Emil F.
Davidson, John C.
Davis, Dick
Deise, Sam
Farrar, Robert E.
Felger, Willard
Froebe, Jack A.
Green, Lester C.
Haar, Florence
Hartman, Louis S.
Honeywell, JoAnn
Hoopes, David T.
Hyatt, Robert
Imars, Wayne J.
Jennison, Marshall.
Kagy, Edmund M.
Kuehnel, Esther
London, Carol
Matthews, Dorothy A.
McBride, Margaret Gene
McIntyre, Maxine
McLean, Barbara
Mercer, Janet
Miraglia, Joseph
Montgomery, Pat
Mowrey, Jack A.
Patchett, Corabell
Paterson, Berdie
Ray, Myrna
Sauer, Bentley F., Jr.
Short, Evelyn
Silsby, June
Skeel, John L.
Smith, Donald, Sr.
Spielhaupter, Helen

1949
Alderfer, William J.
Arnold, Ray A.
Babcock, Walter C.
Best, Emerson H.
Bond, George E.
Buchanan, Jack C.
Campbell, Alice
Carleton, Clarice

Carlson, Dianne
Carlson, Donna Lee
Cubberley, Peter T.
Clarke, Warren
Darlin, Bill
Davidson, Jean A.
Davis, William H.
Edwards, Janice
Fischer, Jean
Hatcher, Janette
Hladik, Pat
Jackson, Jane E.
Kaserman, Carol
Kennedy, Helen
Kenney, William G.
Kroening, Ann
Lewis, Alice
Melbourne, Judy
Metzko, Bob
Miller, John J.
Minor, Wesley.
Nelisse, Pat
Peterson, Robert G.
Picking, Jay W.
Plazak, Robert
Ralston, Pat
Ritchey, Beverly
Rohrman, Sally Lone
Root, Betty A.
Sailer, Richard F.
Schroeder, Elizabeth
Scott, Robert
Smith, Harry B.
Sparrow, Robert E.
Squire, Jean C.
Stem, Frances
Stratton, Joy
Symes, Janette
Taylor, Wade
Tilton, Ann
Waller, Robert L.
Whitlam, Charlotte

1950
Bailey, Beth
Bond, James
Bowe, Betsy
Brower, Nancy
Chambers, Richard A.
Clarke, George.
Cobbledick, Dorn M.
Cramer, Alan
Crowe, Dick
Draz, Richard
Henry, Janet
Hill, Gene
Imars, Glen
Johnson, Patricia

Kaserman, Mary
Keary, Betty
MacLaren, David S.
McFarland, Carole
Newton, Richard
O'Kane, Michael
Payer, Harry F.
Peterson, Russell P.
Plazak, Doris
Richards, Marjorie
Root, Stuart D.
Ryan, Jack
Seymour, Richard D.
Sheffield, Lou
Shelton, Darrell E.
Shurmer, Mary Lou
Stevenson, Myra
Stoneman, James V.
Tinge, Rolf R.
Van Gorder, Barbara
White, Judy A.
White, Robert M.
Wilson, Frederick M.
Winship, Bob

1951
Anderson, Marjorie L.
Arnold, Robert O.
Babcock, Lynn W.
Barber, Bryan
Behlen, Louise
Carlton, Peg
Doell, James
Dunton, Nancy R.
Ebel, Joan
Eggleston, Thomas
Evans, Donald Keith
Evans, Richard W.
Fitzpatrick, Diane
Green, Jeanette
Griffith, Joanne
Hart, George
Henderson, Raymond
Hill, Betty
Hills, Marilyn
Hine, James W.
Hoekstra, Paul
Hubbard, Tom V.
Kennedy, Donald P.
Kewish, Alan E.
Lake, Harriet
Luckay, Frank
Madison, Joanna
McFarland, Richard
Plzak, Don
Robinson, Jean A.
Rodgers, John B.
Schaaf, Berbara

Short, David W.
Toth, Robert L.
Wiley, Kenneth
Wince, Bevington
Worstell, William R.

1952
Akers, Dick
Apel, Gordon
Babcock, Mary Anne
Barber, Warren
Barriball, Margaret Ann
Bell, Betty A.
Boone, Robert C.
Bowe, Thomas W.
Brichford, Florence
Bull, Ford
Bullock, Barbara
Butler, William J.
Church, Genie
Collier, Rhea
Conway, Tim D.
Cox, Gerry E.
Davis, Jean
Engstrom, Judy
Fitzpatrick, James
Froebe, Jerry M.
Gibson, James K.
Grieme, Betty
Hawthorne, Martin K.
Heck, Douglas E.
Henderson, Thomas J.
Hill, Cecil S.
Hofmann, Carl J.
Hubbard, James
Hurst, John
Imars, Dean
Keal, Merry Lee
Mason, Ginger
Miralia, Benedict P., Sr.
Nelisse, Donald
Pearch, Ann
Pinkett, Susanne
Potter, Marilyn
Robbins, Leora
Rodgers, Thomas
Ryan, Carolyn
Shatford, Anita
Simpson, Raymond
Smith, Lura
Smith, Stephanie
Stanton, John S.
Stevenson, Charles
Stoneman, Patricia
Waller, Doris
White, Rosalyn"
Wilson, Sally
Worley, Julia

1953
Armstrong, Roger M.
Barriball, Roberta
Bradley, Gaynor
Britt, Adrienne
Bullock, Donald L.
Burke, Judy A.
Carlson, Sarah
Clark, Shirley A.
Cowhard, Elbert "Al" Leroy
Crittenden, Bruce, Jr.
Crombie, William P.
Crowe, Barbara
Cubberley, Hal
Curtiss, Shirley
Ebel, David
Ebel, Judy
Farris, David
Fram, Carol
Hartman, Roger C.
Hawersaat, Carol M.
Hawn, Jerry M.
Hemming, Winifred L.
Hills, Shirley
Hoekstra, Karl
Kachele, Larry S.
Keck, Carolyn
Kline, Lois
Lambert, Joan D.
Lawyer, Bill
Luckay, Alice
Matthews, Gary
Matthews, William
McCabe, Kenneth Eugene
McCormick, Ronald J.
McFarland, John Clarence
Moyse, Jim
Nelisse, Sue
Nichols, Gordon C. ,II
Plzak, George
Richards, Dorothy
Robinson, June
Sargent, Eugene A.
Sasak, Jack
Scott, Sue
Simons, Marylin
Spanagel, John David
Stroud, J. P.
Sturges, Leslie
Toth, Donald R.
Weeks, Lisa
Wendl, Bill
Williams, Marie

1954
Best, Eugene F.
Birkin, Sue
Blair, Philip

Brumfield, Wanda
Burton, Raymond D.
Carlton, Michael W.
Cohn, David
Collier, Jayne E.
Cramer, Clark W
Crink, James W.
Cutshaw, Wilma
English, Lynn Suzanne
Engelhardt, Jean
Fitzpatrick, Jon
Fulton, Janet
Green, Susan E.
Hladik, David R.
Hudson, Robert C.
Hunt, Robert P.
Jephson, Richard E.
Keal, Jane
Konyecsni, John M.
Kulcasr, Judy
Lewis, Harry J
McNally, Mike
Miller, John R.
Myers, Nancy M.
Odenweller, Chariss
Pearch, Nancy
Robinson, Kay
Rock, Helene
Schroeder, Nancy
Scott, Carol L.
Shelton, Fredrick T.
Sindelar, Stanley R.
Smith, Glenda Bertine
Steele, Ronald
Stephan, Thomas A.
Tilton, Ward D.
Toso, Trudy
Turner, Bobbie
Ulrich, Lynn
Wendl, Betty
Worley, Jerry W.

1955
Babcock, Roger R.
Banning, Phillip Guy
Barriball, Ruth
Bateson, Georgia
Bodwell, Richard
Bowe, James L.
Bowers, Sonya
Butler, Bob
Carroll, Pat A.
Cleaveland, Phil
Davis, Pat
Dornbos, Jack H.
Engstrom, John A.
Flynn, Alvin D.
Giffhorn, Ann

Greenway, George R.
Harmon, Larry.
Hart, Carol A.
Hawthorne, Carol
Hill, David Allan
Hill, Gordon C.
Hofmann, David C.
Hooker, Roger Allen
Hunt, Robert C.
Hunt, Lindy
Jackson, Joan C.
Jenkins, Charles H.
Jones, Joel M.
Keck, Julia
London, Anne
Mattern, Thomas G.
McBride, Dolores
McClanahan, Ann
Moyse, William C.
Nichols, Marilyn
Otis, Jayne
Reed, Saundra
Reitz, Valerie
Robinson, Ronald G.
Ryan, Margaret
Schwerzler, Sally
Sekeres, Dave J.
Smith, Mark W.
Snow, Robert C.
Stebbins, Sue Ann
Stoneman, Richard
Stoney, Stan
Van Gorder, James
Van Nort, Peter
White, James R.
White, Lloyd E.
Wiley, Larry
Williams, Joan
Wilson, Julie
Wood, Eugene E.
Yunkes, Charles G.

1956
Arnold, Cynthia
Barnhouse, Donald
Bateson, Brenda
Bayless, Myrna
Behnke, Richard
Bradley, Dennis
Brown, Richard.
Bull, Emerson
Camp, George H.
Chapman, Robert Fraser
Cordes, Martha
Curtiss, Gary
Evans, Patricia
Evans, Suzann B.

176

Extrom, Mary
Fischer, Frieda
Fish, Sandra
Givens, Joann
Goodin, Robert W.
Groth, Hugh F.
Grubich, Grace
Harr, Sallyann
Hawn, Roberta
Hoffman, Michael
Hoffman, Michael James
Keal, Thomas
Kelly, Susan
Kewish, Karen
Klifoyle, James K.
Lauterer, Kenneth R.
Loan, Charles J.
Mayner, Kam
Mayner, Kermit A.
Miller, Mary Lynn
Nye, Virginia
Otis, Joel A.
Owens, Lee
Richardson, Leslie
Rink, Kurt K.
Robbins, David W.
Rodgers, Sarah J.
Rogerson, Margo
Rouru, Jack S.
Searcy, William
Shelton, Carol
Shelton, Adrienne C.
Sheridan, Patricia
Shipley, Helen
Smith, Patricia
Solether, Darryl
Sprague, Robert E.
Stanton, Donna
Stanton, Marion
Stebbins, Charles H.
Straka, Allen B
Stratton, James A.
Sutton, Janet
Thoren, William T.
Van Doren, Richard F.
Wilber, Robert
Wilbur, Robert K.
Williams, Charles William
Williams, Nancy
Woodworth, Thomas Wayne
Young, Maurice Richard

1957
Ackland, Ronald
Anderson, Richard L.
Baehr, Adrienne
Baker, Judy
Banning, David A.

Barriball, Barbara
Barriball, Dean
Barton, Marshall
Bowers, Jean
Burns, Dianne
Carlson, Thomas R.
Clark, David Lee
Cummins, Mary Alice
Dodson, Osborne, Jr.
Fisher, Carlton
Fletcher, James P.
Flynn, Virginia M.
Frew, Karen
Harmon, Thelma
Harr, William
Hawersaat, Lawrence H.
Hegerty, Connie
Herbell, Phyllis
Huggett, Tryon Virgil
Johannisson, Eric
Neff, William
Newstead, Robert T.
Nix, George C.
Petras, Janice
Pinkett, Richard
Quillen, Anne
Reitz, Margaret
Rice, George J.
Shelton, Sharon
Short, Harold
Simmons, Mary Lou
Simon, Linda L.
Slavik, Nancy
Spanagel, Virginia
Spielhaupter, Kaye
Thomas, John
Vercoe, David Alan
Wallen, Susan
Willams, Robert L.
Yanko, Irene Mary Jo

1958
Ackland, Tom B.
Bevis, George R.
Bird, Bruce
Blair, William Howard
Brown, Patricia
Bullen, Georgia
Burke, Pat
Criswell, Steve B.
Crittenden, Gale
Cutshaw, Bill
Daggett, Betsy
Dagil, Mary Ann
Day, Carolyn
Fish, William
Fitz, James A.
Fitzgerald, Hester

Foster, Keith
Fusselman, Lee
Guarnieri, Alice
Guilbert, Lynn
Heaps, Janet
Hegerty, Sallie F.
Hentemann, June
Hoekstra, Marta H.
Hudson, Myra
Hurtt, Holly
Jamieson, Nan
Kaserman, Jean
Keary, Bernard
Kermeen, Kathy
Knot, Mary Lou
La Musga, Dianne
Longwell, Galen
Matthews, Joan
McCormick, Gerald
McLeod, Keith D.
McPeak, Ellen
Merritt, Ron
Mitchell, Kenneth
Mogg, Rick H.
Morton, Joe
Morton, Susan
Nall, Carl
Nichols, Bob
Nosol, Agnes
Odenweller, Parks
Otis, Barbara
Palmer, Gary L.
Parmelee, Sally
Picking, Sue
Reed, Paula
Reitz, Robert William
Richardson, Judy
Robens, Judrth
Rock, Penny
Rood, Ron
Schreck, James F.
Schuster, Joan
Schwerzler, Gary
Scott, Winnie
Searcy, Bob
Sherman, David
Sindelar, Al L.
Smith, Claire
Southmayd, Peter B.
Stearns, Bill
Steele, Barbara
Stone, Sharon
Swyt, Robert L.
Thoren, Ann
Van Nort, Steve D.
Williams, Doug L.

1959

Ames, Lawrence E.
Banning, Lorene
Barriball, Patricia
Bauman, Jacqueline B.
Bevis, Roger A.
Brooks, Barbara
Byrne, Phillip M.
Campbell, Donna Kay
Chapman, Donald M.
Church, Hank
Class, Suzie
Clayton, David L.
Cordes, Bill
Crawford, Lee
Davidson, Arthur J.
Di Egidio, Leon
Dunbar, David H.
Farrow, Robert L
Foster, Sandra
Fram, Gloria
Gilson, Sally
Grose, Shirley
Groth, Carolyn
Grubich, Michael
Guarnieri, Fred
Gurney, Jean
Haecker, Karl
Hallstrom, Richard
Hastings, Larry R.
Henry, Thomas K.
Hill, A. Lee
Hill, Julie
Hill, June
Hunt, Marianne
Hunt, Marty
Jones, Robert E.
Kiel, Frederick O.
Knott, Bill E.
Krause, Carl D.
Kreycik, Beverly
Kuhn, Robert
Lambert, Sue
Lamusga, Dennis J.
Lee, Mary E.
Lewis, Jim T.
Lockemer, Bruce
Long, James
Mares, Bill Elton
Mayner, Claudia
McFarlin, Doug
McKibben, Orlo.
Mogg, Janet L.
Moorhead, John
Nagakawa, Nazomu
Neidhardt, Carol Burns
Nichols, Phelps
Nye, Carol
Pealer, Leanne

Petersen, Perry H.
Pickford, Earle A.
Richardson, Jack E.
Rickards, Reese P.
Ricker, Betty Lou
Rigoutat, Ann
Robinson, Charles
Rood, Judy
Rufener, Loretta
Rusch, Robert M.
Sekeres, Bruce
Shipley, M. Joan
Sprague, Carol
Stillman, Richard H.
Stoa, Karen
Strick, Meta
Szitar, William D.
Terry, Carroll
Thomas, Rick
Thompson, Alan R.
Toso, Inge
Wagner, Christine
Wells, Terry W.
Whaley, Ted
Wilson, Bonnie
Yerke, Sandy A
Zugan, Frank G.

1960
Anderson, Norman
Bayless, Peerl
Bair, John C.
Barton, Lynn M.
Benner, Carolyn
Beuoy, Bonnie
Bigler, Carol
Boehm, Roger
Borsani, Horacio
Bowers, Ann
Brown, Lori
Brown, Melissa
Butler, Joan
Cahill, Tom
Clark, Nancy V.
Davis, Lewis C., Jr.
Dewell, Ann
Ebersold, Joan
Freer, Fred S., III
Freeze, Richard Paul
Greenway, Mary
Guarnieri, Tony E.
Guest, Nancy A.
Guilbert, Jennifer
Hallstrom, Ronald
Harden, Pam
Harp, Jeffrey C.
Heimerdinger, William A.
Hill, Barbara

Hope, Phyllis J.
Lloyd, Hugh W.
Hurst, Cynthia
Hurst, Karen
Johannisson, James R.
Jones, Judith L.
Kecso, James
Kilby, David
Kleve, George
Kroening, Elizabeth
Larker, Geraldine
Lauterer, Gerald
Levi, Tom
Lowe, Sherrie
Maves, Julie
McDermott, Francis E.
Miller, Bob D.
Miller, Hayden S.
Mitchell, Don R.
Modica, Judy
Morse, Marlaine
Mullen, Brenda
Nagy, Barbara
Odenweller, Vicki
Odiorne, Nancy
Otis, Diana
Otis, Robert P.
Peterson, Karl
Sagy, Barbara
Shelton, James
Skerritt, Sheila
Steele, John F.
Steele, Paula
Stevenson, Rick
Stiles, Allan
Stroud, Janet
Tenny, Barbara
Tenny, Susan
Theis, Barbara
Thoren, Christine
Vaccariello, Phyllis
Vincent, Mary
Wade, Susan
Warner, Peter
Weizer, Albert Clyde
Weizer, Norman
Wheeler, Barbara
White, Gary E.
Wilson, Beth

Chagrin Falls Schools' Achievement Hall of Fame

1992

Bullock, Donald L. '53
Hubay, Charles A. '36
Kagy, Edmund M. '48
Nichols, Gordon D. '24
Root, Stuart D. '50
Stanton, William '36
Terpenning, Margaret S. '70
verDuin-Palit, Helen '66

1994

Evans, Richard W. '51
Harmon, Robert J. '64
Jones, Joel M. '55
Schregardus, Donald R. '68
Tenny, Allen J. '26
Van Nort, Peter '55

1996

Alcorn-Kelker, Katharin '61
Clemens, George '40
Crawford, A. Lee '59
Draz, Richard '50
Farris, David J. '53
Griffith-Root, Joanne '51
Rodgers, Elizabeth G. '19

1998

Dye, Robert Paul '47
Engel, Margaret '69
Ettinger, Walter H. '70
Finch, Jerald A. '45
Griffith, David C. '46
Harris, Carlyle S. '14
Rosner, Robert S. '25

2000

Albers, Gregg R. '73
Conway, Tim '52
Cubberley, Peter T. '49
Darlin, Bill '49
Mayner-Greenwood, Claudia '59
Sherman, Christopher R. '70
Vecchiarelli, Nancy '68

2002

Bartlett-Hobgood, Linda '71
Boardman, David '75
Kuivinen, Karl Church '66
Maistros, Jack '75
Rodgers, John B., Jr. '51
Sutton-Wright, Suzanne '62
Thomas, John '57

2004

Baker, Douglas '70
Church, John A., Jr. '64
Draz, Captain David Ingraham '44
Pearce-Vasquez, Steffanie '76
Schron, Jack H., Jr. '66
Shafer-Zizzo, Tina '74
Webster, Dr. Denise (Denny) '62

Appendix VI
Chagrin Falls Schools' Athletic Directors

*Prior to 1938, all high school
athletic activities were conducted by the
high school principal in cooperation with
the school superintendent.*

Ted Gurney	1938 - 1966
Ralph Quesinberry	1966 - 1980
Fred Girard	1980 - 1983
Glenn Wyville	1983 - 1991
Lenny May	1991 - 2004
John Farrell	2004 -

Chagrin Falls Schools' Athletic Heritage Hall of Fame 1897-1950

There was a time when the accomplishments of high school athletes were not publicly acknowledged as they are today through modern media. Yet, these athletes' achievements and contributions to their schools were as great as those of any time period.

The Veterans' Committee of the Chagrin Falls Schools' Athletic Hall of Fame has created the Heritage Hall of Fame to recognize those splendid athletes of the past. During their tenure at Chagrin Falls High School, the inductees dominated the competition, establishing records and leading their teams to championships.

A plaque with the athletes' names engraved was presented to Chagrin Falls Schools' Superintendent, Dr. David Axner, on October 2, 2003, at the Chagrin Valley Athletic Club during the Chagrin Falls Schools' Athletic Hall of Fame induction banquet.

Lute Harris-Honorary
Ray Honeywell-1900
Frank Coombs-1910
Lawrence Gates-1911
Harley A. Coombs-1912
Sim Shepard-1912
Lawrence Winchell-1921
Cecil Burnett-1922
Bruce Schwarze-1925
Durwood Nelisse-1926
Britton Tenny-1923
Robert Hopkins-1926
Mildred Isaac-1927
Cecil Hill-1927
Gordon Bradley-1932
George "Sleepy" Seliga-1933
LeRoy Robinson-1933
Ed "Fuzz" Hammon-1937
Ken Shutts, Sr.-1938
Stan Law-1939
John Benbow-1939
Bill Shelton-1940
George Sindelar-1941
Glen Snider-1942
Harry "Baldy" Brooks-1943
Charles Benbow-1944
Don Lumme-1945
Bob Crowell-1945
Joe Hubbard-1947
Emil Danciu-1948
Joe Miraglia-1948

Chagrin Falls Schools' Athletic Hall of Fame

1991
Groth, Jeff '75
Gurney, Ted - Coach/Athletic Director
Lauterer, Ken '56
Nelisse, Elwood '26
Quesinberry, Ralph - Coach/Athletic Director
Robinson, William '31
Shutts, Bob '64
Van Nort, Steve '58
Wise-Beckman, Sue '80

1993
Bistritz, Bob '78
Bradley, Dale '65
Champlin, Tom '75
Edwards, Bill '41
Miller, Dan '72
Phend, Jane '83
Piai, John - Coach
Wyville, Glenn - Coach/Athletic Director

1995
Banning, Dave '57
Crowel, Margaret '43
Fitz, Nancy '85
Hurst, John - Coach '52
Roeder, Bob - Honorary '46
Stanton, Jack - Coach '52
Wiese, Andy '83
Willard, Bob '70

1997
Fitzpatrick Jon '54
Kline, Everett, Jr. '19
Lockemer, Vern '63
Ohlrich, Bob - Coach
Rudolph, Brett '83
Skeel, Jack '48
Slaybaugh, Ray '64
Ward-Curley, Janet '84

1999
Evans, Donald '51
Florkiewicz, T.J. '88
Green, Lester '48
Revelle, David '80
Snavely, Paul '71
Thome-Kennedy, Colleen '87
Wiley, Larry '55

2001
Bartley-Edgington, Carol '80
Bierman-Caja, Anne '81
Bradley, Dennis '56
Burwell, Joe '74
Groth, Douglas '76
Kaye, Ryan '88
Plzak, Robert '49

2003
Bomback, Glenn Jr. '72
Ehrenbeit-Blair, Stacey '88
Groth, Jon '80
Harsh, Eric '88
May, Lenny - Coach/Athletic Director
Speed, Erik '86
Wiley, Ken '51

2005
Conley-Botcher, Shawn '91
Davidson, Art '59
Freshman-Johnson, Rachel '92
Kruse, Travis '95
Shutts, Steve '70
Van Nort, Peter '55
Wise, Warren '67

Chagrin Falls Schools' Ohio Athletic Champions

Ohio High School Athletic Association

Team State Champions
1970	Boys' Cross Country
1991	Girls' Cross Country
1996	Girls' Soccer
1998	Girls' Basketball
2003	Boys' Lacrosse

Team State Runners-up
1970	Boys' Cross Country
1971	Boys' Cross Country
1983	Girls' Basketball
1992	Girls' Cross Country
1993	Boys' Cross Country
1997	Girls' Basketball
2003	Boys' Soccer

Team State Semifinalists'
1956	Boys' Basketball
1979	Girls' Basketball
1981	Boys' Soccer
1982	Girls' Basketball
1983	Girls' Soccer
1985	Boys' Soccer
1986	Boys' Soccer
1995	Girls' Soccer
1997	Girls' Soccer
2002	Boys' Lacrosse

Individual State Champions
1925	Track/Elwood "Bus" Nelisse-mile
1927	Track/Cecil Hill-mile
1931	Track/Bill Robinson-100yd
1959	Track/Art Davidson-100 yd
1982	Track/Andy Weise-1600m
1983	Track/Andy Weise-1600m
1988	Track/Eric Harsh-1600m
1998	Swimming/Diana Munz-2 Events
1999	Swimming/Diana Munz-1 Event
2000	Swimming/Lauren Preyss-1 Event
2001	Swimming/Lauren Preyss-2 Events
2002	Swimming/Lauren Preyss-2 Events
2003	Swimming/Lauren Preyss-1 Event

All-American Athletes
1995	Boys' Soccer/Brye Gerhardt
1996	Girls' Soccer/Katie Carson
1999	Swimming/Diana Munz
1999	Football/Sean McHugh
2001	Swimming/Lauren Preyss
2002	Swimming/Lauren Preyss
2003	Swimming/Christine Collins, Jennifer Henderson, Frances Killea, Lauren Preyss

National Scholar All-American
2002	Girls' Soccer/Britton Lombardi

Appendix X
Bibliography

BOOKS

Babinsky, Jane E. and Miriam Church Stem. *The Life and Work of Henry Church.* Chagrin Falls. Chagrin Falls Schools', Classes of 1974 and 1916

Blakeslee, Chiles T. (1969). *History of Chagrin Falls and Vicinity* (new revised edition). Chagrin Falls: Friends of the Chagrin Falls Library. Originally written (1874). *Chagrin Falls Exponent* (1903).

Coates, William. (1924). *A History of Cuyahoga County and The City of Cleveland.* (Volume 2). New York: The American Historical Society.

Elliott, Rebecca H. (1989). *James A. Garfield- The Early Years 1831-1856.* Moreland Hills: The Moreland Hills Historical Society.

Gorretta, Laura J. (Ed.) (2004). *Chagrin Falls—An Ohio Village History.* Chagrin Falls: The Chagrin Falls Historical Society. Chagrin Falls Schools', Class of 1968.

Gumprecht, Annie Huggett. (1998). *Annie's Anecdotes.* Chagrin Falls: The Chagrin Falls Historical Society. Chagrin Falls Schools', Class of 1942.

Hubbard, Barbara B. and Thomas G. Mattern. (1989). "Oral Histories of Long-Time Chagrin Falls Teachers and Alumni." *Echoes of the Past.* (Volume I). Chagrin Falls: Chagrin Falls Schools' Historical Preservation Society. Chagrin Falls Schools', Classes of 1952 and 1955.

Hubbard, Barbara B. and Thomas G. Mattern (Eds.). (1991). "Pictorial and Oral Histories of Chagrin Falls Schools," *Echoes of the Past.* (Volume III). Chagrin Falls: Chagrin Falls Schools' Historical Preservation Society. Chagrin Falls Schools', Classes of 1952 and 1955.

Johnson, Crisfield. (1974). *History of Cuyahoga County, Ohio.* Cleveland: Greater Cleveland Genealogical Society. (new revised edition). (1879). Cleveland: D.W. Ensign Co.

Mattern, Thomas G. (Ed.) (1997). *Celebrating 100 Years of Chagrin Falls High School Football 1897-1997.* Chagrin Falls: Chagrin Falls Alumni Association. Chagrin Falls Schools', Class of 1955.

Rodgers, Elizabeth G. (1987). "Chagrin Falls Village." *The Encyclopedia of Cleveland History.* Cleveland: Case Western Reserve University. Chagrin Falls Schools', Class of 1919.

Rodgers, Elizabeth G. (1988). *CHAGRIN... Whence the Name?* Chagrin Falls: Elizabeth G. Rodgers. Chagrin Falls Schools', Class of 1919.

Sands, Lewis. (1990). "A Brief Review of the Chagrin Falls Public Schools from 1859 to 1959." *Echoes of the Past.* (Volume II). Chagrin Falls: Chagrin Falls Schools' Historical Preservation Society.

Versteeg, D.D., John M. (1962). *Methodism Ohio Area 1812-1962.* Delaware: Ohio Area Sesquicentennial Committee.

Vincent, D.D., Clarence A. (1976). *Chagrin Falls and Vicinity from 1865-1880 – Early History and Early Memories.* Chagrin Falls: Friends of the Chagrin Falls Library. (Reproduction). Issues November 19, 1930 – January 31, 1931. *Chagrin Falls Herald.*

DOCUMENTS

Church, Austin. (1911) Written Reminiscences.

Naylor, Wendy Hodge and Yolita E. Rausche. (1994). National Register Draft: Chagrin Falls High School/Grade School Building.

Rodgers, Elizabeth G. Papers. Chagrin Falls: The Chagrin Falls Historical Society. Chagrin Falls Schools', Class of 1919.

Walters, Franklin. (1853-1854). Unpublished Diary.

Williams, L.D. [Papers of Elizabeth G. Rodgers]. Chagrin Falls: Chagrin Falls Historical Society. Chagrin Falls Schools', Class of 1919.

LECTURE

Rausche, Yolita E. (October 7, 1995). "Aristarchus Champion, The Champion Library Hall," Western Reserve Symposium: Case Western Reserve University.

LETTERS

Blazer, John. Letter. February 7, 2004. Fairfax, VA. Chagrin Falls Schools', Class of 1967.

Finch, Jerald A. Letter. 1995. Richmond, VA. Chagrin Falls Schools', Class of 1945.

Foote, Janet Henry. Letter. January 6, 1993. Athens, Alabama. Chagrin Falls Schools', Class of 1950.

Foster, Paul. Letter. April 29, 1997. Bay Village, OH. Chagrin Falls Schools', Class of 1937.

Ruch, Douglas E. Letter. April 22, 1999. Casa Grand, AZ. Chagrin Falls Schools', Class of 1936.

Sheldon, Newton S. Letter to cousin. December 9, 1848. Chagrin Falls: Student of Asbury Seminary.

Szitar, John Jr. Letter. July 7, 1995. Mayfield Hts., OH. Chagrin Falls Schools', Class of 1925.

Weber, Ruth Barriball. Letter. January 15, 1998. Rockledge, FL. Chagrin Falls Schools', Class of 1955.

MAGAZINES

Lupold, Harry Forrest. (July/August 1980). "The Civil War Journal of a Western Reserve Soldier." *The Western Reserve Magazine.* p. 36.

"Chagrin Falls Methodist Church Past and Present". (May 1, 1896). *The Methodist Times,* Volume V, number 18. Courtesy of Mrs. C.S. Harris.

NEWSPAPERS

Chagrin Valley Herald (1946-1968). Tenny, Allen J. [Ed. & Pub.] Chagrin Falls: Chagrin Falls Public Library.

Chagrin Valley Times. Chagrin Falls: Chagrin Falls Public Library.

Chagrin Falls Exponent. (1874-1963). Stranahan, J.J. [First Publisher and Proprietor]. Chagrin Falls, OH: Cuyahoga County Public Library-Chagrin Falls Branch; The Ohio Room. [Microfilm].

Cleveland Newspaper Digest. Annals of Cleveland (abstracts from articles in Cleveland newspapers dealing with Chagrin Falls, 1818-1875).

Echo. (1922-1956). [Chagrin Falls High School newspapers].

The Geauga Republican and Whig, Volume I. (September 9, 1843). "Asbury Seminary at Chagrin Falls."

Tiger Rag. (1957-1960). [Chagrin Falls High School newspapers].

Newspaper clippings from: *The Chagrin Valley Herald, Chagrin Herald Sun, Chagrin Falls Exponent and Chagrin Valley Times.* Chagrin Falls: Chagrin Falls Public Library; The Ohio Room.

PERIODICALS

Bottomy, Marjorie Black. (January, 1995). *Tiger Tales*, Volume V, Issue 1. Chagrin Falls Schools', Class of 1933.

Solether, Mike. (August, 2002). *Tiger Tales*, Volume XII, Issue 2. Chagrin Falls Schools', Class of 1969.

Vittek, Jim. (August, 1994). *Tiger Tales*, Volume IV, Issue 3. Chagrin Falls Schools', Class of 1968.

PERSONAL INTERVIEWS

Blair, Audre. Personal Interview. June 11, 1997. Chagrin Falls Schools', Class of 1933.

Clemens, Peter. Personal Interview. 1998. Chagrin Falls Schools', Class of 1938.

BOARD MINUTES

Record Books of the Chagrin Falls Public Schools. (1849-1963). Handwritten by district clerks, secretaries and treasurers. Made available to the Alumni Association office as follows:

"Board Minutes". (May 25, 1849-March 30, 1877). Chagrin Falls, OH: Chagrin Falls Board of Education.

(MISSING) "Board Minutes". (April 1, 1877-April 30, 1891). Chagrin Falls, OH: Chagrin Falls Board of Education.

"Board Minutes". (April 20, 1891 – November 5, 1909), (November 12, 1909-December 18, 1923), (January 7, 1924-August 24, 1931), (August 31, 1931-October 17, 1938), (October, 26 1938- January 6, 1941), (January 6, 1941-September 8, 1947), (October 13, 1947-November 9, 1953), (December 14, 1953 – December 3, 1956), (December 8, 1956-May 20, 1963). Chagrin Falls, Ohio: Chagrin Falls Board of Education.

YEARBOOKS

Annual. (1911-1924). [Chagrin Falls High School yearbooks].

Zenith. (1925-1960). [Chagrin Falls High School yearbooks].

PHOTOGRAPHIC CREDITS

Chagrin Falls Historical Society - Photo Archives

Chagrin Falls Alumni Association - Historical Room

Chagrin Falls High School - 1911-1960 yearbooks

The Church Family - Sketches of Early Chagrin Falls Schools by Henry Church, Jr.

Chagrin Valley Herald

The Plain Dealer

Tag Art Studio: *Terry Taggart '62* created these "Photages™" from photographic resources

History Of The Chagrin Falls Schools
*Volumne One 1833-1960*__ dust jacket
The Early Years__ inside front panel
School Display__ PAGE i
Rings, Pins & Things__ PAGE ii
Skippie & Capes__ PAGE X
Author's Note__ PAGE xii
Introduction__ PAGE xiv
1911-1920 Yearbooks__ PAGE xvi
Schools__ PAGES 8-9
Fairgrounds__ PAGES 16-17
Triangle__ PAGE 22
Plays__ PAGES 34-35
Students__ PAGES 42-43
Time Capsule__ PAGE 49
Candid Photos__ PAGE 56
1931-1940 Yearbooks__ PAGE 68
Proms__ PAGE 74
Cartoons__ PAGES 84-85
Art__ PAGES 96-97
1941-50 Yearbooks__ PAGE 102
Teacher & Staff__ PAGES 114-115
1950-1960 Yearbooks__ PAGE 118
Sports__ p134-135
Newspaper Clippings__ PAGE 149
An Unidentified Class__ PAGES 188-189
The Later Years inside__ back panel

www.tagartstudio.com

1950-51 - ROOM 102 - PRIMAR

guy would end up
ing across the street
for the rest of
his life

MISS M. RUTH GUTHRIE

ding: Gifford, Friebe; Smith, Maiden, Lee,
ted; Ransford, Lemner, Behlen; Mid
k, Conrad, Myers; Bottom row; Fitz; Key